Masterir
Primary
Music

Mastering Primary Teaching series

Edited by Judith Roden and James Archer

The *Mastering Primary Teaching* series provides an insight into the core principles underpinning each of the subjects of the primary National Curriculum, thereby helping student teachers to master them. These comprehensive guides introduce the subjects and help beginner teachers know how to plan and teach effective and inspiring lessons that make learning irresistible. Each book follows the same sequence of chapters, which have been specifically designed to assist teachers in developing pedagogical excellence in each subject. Examples of children's work and case studies are included to help illustrate what is considered to be best and most innovative practice in primary education. The series is written by leading professionals, who draw on their years of experience to provide authoritative guides to the primary curriculum subject areas.

Also available in the series

Mastering Primary English, Wendy Jolliffe and David Waugh

Mastering Primary Languages, Paula Ambrossi and Darnelle Constant-Shepherd

Mastering Primary Physical Education, Kristy Howells with Alison Carney, Neil Castle and Rich Little

Mastering Primary Science, Amanda McCrory and Kenna Worthington

Forthcoming in the series

Mastering Primary Art and Design, Peter Gregory, Claire March and Suzy Tutchell

Mastering Primary Computing, Graham Parton and Christine Kemp-Hall

Mastering Primary Design and Technology, Gill Hope

Mastering Primary Geography, Anthony Barlow and Sarah Whitehouse

Mastering Primary History, Karin Doull, Christopher Russell and Alison Hales

Mastering Primary Mathematics, TBC

Mastering Primary Religious Education, Maria James and Julian Stern

Mastering Primary Music

Ruth Atkinson

Bloomsbury Academic
An imprint of Bloomsbury Publishing Plc

B L O O M S B U R Y

LONDON · OXFORD · NEW YORK · NEW DELHI · SYDNEY

Bloomsbury Academic

An imprint of Bloomsbury Publishing Plc

50 Bedford Square	1385 Broadway
London	New York
WC1B 3DP	NY 10018
UK	USA

www.bloomsbury.com

**BLOOMSBURY and the Diana logo are trademarks
of Bloomsbury Publishing Plc**

First published 2018

British Library Cataloguing-in-Publication Data
A catalogue record for this book is available from the British Library.

ISBN: HB: 978-1-4742-9680-9
PB: 978-1-4742-9679-3
ePDF: 978-1-4742-9681-6
ePub: 978-1-4742-9682-3

Library of Congress Cataloging-in-Publication Data
A catalog record for this book is available from the Library of Congress.

Series: Mastering Primary Teaching

Cover design by Anna Berzovan
Cover image © iStock (miakievy/molotovcoketail)

Typeset by Deanta Global Publishing Services, Chennai, India
Printed and bound in Great Britain

To find out more about our authors and books visit www.bloomsbury.com. Here you will find
extracts, author interviews, details of forthcoming events and the option to sign up for our
newsletters.

*This book is dedicated to children's music education.
If one more teacher enables one more class to experience enjoyable
music-making, then this book has been worth writing.*

Contents

List of Figures

(All images are the author's unless otherwise stated)

Morse, S. (2009). *American Taiko Team Celebrates Ten Years of Cultural Exchange.* Available at: http://www.misawa.af.mil/News/Photos/ igphoto/2000598955/ (Downloaded 5 May 2017).
Attribution: By Staff Sgt. Samuel Morse. Open use.

Bragadini, A. (2009). *Haka.* Available at: https://upload.wikimedia.org/ wikipedia/commons/2/24/Haka.jpg (Downloaded 19 December 2016).
Attribution: By Alessio Bragadini from Milan, Italy (Haka) [CC BY-SA 2.0 (http://creativecommons.org/licenses/by-sa/2.0)], via Wikimedia Commons.

Bergman, B. (2008). *A Small Group Playing Great Music.* Available at: https://commons.wikimedia.org/wiki/File%3ADenton_Arts_and_Jazz_ Festival_-_A_Small_Group.jpg (Downloaded 23 December 2016).

Series Editors' Foreword

A long and varied experience of working with beginner and experienced teachers in primary schools has informed this series since its conception. Over the last thirty years there have been many changes in practice in terms of teaching and learning in primary and early years education. Significantly, since the implementation of the first National Curriculum in 1989 the aim has been to bring best practice in primary education to all state schools in England and Wales. As time has passed, numerous policy decisions have altered the detail and emphasis of the delivery of the primary curriculum. However, there has been little change in the belief that pupils in the primary and early years phases of education should receive a broad, balanced curriculum based on traditional subjects.

Recent OFSTED subject reports and notably the Cambridge Primary Review indicate that, rather than the ideal being attained, in many schools the emphasis on English and mathematics has not only depressed the other subjects of the primary curriculum, but also narrowed the range of strategies used for the delivery of the curriculum. The amount of time allocated to subject sessions in Initial Teacher Education (ITE) courses has dramatically reduced which may also account for this narrow diet in pedagogy.

The vision for this series of books arose out of our many years of experience with student teachers. As a result, we believe that the series is well designed to equip trainee and beginner teachers to master the art of teaching in the primary phase. This series of books aims to introduce current and contemporary practices associated with the whole range of subjects within the Primary National Curriculum and religious education. It also goes beyond this by providing beginner teachers with the knowledge and understanding required to achieve mastery of each subject. In doing so, each book in the series highlights contemporary issues such as assessment and inclusion which are the key areas that even the most seasoned practitioner is still grappling with in light of the introduction of the new primary curriculum.

Readers will find great support within each one of these books. Each book in the series will inform and provide the opportunity for basic mastery of each of the subjects, namely English, mathematics, science, physical education, music, history, geography, design and technology computing, art and design and languages and religious education. They will discover the essence of each subject in terms of its philosophy, knowledge and skills. Readers will also be inspired by the enthusiasm for each subject revealed by the subject authors who are experts in their field. They will discover many and varied strategies for making each subject 'come alive' for their pupils and they should become more confident about teaching across the whole range of subjects represented in the primary and early years curriculum.

Primary teaching in the state sector is characterized by a long history of pupils being taught the whole range of the primary curriculum by one teacher. Although some schools may employ specialists to deliver some subjects of the curriculum, notably physical education, music or science, for example, it is more usual for the whole curriculum to be delivered to a class by their class teacher. This places a potentially enormous burden on beginner teachers no matter which route they have taken to enter teaching. The burden is especially high on those entering through employment-based routes and for those who aim to become inspiring primary teachers. There is much to learn!

The term 'mastery' relates to knowledge and understanding of a subject which incorporates the 'how' of teaching as well as the 'what'. Although most entrants to primary teaching will have some experience of the primary curriculum as a pupil, very few will have experienced the breadth of the curriculum or may have any understanding of the curriculum which reflects recent trends in teaching and learning within the subject. The primary curriculum encompasses a very broad range of subjects each of which has its own knowledge base, skills and ways of working. Unsurprisingly, very few new entrants into the teaching profession hold mastery of all the interrelated subjects. Indeed for the beginner teacher it may well be many years before full mastery of all aspects of the primary curriculum is achieved. The content of the primary curriculum has changed significantly, notably in some foundation subjects, such as history and music. So although beginner teachers might hold fond memories of these subjects from their own experience of primary education, the content of these subjects may well have changed significantly over time and may incorporate different emphases.

This series, Mastering Primary Teaching, aims to meet the needs of those who, reflecting the desire for mastery over each subject, want to know more. This is a tall order. Nevertheless, we believe that the pursuit of development should always be rewarded, which is why we are delighted to have so many experts sharing their well-developed knowledge and passion for the subjects featured in each book. The vision for this series is to provide support for those who are beginning their teaching career, who may not feel fully secure in their subject knowledge, understanding or skill. In addition, the series also aims to provide a reference point for beginner teachers to consult repeatedly over time to support them in the important art of teaching.

Intending primary teachers, in our experience, have a thirst for knowledge about the subject that they will be teaching. They want to 'master' new material and ideas in a range of subjects. Teaching the primary curriculum can be one of the most rewarding experiences. We believe that this series will help the beginner teachers to unlock the primary curriculum in a way that ensures they establish themselves as confident primary practitioners.

Judith Roden
James Archer
June 2017

How to Use This Book

This is one of twelve books that together help form a truly innovative series aimed to support your development. Each book follows the same format and chapter sequence. You will find a wealth of information within each chapter that will help you to understand the issues, problems and opportunities that teaching the subject can provide you as a developing practitioner in the subject. Crucially, each chapter provides opportunities for you to reflect upon important points linked to your development in order that you may master the teaching of music.

Each chapter has been carefully designed with key features to help you develop your knowledge of the subject systematically. Chapter objectives clearly signpost the content of each chapter and these will help you to familiarize yourself with important aspects of the subject and will orientate you in preparation for reading the chapter. The regular 'pause for thought' points offer questions and activities for you to reflect on important aspects of the subject. Each 'pause for thought' point provides you with an opportunity to enhance your learning beyond merely reading the chapter. These will sometimes ask you to consider your own experience and what you already know about the teaching of the subject. Others will require you to critique aspects of good practice presented as case studies or research. To benefit fully from reading this text, you need to be an active participant. Sometimes you are asked to make notes on your response to questions and ideas and then to revisit these later on in your reading. We strongly urge you to engage with the 'pause for thought' activities. It is our belief that it is through these moments that most of your transformational learning will occur. At the end of each chapter, you will find a summary of the main points from the chapter, along with suggestions for further reading.

We passionately believe that learners of all ages learn best when they work with others, so we would encourage you, if possible, to work with another person, sharing your ideas and perspectives. The book would also be ideal for group study within a university or school setting.

This book has been authored by Ruth Atkinson, who is an experienced and highly regarded professional in her subject area. Ruth is a strong voice within the primary music community. This book will enable you to benefit from her rich knowledge, understanding and experience.

Acknowledgements

Many people have helped to shape and improve this book.

I thank my family for encouraging me musically and my colleagues for encouraging me in my writing. My partner Mark Wilson has supported me as a true critical friend through the entire project, reading and re-reading my developing book and offering plenty of astute feedback and cups of tea. Kip Pratt, Hilary Lade, Jane Mayers and Connie Koch Rasmussen all read sections of the draft version of the book and made useful suggestions. Benji Rogers supported me with the preparation of some of the figures. I have also valued the support of the series editors and the publishing team at Bloomsbury Academic.

My special thanks go to Noelle Boucherat, Jessica Rowe and the children of Wembury and Montpelier Primary Schools for kindly allowing me to photograph their music lessons. I would also like to thank past and present student teachers at the Plymouth Institute of Education, Plymouth University, UK, whose experiences have informed me in all manner of ways. Particular thanks go to those students who have allowed their photos, words or research to be included in this book.

Any remaining errors, omissions and confusions are entirely mine.

List of Abbreviations

OFSTED – Office for Standards in Education, Children's Services and Skills
PCK – pedagogic content knowledge, the specific knowledge and expertise needed by a teacher within a given subject or discipline (Shulman 1987)

Introduction

This book is the distillation of many years of experience in primary education generally and in primary music education in particular. While the details of music curricula change over time, the essence of good teaching does not.

In this book you will find the subject knowledge you need to teach the entire primary music curriculum. The other main component of the book is advice on effective ways to teach primary music – sometimes referred to as 'pedagogic content knowledge' or PCK (Shulman 1987). This includes a range of teaching strategies, perhaps none more important than your *modelling* of certain attitudes such as enthusiasm, perseverance, enjoyment, a positive reaction to 'mistakes' and an inclusive disposition demonstrated by overtly valuing everyone in the room and welcoming participation.

You may never have seen a music lesson being taught in a primary school. If so, you are not alone (Ellison and Creech 2010, pp. 219–20). Trust your instincts as a teacher who knows what engages and inspires your pupils. Enjoy what you do, together.

The suggestions in the book are designed to suit those who might be feeling rather cautious, as this is often what less experienced teachers want to begin with. Although there is a wealth of ideas here, the main message for you is, 'Have a go!' Pick something that looks possible and start with that. Take small steps and your confidence will grow. It's like the moment when you go abroad and order a drink in another language … and a drink arrives!

Once you feel a bit more confident by all means do things differently. Allow more space and possibility into your plans. Respond to what the children find interesting and engaging. Let them take more control over their learning. You will find you are successfully covering the curriculum as long as your music provision is rich, varied and immersive. Dare to improvise! In other words, trust in your abilities as a teacher to observe, adjust and ask questions that push children's musical understanding. The important thing for the children is to allow them to learn music musically, as other musicians do (like writers learn to write, or footballers learn football).

The difference between teaching music and not teaching music is the courage to 'have a go'. Teachers who avoid teaching music often hold the misconception that they *can't* teach it. If they themselves are not great singers or saxophone players they think they are somehow exiled from involving themselves in music education.

Figure 0.1 Your confidence will grow

In fact there is no such separation into 'those who can' and 'those who can't': music is a universal thing. There is no gene for music. The teachers who shy away from music would probably have a go at teaching art or geography, yet the issues are the same. In avoiding music, they deny their pupils entitlement to the full curriculum. They also reveal a rather egocentric attitude. Whose musicianship are we really interested in, after all – that of the teacher or the children? 'To be human is to be musical, and to be offered the opportunities for musical engagement is every child's right' (Welch and Ockelford 2010, p. 50).

Teachers who are not expert musicians can teach excellent, inspiring, effective, enjoyable primary music lessons. We especially need these teachers, so that we can counteract the misconception that music is 'for the few'. It is for everyone and it needs to be with everyone and by everyone. I hope that you will enjoy your development as a 'can-do' teacher of inclusive primary music. It needs champions!

Pause for thought

Is there something about the thought of teaching music that scares you? Make a note of it now and return to it later. On your return, reflect on whether you have come across any strategies in the book that might help you.

Pause for thought

What do you think could be a 'way in' to music teaching, for you? It could be something that seems very modest (for example, allowing children to hear recorded music at some point in the day, or organizing an informal visit from a musician). Make a note of your ideas now, and add to them after you have spent time exploring the book.

You may want to read this book from cover to cover. If you prefer to dip in, however, it might help to know that

Chapter 1 explores what music is and why it is important for all children

Chapter 2 outlines the current state of music in primary schools and explains how you can make a real and positive impact in children's musical lives

Chapter 3 looks at two ways in which music is irresistible for children and introduces some useful terminology

Chapter 4 begins a three-chapter focus on music-related skill development, focusing on important personal skills, interpersonal skills and the use of language

Chapter 5 continues to look at music-related skill development with a focus on more specific skills of listening, audiating (i.e. using aural imagination), singing, playing and music-reading

Chapter 6 also focuses on music-related skill development by showing how to support children's creative work

Chapter 7 explains how to notice and assess children's musical learning over the short, medium and long term

Chapter 8 looks at how to plan and resource music lessons, how to relate them to other aspects of children's school experience and what to do about one's own possible lack of singing proficiency.

There are cross references between the chapters so that you should be able to follow a thread of interest once you have begun. The case studies in the book are all based on real events, though details have been changed.

Having begun to feel comfortable teaching primary music themselves, here's what some of the BEd students from Plymouth University wanted to tell you:

- Children aren't critical – they will want you straight on X Factor.
- Force yourself to do it!
- What's the worst that can happen?
- Don't be scared of singing.
- Just take the risk!

Although this book contains enough information to support you in teaching the primary music curriculum, you may find that you also want to develop your own musicianship. Chapters 2 and 8 give some ideas for accessible things you can do: enjoy!

One more thing. This book is full of words, but the best music lessons aren't. They are full of sounds, frowns of concentration, smiles, groans, wide-eyed moments, laughter and applause. They involve everyone, building on what each child can contribute and enabling each child to learn more. They allow children to feel and behave like the musicians they are. I am indebted to all those who have shown me what that means.

Figure 0.2 Why not try something new in music?

Morse, S. (2009). *American Taiko Team Celebrates Ten Years of Cultural Exchange.* Available at: http://www.misawa.af.mil/News/Photos/igphoto/2000598955/ (Downloaded 5 May 2017). Attribution: By Staff Sgt. Samuel Morse. Open use.

Chapter 1
An Introduction to Primary Music

Chapter objectives

- to introduce a broad definition of music
- to assert that everyone has musical potential
- to explore the many ways in which people can be considered musical
- to assert the importance of primary music in the curriculum
- to introduce the current Primary National Curriculum for Music
- to consider the intrinsic and transferable benefits of primary music for children's learning and development

What is primary music?

Pause for thought

How does music feature in your life? Write down as many ideas as you can.

Pause for thought

What does the word 'music' mean to you? Write down your ideas.

Pause for thought

What kinds of music do you like?

Pause for thought

Why do you think you have come to have these musical preferences?

If you can, share and compare your thoughts with a friend.

Music is part of the fabric of our lives. It plays a central role in most important occasions; we turn to it deliberately for solace, pleasure and joy; and it infiltrates our days in countless ways. People have their own musical preferences and each person lives in a particular musical world where he or she will encounter some kinds of music and not others. We are inducted into our individual musical worlds through a process of enculturation, starting before we are even born (Parncutt 2006).

Figure 1.1 Enculturation to one's 'sound-world' begins before birth – the unborn baby Robbie will already recognize his mother's voice and may also be able to hear the sea

Since we all know what music is, you would think that defining it would be straightforward. But when you try, lots of questions come to mind. Here are just a few:

- Does music have to have a tune?
- Does it have to have a beat?
- What about atmospheric film-scores?
- Is birdsong music?
- Is a car-horn music? What if it's the kind that plays a tune?
- Is a wind-chime music?
- Does it have to have a pattern or a structure?
- Does it have to be a complete 'piece'?
- What about video-game music?
- If I sample the sound of a car-horn and use it in my composition, is it music?
- What is music for?
- What about music I don't like?

To get closer to what *primary music* is, it is helpful to try to establish a broad, inclusive definition of *music* itself, built from some first principles.

To begin with, it has to do with *sound*. It is sonic. In fact, if the very mention of the word 'music' in the curriculum sends you into an anxious sweat, try substituting the word 'sonic'. Listening, making sounds, exploring sounds, sharing sonic creations and talking about sounds are all involved in teaching primary music. Thinking about what you are teaching as 'sonic' education can also help to remove potentially unhelpful value judgements about what the children are producing, which come from your own musical enculturation and preferences. You can listen to their sonic creations with less biased ears, hearing what *is* rather than what is *not*. As Dizzy Gillespie, a famous jazz trumpeter and composer, said: 'I don't care too much about music; what I like is sounds' (Taylor 1993).

Music also has to do with *people*: there would be no music without them, and wherever they are there is music. 'The appreciation of music is a universal feature of humankind; music-making is found in all societies and it is normal for everyone to participate in some manner' (Mithen 2006, p. 1).

So far so good. However, not all sounds that people make or hear are music. The driver who sounds a car-horn as a warning to another road-user is not making music. The hammering of the do-it-yourself enthusiast next door is not appreciated as music even if it has a regular rhythm. A third defining principle therefore has to do with *intent*. A child humming in the back seat of a car, a football supporter swelling the sound of the team's anthem, a trombone player in an orchestra, a busker in a shopping centre, an adult singing to a sleepy baby – they all are making music, because that is their intention.

Figure 1.2 Lullaby from a great-grandmother

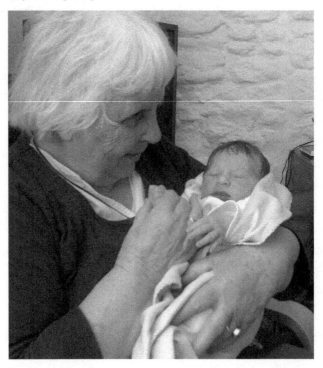

The sounds made by people in these examples are not random, either. They are put together into 'sonorous shapes' (Swanwick 2012, p. 2) that *mean* something to the people making them. As a visual analogy of this, think of what happens perceptually when two dots and a curvy line are drawn on a paper and suddenly they 'mean' a face. A verbal analogy would be putting letters together into meaningful words. The same happens in music. For example, there is a group of sounds which, when heard in sequence, 'mean' 'Happy Birthday To You'. Perhaps your auditory memory is good enough that you can 'hear' that well-known tune in your head right now.

We can also share our pictures, words and sonorous shapes with others to *express* what we mean. And we can *receive* (actively look at and listen to) the expressions of others in a bid to share their meaning. Like language and art, therefore, music is a *medium of communication*. But while verbal language is excellent for communicating semantic meaning, music excels at *communicating emotionally and socially*. Typically, a verbal communication involves turn-taking and dialogue, whereas music allows participants to act simultaneously, often synchronizing their participation to a beat or pulse (known as 'entrainment') (Cross 2011, p. 6). People share musical meanings, feelings, movements and impulses together *simultaneously* as the music is happening. This shared, co-created experience is a very special feature of the medium and it reaches out to include listeners too (Overy 2012).

Figure 1.3 Haka: a shared, co-created, simultaneous experience

Bragadini, A. (2009). *Haka.* Available at: https://upload.wikimedia.org/wikipedia/commons/2/24/ Haka.jpg (Downloaded 19 December 2016). Attribution: By Alessio Bragadini from Milan, Italy (Haka) [CC BY-SA 2.0 (http://creativecommons.org/licenses/by-sa/2.0)], via Wikimedia Commons

Different meanings are best expressed through different media. Eisner (2005) puts it well:

> There are ideas, images, and feelings that can only be expressed through visual form. … The expressive content of the visual arts cannot be duplicated in music; the expressive content of music cannot be duplicated in poetry; and poetry is no substitute for science. … The nature of these [auditory, visual, discursive] modes defines the parameters of conceptual possibility. For example, consider how easy it is to conceptualize and express suspense in music and how difficult it is in visual art. Suspense is a temporal phenomenon, visual art is not. (Eisner 2005, p. 65)

Above all, music *matters* to people. Music exists in every human culture and society, despite the fact that it is not needed for immediate survival or safety. There are profound links between music and emotion. You can probably name music that makes you feel happier or sadder – in fact just thinking about that music can begin to have an emotional effect. There is also a deeply social dimension to music: if you have been in the audience of your favourite group at a music festival, for example, you will have experienced this. There seem to be deep-rooted links with belonging, group identity and cooperation. This 'mysterious, wonderful and neglected feature of humankind' (Mithen 2006, p. vii) is unique to music. So although it may not be necessary for survival, music is life-enhancing for individuals and for groups of people. (See Chapter 3.)

One final thing. Music *happens*: it is temporal, a transient occurrence in time. Although we can 'capture' music to hear it again in the future by recording it, noting it down somehow or learning it off by heart, it only exists as music when it is played and listened to again. Many philosophers consider music to be a verb just as much as – or more than – a noun (Small 1998; Elliott and Silverman 2005). Think of the analogy with the word 'dance', which works equally well as a verb and as a noun. It is interesting to experiment with using the word 'music' as a verb. Small (1998) adopted the word 'musicking' to represent the happening of music. He felt that people can be involved in musicking in many ways: as performers, listeners, producers, composers, event organizers and joiners-in. 'Music is an *activity* that is universally accessible' (Ellison and Creech 2010, p. 211: my italics). Notice that listening is a way of musicking, too. If I listen to birdsong, a wind-chime or a photocopier with musical intent, I can hear them as music. In fact I can't help moving in time to a photocopier – how about you?

Conceptualizing music as a verb (as activity, doing, happening, experiencing) as well as a noun (the 'products' of music-making, which may or may not be replicable in the future) is a bit like the way people conceptualize the English language and English literature. English language is a happening thing. It is about the need or desire for communication, using a verbal medium to express and receive ideas. It is about sharing purposes and meanings in particular contexts. English literature, in contrast, is concerned with objects – verbal artefacts that can be examined, analysed, compared, contrasted and emotionally reacted to. Some human societies and cultures may not have a 'body of literature' but all have language.

The same is true for music. Because in our Western culture we *do* have several 'bodies of music' – hit singles, rock albums, jazz standards, traditional folk music, classical music – our own modest identities as musical people can be overshadowed. But anyone who enjoys listening to music, who taps a foot to a beat, who has musical preferences and maybe hums along to the car radio is demonstrating musicality. It is important that we recognize this. Musicality is not solely to be found in an elite group of people. In her highly accessible book of everyday songs for everyone to sing Cerys Matthews says, 'We are not going to be singing Handel's *Messiah* or Wagner's "Ring Cycle". We are not the marathon runners of opera, we are merely park wanderers. … So don't worry. At all' (Matthews 2014, p. 11). Park wandering is, after all, a lovely life-enhancing thing to do. 'Musicality' is explored further in the next section.

In summary, music is a distinct and meaningful medium of communication which is important to people socially and emotionally. We can use the word 'music' as a noun, describing the 'artefacts' created by people in this medium. We should also conceive of the word 'music' as a verb, referring to all the ways people can take part in and experience musical happenings. One of music's special features is that it allows people to participate simultaneously, which can engender strong feelings of enjoyment, belonging and the desire to cooperate. There are things that can be said, heard and felt musically that cannot be shared in any other way. Everyone is musical at some level and everyone can develop their musical understanding and musicianship.

This broad definition of music is not culturally specific. (Later in the chapter we will look briefly at children's musical enculturation.) The definition does not specify

Figure 1.4 Everyone is musical at some level

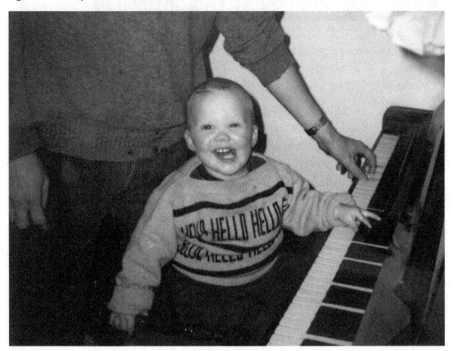

tunes or rhythms or instruments. It is wide enough to embrace very young musicians and those with no particular performance skills, as well as those with high levels of musical understanding and expertise. It includes your pupils and it includes you.

Pause for thought

How much of primary music do you feel should be about musical **activities** such as listening, playing, singing, creating and composing? How much should it be about investigating and getting to know existing musical **products**? (Try to disregard what you think you could *teach* for the moment – what do you think children deserve to *learn*?)

Pause for thought

Take a look at the current National Curriculum for Primary Music (Department for Education 2013). Which parts of the curriculum treat 'music' more as a noun and which ones treat it more as a verb?

What does it mean to be musical?

Apparently, organizers kept Elvis Presley from joining his school's glee club. They said his voice would ruin their sound.

(Robinson and Aronica 2010, p. 11)

Many people say they are not musical. A prominent reason for this is that although most people enjoy music and take part in musical activities such as informal singing (around the house, at concerts, festivals, in the team bus, at parties) and responding to music (at discos, dances, aerobics classes) they do not consider this 'being musical'. They think instead that their lack of the 'technical aspects of performance' (Hargreaves, MacDonald and Miell 2012, p. 130) or their lack of musical knowledge (Henley 2016) precludes them from calling themselves 'musical'.

However, research strongly suggests that everyone is musical. 'The ability to make music in some form, to notice distinctive features in musical structures, to be moved emotionally by particular pieces of music – these are all examples of a species-wide capability' (Welch and Adams 2003, p. 6). 'All humans have the potential to make music and … musicality is as universal as linguistic ability' (Hallam 2006, p. 104). 'We are all musical' (Hargreaves, MacDonald and Miell 2012, p. 129).

So what is musicality?

Pause for thought

What is your view? Complete the statement 'Being musical is …' before reading on.

Hallam and Prince (2003) asked over 400 people (adults and children, some actively engaged with music and some not) to complete the statement 'Being musical is …'. They had a wide variety of responses and concluded that 'conceptions of musical ability … were complex and multi-faceted' (p. 17). Further analysis revealed several strands to 'being musical', with those most often cited shown here in bold:

- receptive responses to music
- understanding
  - having knowledge about music
  - active responses to music
  - appreciation and evaluation of music
- aural skills
  - having a musical ear
  - **rhythmic ability**

- generative activities
  - ○ performing
  - ○ being able to play an instrument or sing
  - ○ being able to read music
  - ○ developing technical skills
  - ○ emotional sensitivity
  - ○ **communication** and interpretation
  - ○ **performance in a group**
  - ○ composition/improvisation
  - ○ **organization of sound**
  - ○ creativity
- **the integration of a range of skills**
- **personal qualities**
  - ○ **motivation**
  - ○ personal expression
  - ○ immersion in music
  - ○ total commitment
  - ○ metacognition (being able to learn to learn)

Hallam and Prince (2003, p. 17)

In broad terms then, being musical is about wanting to be involved in musical happenings whether by making music, listening to music or both. It does not necessarily have to include proficiency in singing or playing. You are musical if you enjoy music *with* people – you don't have to be able to sing or play *to* people.

Hallam and Prince (2003) is just one study investigating the concept of musicality. Reviewing pertinent literature, Henley (2016) finds there is a consensus that being musical means being actively engaged *in* music rather than having knowledge *about* music. Practically everyone is musical, in the same way that practically everyone has language. Not everyone is a skilled orator, poet or author and not everyone is well-read, but we can all speak, listen and communicate. In teaching primary music we are aiming to nurture children's musicality through basic musical speaking, listening and communicating: in other words, active musical engagement. Skills and knowledge will grow, gradually, from this important beginning.

The distinctions between making music *with* people and *for* people, and between learning *in* music and *about* music, are important and will be discussed further in the next chapter. For the sake of clarity, here are the definitions of certain key words as I use them in this book:

Musicality is a noun that refers to the entirety of a person's engagement *in* and *with* music, including 'expressive' and 'receptive' aspects.

Musical is an adjective to describe a person's musicality. A person can be musical without ever making a musical sound.

Musical potential is the capacity of a person to grow and develop his or her musicality. We all have it, just as we all have language potential.

Musicianship is used to refer to the outward signs of a person's musicality, that is, their musical behaviours.

Musical talent, skill, proficiency are ways to describe these 'expressive' aspects of a person's musicality.

Musical understanding, knowledge, awareness, appreciation, sensitivity are ways to describe the internal aspects of a person's musicality.

Declarative musical knowledge is what a person can put into words (declare) *about* music. Although not essential to musicality, it can deepen and enrich it.

Pause for thought

The question is not 'Are you musical?' but 'How are you musical?' Select from the list of ideas collated by Hallam and Prince (2003) above to describe your own musicality – and add any other points you wish to.

Notice the wording of this pause for thought. Keep in mind that everyone has musical potential and that everyone can develop their musicality (Tafuri 2008). For example Welch (2006), focusing on singing, discusses the strong evidence that singing is 'normal developmental behaviour that can be enhanced or hindered, particularly by the events and experiences of childhood' (p. 312). Henley (2016) too asserts that children 'are not fixed entities who arrive in school with an innate ability to either do or not do music; that being musical is part of our human design' (p. 11).

Our musicality is in part developed unconsciously by a lifetime of musical experiences, through a gradual process of *enculturation*. We are 'shaped by the sound-world and local culture into which we are born and raised. Consequently, young children are likely to enter school having experienced a range of different musical genres and having developed sensitivity to key features of the music(s) within their home and community culture. … Children also have begun to develop preferences for particular musical styles' (Welch and Adams 2003, p. 6). People demonstrate their musical understanding through expressing musical likes and dislikes, influenced by their musical enculturation.

Simple exposure to music also allows people gradually to internalize awareness of **beat** (the steady pulse underpinning much music), **rhythm** (patterns of long and short sounds), **melody** (patterns of higher and lower sounds) and so on. Some people grow up in more musically rich environments than others so they have more opportunities to develop this musical awareness. Some people are also encouraged and supported to learn specific skills such as singing or playing. So although 'nature' gives us all a good start, 'nurture' is not as equitable.

Why should music be part of the primary curriculum?

Leading on from the previous paragraph, the first argument in favour of primary music is one of social justice. As we have seen, all children have a natural propensity for music (Tafuri 2008). Marsh and Young (2006) say that 'all young children are prodigious producers of a rich variety of spontaneous musical play' (p. 294). Effective primary music education should respect this propensity and work in harmony with it. Tafuri (2008) argues that children need a musically rich environment just as they need a language-rich environment if their innate propensities are to blossom. As others warn of 'language deprivation', Tafuri alerts us to the effects of 'musical deprivation' (p. 87), which can hinder children's musical development in an analogous way. One reason why music deserves its place in the primary curriculum is therefore to nurture the musicality of all children. Put simply, music needs to *happen* in primary schools, to be part of children's lives, otherwise we are not 'nurturing' children's musical 'natures'. Chapter 3 contains some suggestions for this, including ensuring the inclusion of all children in primary music. Chapter 7 looks at how to find out whether children's musicality is developing over time.

A second important argument for primary music concerns how we know and understand ourselves, each other and our worlds. If subjects such as science, mathematics, language, geography, physical education and art deserve their place in the curriculum because each offers a distinctive and valuable way of experiencing and knowing the world and of engaging in it, then so does music. Paynter (2002) explains that 'music itself is a form of knowledge; not of the same kind as [say] historical or scientific knowledge … but an important way of knowing, nevertheless' (p. 219). This echoes Eisner's (2005) point that there are things that can best (or only) be communicated musically. 'It has a power and meaning beyond words. Music takes over where words leave off' (Young 2015, p. 183). This is something that has always been known: for example, Victor Hugo is famously quoted as saying, 'Music expresses that which cannot be said, and on which it is impossible to be silent'. Incorporating genuine purpose into children's musical work, by offering opportunities to express things musically, is of central importance and Chapter 4 will consider this in detail.

Third, it is worth re-stating that music is a sonic medium. Just as it is important for children to get to know, explore and manipulate the physical and visual dimensions of their environments by looking, touching and moving, so it is important for them to get to know, explore and manipulate the dimension of sound. Although some aspects of sound are a focus when learning to speak, read and spell, and although music may occur incidentally elsewhere in the curriculum, it is in primary music that sounds and listening are placed centre stage. The focus is on hearing; on developing auditory awareness, discrimination, memory and imagination; on gradually learning musical terminology so as to be able to talk about sounds; and on having the chance to give full attention to sounds and the pleasure that working in sound can bring. Chapter 3 introduces useful terminology and Chapter 5 includes ways to develop auditory skills.

The fourth argument centres on acquiring musical awareness and understanding. Some groups of sounds are sounds, and some groups of sounds are music. The difference is in the meaning conveyed. Just as some vocal sounds are meaningful words and some are not, some 'sonorous shapes' (Swanwick 2012) carry emotional, predictive or social connotations. What is meaningful in one culture may not be in another – again, think of the analogy with verbal language. Children deserve to become more aware of what makes music music, to explore their musical cultures, to consider in more depth the types of music that are familiar to them and also to extend their musical experiences. They should gradually become aware that they *are* musically enculturated, so that they can be critical listeners and 'consumers'. Children's entitlement to learn *about* music as well as *in* music is discussed in Chapter 3, where ideas are given to support children's explorations.

Children also need opportunities and reasons to develop and express their own musical ideas. This is an argument for supporting children to develop their creative skills in music. Accessible digital technologies now enable children to express themselves musically without being limited by their levels of vocal or instrumental skill (Webster and Hickey 2006; Watson 2011) so this is an exciting time to be a creative young musician. The important area of creativity is the focus of Chapter 6, which looks in detail at how to support creative work in primary music.

However it is also important to help children develop skills in producing musical sounds by singing and playing. Children love to acquire and master new skills – you only have to look at the success of computer games, for example, to appreciate this. Tafuri (2008) is among many writers who point out that although we all have the potential to learn skills such as singing and playing, they take time to acquire and become 'stable'. It is outrageous that so many adults say they can't sing because when they were younger someone said or did something that signalled to them that they couldn't. The natural reaction to such a signal would be to stop trying – to stop acquiring the skill. This is a classic example of a self-fulfilling prophecy. Singing and playing need the same support and encouragement over time as any other skill. For example Welch et al. (2011) show clear evidence that 'a programme of sustained singing education can have a positive benefit on children's singing behaviors and development' (p. 83). By the way, it is never too late to decide to learn how to sing and play an instrument yourself: treat it like learning another language and take it gradually. Chapter 5 focuses on the development of singing and playing skills in the context of curricular classroom music, while there is some advice in Chapter 8 on how to improve your own singing.

Figure 1.5 Acquiring the skill of playing an instrument takes time, like any skill

A further strong reason for teaching primary music is that it can be such a source of communal cohesion, pleasure and pride. It is exhilarating to take part in a class performance and it can offer children a particular way to 'shine'. I can't remember seeing any child's family members shed happy tears over their mathematics achievements, but I have seen many reaching for their hankies during musical performances. There is more on this aspect in Chapters 3 and 4.

Finally, a good primary music education is enjoyable and will often spark a lifelong passion, so that children may grow up to join the tens of thousands of people who make a living in some part of the music business. Or they may join the much larger number of people who take pleasure from engaging in music as amateurs, that is, because they love it. Music can enhance people's entire lives by giving pleasure, connecting with emotions and adding social richness. If you have ever sung in a choir or played in a group you have probably experienced the awe of participating in something that seems to be 'more than the sum of its parts' in a joyful way. Perhaps you have been in a position where you needed to perform solo: the nervousness beforehand and the exhilaration afterwards are memorable feelings. Good primary music can act as a foundation for such transformational experiences. If you are one of the many adults who were unfortunately put off music by negative past experiences,

Chapter 2 might inspire you to rebuild your confidence and enthusiasm so that your pupils do not suffer as you did.

The National Curriculum itself argues strongly for the inclusion of music, saying:

> Music is a universal language that embodies one of the highest forms of creativity. A high quality music education should engage and inspire pupils to develop a love of music and their talent as musicians, and so increase their self-confidence, creativity and sense of achievement. As pupils progress, they should develop a critical engagement with music, allowing them to compose*, and to listen with discrimination to the best in the musical canon**. (Department for Education 2013, p. 1)

*To **compose** means to make up music: to invent, create, develop and refine musical ideas.

The **musical canon is the music – of different kinds/genres – that has stood the test of time.

Having said all this, school music is only one part of most children's musical worlds. As primary teachers we cannot do everything, but what we can do is to ensure that children continue to develop musically in ways that keep their options open and preserve their self-belief – by believing in the musical potential of each child ourselves. As Pitts (2000) puts it. 'We need to be modest about the place of school music in the overall musical development of the child, and yet be ambitious about its provision, resourcing and variety, if all children are to have the opportunity to discover its potential for themselves' (p. 41).

Pause for thought

Looking at all the reasons above for including primary music in the curriculum, how would you rank them in order of importance?

Pause for thought

How might your response to the previous pause for thought influence your own approach to teaching primary music?

The National Curriculum for Music

The National Curriculum for Music is a very compact summary of what might reasonably be achieved by the *end* of each stage after many sessions of teaching, learning and music-making. Later in this book (and particularly in Chapters 7 and 8) guidance is given about how to create much more specific and short-term learning objectives that will help children to learn and develop musically so that, over time, they accumulate the musical experience, skills, knowledge and understanding to meet the end-of-key-stage attainment targets.

There is some terminology in the National Curriculum that you may not be familiar with. As well as 'composing' and the 'musical canon' (see above), it mentions the 'inter-related dimensions of music'. These dimensions are **pitch, tempo, dynamic, duration, timbre, texture, structure** and – many people would argue – **silence**. These terms are all explained in Chapter 3. Knowing the words and being able to describe sounds in these terms is a central part of your music subject knowledge. Another phrase that may be new to you is 'staff notation' (in Key Stage 2). This is not, as one Plymouth student reasonably guessed, things that a teacher writes on the board. **Staff notation** is just one way of writing music down on paper, using five horizontal lines with blob-and-stick notes positioned upon them (see Chapter 5).

Pause for thought

Take another look at the National Curriculum for Music, Key Stages 1 and 2 (Department for Education 2013).

Does any of it surprise you?

Write any surprising parts down and revisit them once you have spent time with this book, to see if your views have changed.

Pause for thought

Do you understand what each phrase and sentence in the National Curriculum for Music actually means? Make a note of the ones that are not clear at the moment.

Pause for thought

Can you begin to think of what kinds of resources might support teaching? Start a list.

Pause for thought

Can you begin to visualize the kinds of learning activities that children might engage in? Start another list!

It will be interesting for you to return to your answers at a later date, as you will be able to develop each one in the light of your increased knowledge and experience.

I find it helpful to think of the music curriculum as boiling down to three simple aspects: skills (the 'how' of music); knowledge (the 'what' of music); and purposes (the 'why' of music).

- **skills** – all the things children (and other musicians) *do* in engaging with music
- **knowledge** – of how music is constructed and about a range of existing music
- **purposes** – what music is *for*; how it is used by individual people and groups, informally and formally; reasons why music is created and listened to

---

Pause for thought

Write three headings: MUSIC-RELATED SKILLS, MUSICAL KNOWLEDGE and PURPOSES OF MUSIC.

Drawing only on your own current knowledge of music, how many items can you list under each heading?

The skills and knowledge covered in the primary National Curriculum for Music are set out in more detail in Figure 7.2.

Pause for thought

There is much more throughout this book about skills, knowledge and purposes. For now, consider whether you find it useful to conceive of the music curriculum in this way.

How can music contribute to a child's whole education?

Without music, we cannot be seen to be educating the whole person. The inclusion of music in education allows us to celebrate one of the unique attributes of humanity while, at the same time, developing, deepening and extending our range of available musical behaviours. When we engage with music, we involve our inner emotional world (whether as listener, performer or composer) and foster expressive behaviours and creative imagination. We also experience music as a form of language, as a symbol system, as patterns of sound in which we perceive organization and meaning, and as part of our individual, group and community identity. (Welch and Adams 2003, p. 4)

As we have seen, music is intrinsically valuable in its own right. Additionally it is an excellent context for nurturing valuable 'transferable' skills, attributes, attitudes and values, such as learning to listen, to work in a group and to learn things 'by ear'.

Young (2011, pp. 160–1) points out that if music is taught well for its own sake, such 'transferables' will develop naturally.

Hallam (2015) synthesized a number of studies in a survey of possible transferable benefits. For individual children these benefits include improved aural perception, improved language and literacy skills, improved auditory memory and increased creativity. Personal development and self-belief can also be enhanced through the acknowledgement of and constructive feedback on musical contributions (Hallam 2015). For children who do not excel at verbal, physical or artistic activities, this can be a particularly important way of helping to raise self-esteem and confidence. Hallam also found some evidence for personal benefits in terms of spatial reasoning, attention, self-regulation, 'general attainment', perseverance, determination, feelings of well-being and management of emotions, as well as tolerance and development of socially ethical attitudes.

In relation to groups of children, making music together increases social cohesion, feelings of inclusion and affiliation. This seems to be particularly true for disaffected children. Teamwork, collaboration, turn-taking, improved relationships, group identity-building and solidarity can all be enhanced (Hallam 2015). Rhythmic activities, in particular, seem to encourage pro-social behaviour (Kirschner and Tomasello 2010). Music is an excellent domain in which to support children's emotional and social development and to develop feelings of belonging and

Figure 1.6 Singing a sea-shanty to aid teamwork (photograph by Jessica Rowe)

community in the classroom (and the school). Investigating different musical genres can support cultural cohesion and understanding.

Singing can make its own specific contribution too. 'Humans sing to express emotions beyond mere words. … Even very young children can, and do, express inexpressible feelings in song. … Singing is the birthright of every child' (Smith 2006, p. 28). There is a growing body of research into the specific benefits of singing, when it is handled positively. Saunders, Varvarigou and Welch (2010) summarize recent studies showing that participation in singing:

- engenders a strong sense of community
- improves cardio-physiological fitness
- positively influences the immune system
- improves singers' mood states
- helps infants to bond emotionally
- generates feelings of being positive, alert and spiritually uplifted
- benefits reading and general knowledge via the lyrics (words)

Pause for thought

What can you remember about your own music education in primary school?

Pause for thought

If your own primary school music did not have any of the beneficial impacts described above, why do you think that was?

Although the general benefits of good primary music will positively affect a child's whole education, this is not reason enough to include it in the curriculum. It deserves its place because of its intrinsic worth as a uniquely and universally human way of knowing, feeling, being and connecting, with its immense and immediate power to affect us through meaningful sound.

Summary

Music has been defined in a broad way that emphasizes its nature as activity that happens and includes the many genres and styles found in different places, times and cultures. It is a distinct and meaningful sonic medium of communication which is important to people socially and emotionally. The word 'music', like the word 'dance', should be understood as both verb and noun, denoting the activity and experience of taking part in musical communication expressively and receptively as well as referring to pieces of music. Music allows people to participate together in synchrony, which can be a powerful means of helping them to feel good about themselves individually and as a group.

All humans are born with musical potential, though some are able to develop this potential more than others as a result of their life chances. Everyone is musical to some extent, even if they are not performers, since every person is a product of his or her musical upbringing with at least tacit knowledge of their musical culture/s and with personal musical preferences and responses. There are many ways of being musical, not all involving high levels of skill or knowledge, and musicality is not fixed, but amenable to growth and development.

It is important that music forms part of the curriculum because it is a distinct and valuable way of knowing and feeling about our worlds. All children deserve the chance to develop their musical potential so that they can access and participate in this unique medium of human communication and bonding now and in the future. Primary music is also important for exploring the medium of sound and developing auditory perception and memory. The main aim is to develop children's musicality, with the development of declarative musical knowledge very much in support of that aim.

Enjoyable and challenging primary music education contributes significantly to children's personal, emotional and social development. The music classroom offers golden opportunities to nurture a wide range of important lifelong learning skills and attributes. Effective music teaching can transform children's lives by giving them a sense of self-worth and belonging within their class and school. It may also help children to self-identify as musical and underpin a lifelong passion for music.

Recommended reading

Department for Education (2013). *Music programmes of study: Key Stages 1 and 2 National Curriculum in England.* Available at: https://www.gov.uk/government/uploads/system/uploads/attachment_data/file/239037/PRIMARY_national_curriculum_-_Music.pdf (Accessed 19 December 2016).

Elliott, D. J. and Silverman, M. (2015). *Music Matters: A Philosophy of Music Education*, 2nd edn. Oxford: Oxford University Press.

Hallam, S. (2006). 'Musicality.' In McPherson, G. (ed.), *The Child as Musician: A Handbook of Musical Development.* Oxford: Oxford University Press.

Hallam, S. (2015). *The Power of Music: A Research Synthesis of the Impact of Actively Making Music on the Intellectual, Social and Personal Development of Children and Young People.* London: Music Education Council.

Matthews, C. (2014). *Hook, Line and Singer: 125 Songs to Sing Out Loud.* London: Penguin Books.

Robinson, K. and Aronica, L. (2010). *The Element: How Finding your Passion Changes Everything*. London: Penguin.

Tafuri, J. (2008). *Infant Musicality: New Research for Educators and Parents.* Welch, G. (ed.), SEMPRE studies in the psychology of music. Farnham: Ashgate.

Young, V. (2015) 'An introduction to music.' In Driscoll, P., Lambirth, A. and Roden, J. (eds), *The Primary Curriculum: A Creative Approach.* 2nd edn. London: SAGE Publications.

Chapter 2
Current Developments in Primary Music

Chapter objectives

- to outline briefly how primary curriculum music has evolved
- to explain why instrumental tuition is not part of the primary music curriculum and how it can be provided for
- to outline research evidence about the current quality of primary music provision
- to explore teachers' confidence in their own musicality
- to demonstrate that non-specialist teachers can teach primary music well

What is the state of primary music?

Music's power to bring people together and to confer a sense of belonging and shared purpose has long been harnessed in the wider life of schools. But the character of music as a *curriculum* subject has evolved and shifted with changing opinions about what should be learnt. 'Music's status as a curriculum subject in Britain has almost always been ambivalent … always there, but somehow conditional; the diversity of justifications for the subject ranging from the severely practical, to the high flown' (Cox 2010, p. 26). In the late nineteenth and early twentieth centuries, the focus was purely on singing. Musical appreciation and the playing of instruments appeared on the school curriculum between the two World Wars and by the 1960s some children were also composing their own music (Cox 2010). Schools have varied greatly in their provision, however. After some debate about whether to do so, music was included in the first National Curriculum for England in 1989. This has meant that it has been a statutory curriculum entitlement for several decades.

What should a music curriculum include? There continues to be tension between those who stress the importance of knowing about, reading and performing the best musical 'products' of the Western music tradition and those who take a more 'process'-oriented perspective involving experimentation, creativity and the experience of different genres and styles (Cox 2010; Finney 2011; Young 2011). These two perspectives have been characterized as 'subject-centred' and 'child-centred', 'traditional' and 'progressive' or even 'knowledge' and 'knowing'. At their origin, they differ in the stress they place on music as a collection of artefacts versus musicking, that is, the activities involved in engaging musically (see Chapter 1).

The National Curriculum for Music has, since its inception, been predominantly 'progressive' thanks in particular to the work of John Paynter and Keith Swanwick (Cox 2010, p. 24). However, in the current version of the curriculum some 'traditional' features have made an appearance once again. This change reflects the stance of the government in the early 2010s, with the secretary of state for education stating: 'Government priorities recognize music as an enriching and valuable academic subject with important areas of knowledge that need be learnt, including how to play an instrument and sing' (Henley 2011, p. 4). So as well as the skills of singing, playing, listening, composing and appraising which constituted the previous version of the curriculum, there is now an expectation that children in Key Stage 2 will be taught the basics of music notation and will begin to develop a knowledge of the history of music. (All these things will be explored in later chapters.)

Though the curriculum stipulates a mix of learning *in* music and learning *about* music, the strong consensus among music education researchers, educators and OFSTED (Office for Standards in Education, Children's Services and Skills)

Figure 2.1 Music should predominantly be a practical subject

inspectors (2009b, 2012a) is that classroom music should continue to be a predominantly *practical* subject and that learning about music should be done 'from the inside out and with a real purpose' (Daubney and Mackrill 2015, p. 250).

Generalist primary teachers need to be capable of teaching curricular music as described above, and the focus of this book is on helping you do just that. However, instrumental tuition falls outside the remit of non-specialist teachers. It simply is not feasible to include it within the curriculum. Most instruments are difficult to play, so learners require specialist teachers for many lessons, which is expensive and time-consuming. Traditionally such teaching has been paid for by families and depends on the availability of suitable teachers as well as sufficient financial resources. (In class music lessons it is possible to bypass the need for expertise on instruments by using simple-to-play acoustic instruments, voices, body percussion and digital sound-makers — see Chapters 3, 5 and 6 for more on this.)

Nevertheless, skilled performing is an important part of musicianship for many people and there are plenty of children who want to learn an instrument beyond the level that curricular music lessons can accommodate. So even though you are definitely *not* expected to teach children how to play trombones, violins or bass guitars, it is worth knowing how schools are encouraged to support those children who wish to learn them. Here is a brief outline of how instrumental tuition is commonly organized.

Over the last few years considerable efforts have been made to address the issue of instrumental tuition in a way that it is less dependent on families' abilities to pay. Following a major national review of school music provision (Henley 2011) the *National Plan for Music Education* was published (Department for Education and Department for Culture, Media and Sport 2011). As a result of this plan, there is now a network of 123 Music Education Hubs across the country which receive funding from Arts Council England to act as sources of guidance and help for all schools (Arts Council England, no date). Data suggest that in practice, Hubs are involved with almost 90 per cent of primary schools (National Foundation for Educational Research 2016, p. 19).

As well as being a source of advice for classroom teachers who want support with curriculum music, the Hubs are responsible for coordinating those aspects of music that fall outside the curriculum:

- they provide specialist teachers and instruments for 'first-access' instrumental tuition, so that every child can receive free whole-class lessons in playing a particular instrument for at least a term sometime during Key Stage 2 (often in Year 4 or Year 5)

- they organize and facilitate ensembles – groups, bands, choirs and orchestras – so that there is a progression route for those children who are keen to continue their instrumental/vocal learning beyond first-access

- they cater for the further progression of those at more advanced levels of expertise

- they promote and support singing in all schools, including providing opportunities for children to get together in inter-school singing projects.

The idea is that running alongside curricular music lessons there are routes by which children can learn an instrument and get more involved in singing. The Hub-related activity you are most likely to notice in your school is a series of at least ten free instrument lessons, taught during school time by a visiting specialist to a whole class of Key Stage 2 children. Many schools work with Hubs to extend this opportunity to thirty lessons. Children can then, if they wish, continue with further tuition and playing opportunities, though at this point their families have to start paying the tuition fees and often the transport costs for children to attend ensembles taking place in different locations outside school time. Recent data indicate that about 25 per cent of children do continue to play after their first-access experience (National Foundation for Educational Research 2016, p. 15).

You may also notice that your school subscribes to an online resource known as 'Sing Up' (Sing Up 2016). This was also developed in response to the National Plan for Music and is an excellent source of songs, complete with teaching notes, recordings and much more. It is mentioned in various places in this book.

In some respects then, 'music education in the UK in the twenty-first century is thriving' (Adams, McQueen and Hallam 2010, p. 31). However, Cox (2010), Young (2011) and Finney (2015) are among those who feel that while these various

Figure 2.2 Many children want to learn to play technically difficult instruments, but this is not part of the primary music curriculum

initiatives are welcome, they may inadvertently introduce further tensions. For instance, sometimes the first-access instrumental lessons have been the *only* class music provision, with schools arguing that there is not enough time to provide that *and* the kinds of curricular music sessions that this book is concerned with. In other words, what was designed to complement good curricular music education has at times overshadowed it. OFSTED (2012a, 2012c, 2013) also found that there is often insufficient liaison between class teachers, schools, instrumental teachers and Hubs, with the result that children's overall music education is piecemeal rather than developmental.

What does all this mean for you as a classroom teacher? The most important point is that *curriculum* music (the focus of this book) is a statutory entitlement for all children, so please ensure that your pupils are receiving their entitlement. In addition, there should be times when there is a focus on good-quality singing and – in Key Stage 2 – someone should come in and teach your class a series of at least ten lessons devoted to learning an instrument. It is highly beneficial if you can join your children in these sessions: you gain more musical experience; the teachers can build on your knowledge of your children; and the children see that you have 'voted with your feet', sending a powerful and positive message to them about music.

It may be that your 'PPA time' (weekly non-contact time for planning, preparation and assessment) is covered by someone who teaches the curriculum music to your class. While the teaching may be fine, the danger here is that your personal involvement with your own pupils' musical learning and development is much reduced. This can make it difficult to include music in cross-curricular work, as you may have little knowledge of your pupils' musical needs, strengths or interests (OFSTED 2012a). In this situation it will also be harder for you to develop your own skills and confidence in teaching class music. I would urge you to try to find ways to keep in touch with what your pupils are doing, so that you will feel you can build on it elsewhere in the timetable.

Pause for thought

Think about a primary school you know. How much involvement do the class teachers have with their own pupils' music education?

Pause for thought

If other adults are involved in pupils' music education, how do the class teachers keep track of the musical learning and development?

What does the research say?

There are some rather sobering research findings about the current quality of primary music provision, but there is also strong positive evidence about generalist classroom teachers' potential to improve the situation significantly.

First the bad news. OFSTED (2009a, 2012a) has repeatedly found that the quality of primary music provision across England is patchy. In their latest published survey they reported that only 37 per cent of 90 primary schools inspected were providing good or outstanding music teaching. This figure compares poorly with the 70 per cent of primary schools judged good or outstanding overall. As they put it, 'In too many cases there was not enough music in music lessons' (OFSTED 2012a).

In their inspections, about two-thirds of the music lessons were taught by non-specialist teachers or teaching assistants. The other third, which included first-access instrumental tuition (see previous section), were taught by music specialists. More of the specialists' lessons were judged to be good or outstanding, but more were also inadequate. This is because visiting specialists may have good musical skills and knowledge, but weaker general teaching skills and much less knowledge of individual children and their needs.

For many primary teachers it is the other way round: they have good general pedagogic expertise and knowledge of their children's needs, but weaker knowledge of how and what to teach in music. OFSTED (2012a) saw how teachers applied their general pedagogic knowledge diligently, but were not often able to handle music as the dominant 'language' in their lessons. Following the discussion in Chapter 1 you might recognize, in the description here, that the children were perhaps learning *about* music, but not engaging musically to learn *in and through* music:

> Nearly all non-specialist teachers demonstrated professional, efficient lesson organisation and effective class management strategies. However, in too many cases these strategies were not given sufficient musical dimensions. So, for example, while nearly all class teachers planned lessons with engaging starter activities and opportunities for pupils to work in groups and assess their own work, the activities themselves were often unmusical – for example, completing a worksheet, drawing pictures, and talking or writing about musicians. (OFSTED 2012a, p. 19)

Why do non-specialist primary teachers often struggle to put music in their music lessons? Biasutti, Hennessy and de Vugt-Jansen (2015) have drawn together a considerable body of evidence that shows generalist primary teachers tend to have low levels of confidence for music teaching (p. 145). There are many reasons for this lack of confidence. A principle reason is that the amount of training that student teachers receive in relation to teaching music is inadequate, although the quality of that training may be high (Rogers et al. 2008, p. 486). The problem may persist once new teachers take up their first posts. Because of the low priority given to curriculum music in many schools, there may not be any confident teachers among the staff and music lessons may be rare occurrences. So it may not be easy for new teachers to develop confidence to teach music once they are in school.

However, this cannot be the only reason for teachers' lack of confidence in music. Time given to other foundation subjects is usually just as scarce during a teacher's training, yet teachers rate music as the subject they feel least confident to teach (Hennessy 2000; Stunell 2010; Welch and Henley 2014). It seems that because of their own past experiences many primary teachers perceive music to be a difficult subject to teach, believing that a high degree of performance skill and knowledge is necessary (see Chapter 1).

This research is echoed by my own observations as a primary teacher and now a teacher educator. My colleagues and I frequently encounter low confidence about teaching primary music among undergraduate and postgraduate student teachers and practising class teachers. While there is a strong consensus that music education is important for primary-aged children, many teachers do not think that they themselves can provide that education. Stunell (2010) made an in-depth study of four experienced and generally confident primary teachers who nevertheless lacked confidence in teaching music, to explore this disconnect. I certainly know teachers with 'profiles' similar to this:

> As an adult, Kate was engaged with music at home as a listener. She also sang and danced with her daughter, and took her to mother-and-child music activities. Despite this, she expressed minimal confidence in her own musical identity. When asked what she regarded as the marks of a 'musical' person, she talked of knowledge and understanding rather than any innate ability. She did not regard herself as having this to any degree and saw herself existing in a different world from 'musicians', who would be 'put up there on a platform!' (Stunell 2010, p. 88)

Pause for thought

Think about the subjects in the primary curriculum. List them in order of your present level of confidence to teach each one.

Which subjects do you feel most confident to teach? Why do you think this is?

Which subjects are you least confident to teach? Why might this be?

Ironically, having first-access specialists in school, whose role is purely to teach specific instrumental skills, may have exacerbated the belief among some non-specialist teachers that music can only be taught by skilled musicians, even though the rationale for first-access teaching is to complement – not to compete with — the musical work of class teachers (see previous section). It reminds me of the not-so-hidden message associated with inviting a school nurse in to talk to Year 6 pupils about the 'facts of life': teachers and pupils alike come to perceive the topic as specialist, rarified, different – no longer something that they can broach in a normal and natural way. In effect, they have been excluded.

So much for the bad news. The good news is that non-specialist teachers *are* perfectly able to teach primary curriculum music effectively (Rogers et al. 2008; Lamont, Daubney and Spruce 2012; Henley 2016). The fundamental step is to realize that primary music is *not* about high levels of performance skill, but about children. Children exploring sounds, joining in, enjoying making music, having frequent musical experiences that over time enable them to feel and play a steady beat and increasingly sing in tune, developing a vocabulary with which to talk about the qualities and dimensions of sounds (long, short, loud, spooky, etc.) and recognizing music as a positive part of the fabric of their school lives. Teachers can side-step the issue of not having particular singing/playing skills by letting digital technology provide the musical models (more on this in later chapters). Rather than thinking of music as an exclusive club, primary music is all about inclusion (of teachers too).

How can teachers achieve this fundamental 'reframing' or mindset-shifting, so that they feel able to tackle the teaching of primary music just like any other part of the curriculum? It can be through professional development activity, observing good practice or simply deciding to ignore their own negative beliefs about teaching music and take the plunge anyway. When I asked the student teachers I work with what I

Figure 2.3 Take the plunge!

should write in this book, the message they wanted me to convey most strongly was 'Have a go!'

Rogers et al. (2008) focused on singing. They showed that teachers' participation in professional development activities had a positive effect. They concluded: 'The evidence from this research indicates that generalist teachers can develop the skills they need to teach music in the primary school' (p. 496). Lamont, Daubney and Spruce (2012) reach similar conclusions: 'Singing is a musical activity which all children can join in with, and which all staff can develop the confidence to support and lead' (p. 262).

In both these studies, success was related to the presence of influential people who were enthusiastic about children singing, whether these were singing coaches, music coordinators or head teachers. Ultimately, however, the actual difference was made by class teachers gaining the confidence to use singing in their classes. 'For this to work, you've got to have a teacher in school that will push it on, and have that genuine love of wanting to keep the singing going in school. It doesn't have to be someone who's fabulous at singing, it just has to be somebody who wants it to happen' (Lamont, Daubney and Spruce 2012 p. 259).

What works for singing can work for all aspects of primary music. In Stunell's (2010) study, simply talking about teaching music was enough to make a difference:

> As the interviews proceeded, Kate began to see that knowledge about music could be structured so that she could access it. An embryonic musical self-efficacy belief, nurtured by the researcher, allowed her to see herself as a teacher of music in some very small measure and she began to be more pro-active in organising children's music experiences, using her pedagogic skills with music materials and accepting (as she was able to do in other subjects) that complete 'success' in achieving the objective of the lesson was not essential to children's progress within the field. (Stunell 2010, p. 100)

In this case the 'influential person' was the researcher. It is even possible for a teacher to be his or her own 'influential person', as shown here by a recent Plymouth BEd student conducting her third-year research project.

CASE STUDY

Despite being a final-year BEd undergraduate taking a substantial music specialism, Bethan confessed to lacking confidence in teaching primary music. She had wanted to have English as her specialism but that course had been full! Being a motivated and aspirational student teacher, she decided to put her own lack of confidence under the spotlight for her extended research project.

Bethan designed her research so that she could gather data on her own confidence whenever she taught class music on her final school placement in the Spring Term of 2016. Immediately after each occasion of teaching music, Bethan made detailed reflective notes. These helped her to see what she needed to focus on as a developing teacher in order to plan effective subsequent lessons. She also made a subjective plot of how her confidence had risen and fallen moment by moment through each lesson: a kind of 'confidence graph', which she annotated with her fresh memories of what had caused each fluctuation. She kept a reflective journal where she took a longer-term view on how and why her confidence was changing.

As part of her research Bethan also proactively took steps to address her identified lack of confidence in particular areas as they arose, reflecting on the extent to which these were helpful. Singing was the scariest part of the primary curriculum for her, so she joined a local choir. Later in her placement she introduced more singing into her teaching, not just in music but across the curriculum. She also started and ran a recorder club for Year 1 children.

Bethan was able to pinpoint and learn from a number of influences on her confidence, including

- negative memories of playing in public as a child and the fear of judgement;
- the positive effect of praise from teachers in her placement school;
- the boost when teaching went well;
- the pleasant impact of informal musical experiences such as choir and recorder club;
- anxiety when being observed;
- negative feelings about having to teach music without time to plan;
- anxiety at not having planned an extension activity or extra challenge;
- the boost from children's positive reactions;
- the link with security of subject knowledge;
- the link with understanding of suitable pedagogic approaches;
- perceived complexity of the teaching challenge;
- which aspect of the music curriculum was being taught.

Importantly, she also found that as a result of conducting her research, her confidence in teaching primary music had risen substantially.

Bethan had engaged in a self-directed series of experiential learning cycles (Schön 1987, 1991; Kolb 1984), alternating reflection with experimentation. Her project-based learning (Kaschub 2014) illustrates a powerful and manageable approach to professional development for both student teachers and those in post. This type of self-study (Campbell 2014) is in line with the growing emphasis on teacher-as-researcher particularly within action research frameworks (Cohen, Manion and Morrison 2011). Bethan had wanted to improve her practice and had deliberately set out to overcome her own fears, with great success. You could do this, too.

In writing this book, I hope I can be an 'influential person' for you. If you have ever sung in the shower or in your car or at a festival or football match; if you have ever danced at home or with others; if you find yourself tapping your foot to music; if you have musical likes and dislikes; if you can recognize a voice on the phone before they say who they are (and maybe even detect whether the person is smiling as they talk); if you use music to cheer yourself up, get going in the morning, relax or help you work through anger or sadness … then you are musical. You could follow Bethan's lead and take further musical steps. For instance, why not:

- join a local fun choir
- sing more – why not try one of the songs listed in Chapter 8?
- join a drumming group
- join a dance class
- help with a music club for children
- explore musical apps and software
- make up a verse for a song you like
- teach yourself how to play the ukulele from a book or from the internet
- try going to a different kind of gig or concert and reflect on what you hear.

Figure 2.4 Go to an unfamiliar kind of music event

Bergman, B. (2008). *A Small Group Playing Great Music.* Available at: https://commons.wikimedia. org/wiki/File%3ADenton_Arts_and_Jazz_Festival_-_A_Small_Group.jpg (Downloaded 23 December 2016). Attribution: By Brian Bergman from Humidville (Fort Worth), Texas, USA (A Small Group Playing Great Music) [CC BY 2.0 (http://creativecommons.org/licenses/by/2.0)], via Wikimedia Commons

Ultimately the most 'influential people' should of course be the children. They can learn well in music in lots of ways, not at all dependent on teachers being highly skilled performers. Hennessy (2000) makes an important point: 'A greater focus on children's music-making ... rather than the teacher's also helped to make students less anxious about their own skills' (p. 192). Swanwick (2008) also directs attention away from the teacher to the children: 'The good-enough music teacher is able to facilitate students' immersion in this environment of the symbolic world and promote the growth of their musical autonomy' (p. 12).

Figure 2.5 The focus is on the children's musicality, not the teacher's

Pause for thought

Consider the fact that across much of the world and through much of history, people have not been taught music, they have just learnt it. How?

You might be interested in investigating theories of informal learning such as those discussed by Lave and Wenger (1991) and Rogoff (2012). They are mentioned in the next chapter.

Figure 2.6 Teacher modelling behaviour and positivity while teaching a song

In summary, gaining the confidence to teach primary music seems to be helped by:

- self-identifying, in however modest a way, as 'musical' – that is, as feeling entitled to belong to the world of people who enjoy having music in their lives
- understanding, through observation, experience or reading books like this one, that primary curriculum music can be taught effectively by non-specialist teachers because the subject knowledge involved can be acquired just as for other subjects – it is not necessary to be a skilled player or performer
- realizing that the focus is on the children, not the teacher
- making a conscious commitment to have a go and taking it from there.

How can teachers contribute positively to children's enjoyment of music?

In subsequent chapters there is a lot of practical advice on this. Here I would like to emphasize the central importance of the teacher's attitude.

Let me give a personal example.

CASE STUDY

In my first year of primary teaching, the subject I felt least confident about was physical education, particularly gymnastics. I had visions of children falling from high bars and breaking bones, or being uncontrollably wild in the vast unstructured space of the school hall. I was fortunate that the adviser who visited me that first year was a physical education specialist. He offered to teach a lesson while I observed, in my own school hall with my own class.

He arranged the large apparatus before the lesson. (Dust had to be wiped from some of it because I was not the only teacher lacking the confidence to make use of it.) His behaviour management was firm. The children were to sit without touching even a mat while he gave his instructions. There was to be no talking at all during the lesson, as personal concentration was needed. Anyone who talked would have to sit out for two minutes. If he said 'Stop' children were to do so immediately, making themselves safe where they were. Their challenge was to invent and refine interesting ways to move between pieces of apparatus. If another child was in the way of travel, this was not a problem but an opportunity to be creative, to find a new route, a new move.

That was it. The children were clear about the challenge and the rules. The rest of the lesson was over to them and they loved it, working very hard and sensibly. The adviser watched, moving about the space without interrupting. Only once or twice did any child have to take a two-minute timeout, as they quickly realized he meant what he said. He used quiet questions that opened individual children's minds to possibilities. 'How else could you move from here to there?' 'Which part of your body could take your weight at this point?' Once or twice he said 'Stop', praised the children's response, then asked them to sit in a space while he invited individual children to share what they had been doing. Through giving constructive feedback on their contributions he highlighted what he wanted to see more of: controlled movements, variety in the modes of travel, interesting routes. He never stopped the class for long.

What I experienced in that short time completely transformed my attitude. The lesson was exciting, not scary. I wished I was one of the children! I learnt a number of things, all of which are equally applicable to teaching primary music and compatible with OFSTED (2009b) guidance about how to do it effectively:

- the children should be the ones working hard
- the teacher's job is to enable learning to happen by giving a clear framework, resources and purpose – and then to stand back
- children appreciate a teacher who is strict *for* them so that they are in a predictable environment and clear about what they can and cannot do
- the teacher needs to know the curriculum – the adviser's facilitating questions were all designed to extend children's learning along curricular lines

- the teacher never loses control of the class, because of the clear, shared, enforced expectations
- the learning challenge is inclusive: each child can approach it in his or her own individual way
- we often underestimate children's abilities because we limit what they can do
- there is no one 'right answer': responses are evaluated in the light of the challenge, and used as starting points to extend learning further.

The adviser occasionally modelled a simple move to focus children's thinking on controlling their speed, direction of travel and economy of movement. But I do not remember him ever climbing a rope or bar himself. Yet the children did, assisted by specific coaching advice from him such as, 'trap the rope between your feet, one on top of the other' and 'three of your four limbs need to be holding on while the fourth is moving to a new position'. It is the same when teaching music: the teacher does not have to be a show-off, but an attentive coach and facilitator. The specific coaching points, part of your subject knowledge, can be assimilated over time, as you gain experience.

After watching that lesson, physical education became one of my favourite subjects to teach. It was not because I had suddenly increased my own physical skills: it was about a change of attitude linked to a powerful lesson in pedagogy. In fact the experience improved my teaching across the curriculum.

Learning is an active process. You have to do it for yourself. No one can do children's learning for them, only arrange things so that if children are engaged, learning is likely. Effective teachers minimize 'teaching by telling' because children are passive during such teaching. Instead they maximize the amount of time children are actively doing, talking, thinking and wondering, using a range of pedagogic strategies (expanded from a list by Sewell 2015, p. 17), including

- instructing
- explaining
- questioning
- using correct terminology
- BUT keeping teacher-talk to a minimum
- demonstrating
- modelling
- using gesture, movement, positioning
- coaching
- facilitating
- eliciting
- observing, actively listening and sensing, that is, noticing
- assessing and evaluating

- prompting
- stepping back, allowing time and space
- encouraging
- enthusing about the subject
- reflecting
- sharing expectations
- believing in children's potential
- challenging
- joining in, working alongside
- sharing the learning journey – showing that they are learners too.

Pause for thought

Which of the teaching strategies above did the adviser use in the lesson I observed?

Pause for thought

Which of the strategies could be useful when teaching primary music?

Pause for thought

Which is more important to teaching primary music: being a great teacher or being a great musician?

All children deserve a vibrant primary music education. Non-specialist class teachers definitely have the capacity to provide this for their pupils. A head teacher I used to work with would say, 'Be part of the solution, not part of the problem'. Believe that you can make a difference by taking one small music teaching step at a time and your pupils' enthusiastic responses will give you the courage to continue.

The particular teaching method is nowhere near so important as our perception of what music is and what it does. Running alongside any system or way of working will be the ultimate question 'Is this really musical? Is there a feeling for expressive character and a sense of structure in what is done or said?' To watch an effective music teacher at work (rather than a 'trainer' or 'instructor') is to observe this strong sense of musical intention linked to educational purposes.

(Swanwick 2012, p. 45)

Summary

The current National Curriculum for Primary Music is predominantly process-oriented though there is also factual knowledge to be learnt, just as with other curricular areas.

It is useful to know that, in addition to your curriculum class music lessons, children in Key Stage 2 are entitled to some free instrumental tuition, usually given to a class at a time for a term or more by a specialist teacher. The local Music Education Hub will help schools to organize this. The Hub is also responsible for ensuring there are progression routes available for children who want to continue to learn. Learning an instrument should complement good curricular music teaching, not replace it.

Inspection evidence shows that not all primary school children are receiving a good music education, because many teachers hesitate to work *in* music, preferring to teach *about* music. This is like trying to teach French without any French being spoken in the classroom.

Many primary teachers lack confidence in teaching curricular music. However, this situation is in fact easy to improve. The most important ingredient in moving forward is the courage to have a go, aware that class teachers do not have to be skilled singers or players to provide high-quality music education for their pupils. After all, the focus is on the *children's* musical development.

Recommended reading

Arts Council England (no date). *Music Education Hubs.* Available at: http://www.artscouncil. org.uk/music-education/music-education-hubs (Accessed 21 December 2016).

Daubney, A. and Mackrill, D. (2015). 'Planning music in the national curriculum'. in Sewell, K. (ed.) *Planning the Primary National Curriculum: A Complete Guide for Trainees and Teachers.* Exeter: Learning Matters.

Department for Education & Department for Culture, Media and Sport (2011). *The Importance of Music: A National Plan for Music Education.* Available at: https://www. gov.uk/government/uploads/system/uploads/attachment_data/file/180973/DFE-00086-2011.pdf (Accessed 19 December 2016).

Henley, D. (2011). *Music Education in England.* Department for Education: Department for Culture, Media and Sport. Available at: http://publications.education.gov.uk/. (Accessed 19 December 2016).

Henley, J. (2016). 'How musical are primary generalist student teachers?'. *Music Education Research.* pp. 1–15 doi: 10.1080/14613808.2016.1204278.

Hennessy, S. (2000). 'Overcoming the red-feeling: The development of confidence to teach music in primary school amongst student teachers'. *British Journal of Music Education,* 17(2),pp. 183–96.

Kolb, D. A. (1984). *Experiential Learning: Experience as the Source of Learning and Development.* New Jersey: Prentice-Hall.

Lamont, A., Daubney, A. and Spruce, G. (2012) 'Singing in primary schools: Case studies of good practice in whole class vocal tuition'. *British Journal of Music Education*, 29(2), pp. 251–68.

Lave, J. and Wenger, E. (1991). *Situated Learning: Legitimate Peripheral Participation*. Cambridge: Cambridge University Press.

Office for Standards in Education, Children's Services and Skills (2009b). *Making More of Music: Improving the Quality of Music Teaching in Primary Schools*. Available at: http://webarchive.nationalarchives.gov.uk/20141124154759/http://www.ofsted.gov. uk/resources/making-more-of-music-improving-quality-of-music-teaching-primary (Accessed 5 May 2017).

Office for Standards in Education, Children's Services and Skills (2012a). *Music in Schools: Wider Still, and Wider*. Available at: https://www.gov.uk/government/publications/music-in-schools (Accessed 25 April 2016).

Rogoff, B. (2012). 'Fostering a new approach to understanding: Learning through intent community participation'. *Learning Landscapes*, 5(2), pp. 45–53.

Schön, D. A. (1991). *The Reflective Practitioner: How Professionals Think in Action*. Aldershot: Avebury.

Sing Up (2016). *Sing Up*. https://www.singup.org/ (Accessed 9 July 2016).

Swanwick, K. (2012). *Teaching Music Musically*. Abingdon: Routledge.

Chapter 3
Music as an Irresistible Activity

Chapter objectives

- to advocate for children's entitlement to irresistible music
- to outline two ways in which music is irresistible
- to explore the irresistibility of joining *in* music
- to explore children's curiosity *about* music
- to explore some engaging and manageable teaching strategies
- to tempt you into teaching music

Introduction

Children are born with sophisticated hearing (Trehub 2006) and are naturally interested in and engaged by music. Perhaps you have seen how babies and very young children respond to music, from tiny dancers (MashupZone 2015) to just-verbal rappers (ukroyalpriesthood 2012) and budding performers (uke3453 2009). Music continues to engage children as they grow. Even those who have limited or no verbal language can often respond to and enjoy music (JessiesFund 2014). Intuitively we know that music is important in children's lives. For example, on a child's birthday it is likely to be a key ingredient in the celebrations, with everyone singing 'Happy Birthday' and using music for games like musical chairs, pass the parcel and musical statues, or for a home-grown disco. Music has an irresistible draw and children want to join in.

It is also irresistible because it invites curiosity. Like other aspects of children's surroundings, sounds and music demand exploration, experimentation and enquiry. Children have no inhibitions about immersing themselves in their sonic worlds and will ask a thousand questions to learn more about music. As teachers we do not have to know all the answers, we just need to demonstrate a positive attitude to the questions and to show children how they can discover answers for themselves. Shulman coined the term PCK for the specific knowledge and expertise needed by a teacher within a given subject or discipline (Shulman 1987). Demonstrating a positive attitude is part of your PCK in music.

Half a century ago Bruner wrote about 'the natural energies that sustain spontaneous learning', among which he included both the 'aspiration to emulate a model' and 'curiosity' (Bruner 1966, p. 127). This chapter focuses on these two 'natural energies' of children: the irresistible urge to join *in* music and the curiosity to find out *about* music – and gives you the PCK to support them. Later chapters will explore the pleasures of making music for real purposes, mastering musical skills and being creative with sounds. But first a question.

Why doesn't every adult find music irresistible?

Paradoxically, while music is naturally irresistible for children, a lot of primary teachers find it eminently resistible, as mentioned in the previous chapter. A person's feelings about music – and perhaps especially singing – are rather like their own body image. Self-consciousness can arise in a similar way in both cases. Our culture, including the media, strongly affects how comfortable or uncomfortable we feel about our bodies. We are forced to compare ourselves to images of perfection every day. If we are lucky we will have had a lot of affirmation along the way from important people in our lives. But if just one person makes a tactless expression, gesture or remark, this negative impact can last for years. It is the same with singing and with the self-perception of our musicality generally. The media continually feeds us with examples of perfect music and perfect musicians, against which our own efforts may not measure up well. One ill-judged comment can exile us from feeling we can participate in our own musical culture for a lifetime (Welch 2006). Positive musical self-images depend in large part on the verbal and non-verbal 'messages' we receive from the significant people in our lives as we grow up.

Very young children are blissfully unaware of all this (Austin, Renwick and McPherson 2006, pp. 221 and 223), as they have not yet started to compare themselves with others. However, by Key Stage 2 children will certainly have begun to become self-conscious. We owe it to our pupils to keep the positive, affirmative 'messages' flowing throughout their time in primary school so that we help them feel good about themselves musically, even if we ourselves do not have much musical confidence. We need to believe that children's music is fine and healthy on its own terms, rather than fretting about what it is not. Keep in mind that in primary music we are interested in the inclusive, accessible, 'everyday' kinds of music-making that will nurture a lifelong love of music for everyone and keep options open for those children who may wish to take their musicianship further (Pitts 2016).

We also need to believe – and convey to our pupils – that musicality can and does develop, because children may have come to think that their current ability is fixed for life and they may need support to embrace a 'growth mindset' (Dweck

Figure 3.1 Enjoying music without feeling self-conscious

2016). I hope this chapter will help you to ensure that your pupils' musical curiosity and engagement flourishes and that nothing is done to curb their enthusiasm for music-making or their thirst to find out more. Perhaps you too will start to find music irresistible.

We turn now to two irresistible aspects of music – the urge to join *in* music and the curiosity to find out *about* music. First each one will be introduced and then we will focus on how to harness these two aspects in our teaching.

Why is joining in collective music-making irresistible?

There is something deep and very human about collective, synchronized, musical engagement. No one really knows what it is 'for' but the act of making music together seems to go back a long way. One theory is that music is a sonic extension of body language and that synchronizing this in a communal activity leads to greater mutual trust, the spread of a shared positive emotional state, a blurring of the boundaries of self, an increase in feeling part of a collective or joint unit and a heightened willingness to cooperate (Mithen 2006, pp. 208–17). Schools, like many other institutions, utilize this uniquely human phenomenon to help bond people together through shared singing, so that everyone feels they belong.

> ## Pause for thought
>
> Can you think of any other examples where synchronized music-making is used to increase the positive feeling and conviction of group identity?

In Chapter 1 the distinction between music-making *for* people and *with* people was mentioned. Children generally find making music *with* people irresistible. They badly want to join in. This communal music-making is the opposite of elite: it is for everyone. It very often involves movement of some kind and it feels good to take part. Children smile and laugh, enjoying being part of the collective. There's a strong feeling of belonging. (It's not just children – think of times that music has brought you together with others in this unspoken way.) Later in the chapter there is guidance about how to start collective music-making in your class.

When an entire group makes music together, it often induces feelings of awe and wonder too. There is something special about producing one musical creation together. The whole feels more than the sum of its parts and there is great satisfaction for each person in having contributed to something that no single individual could have created alone. Sometimes it is good to record the occasion, though often the 'product' is not so important (and may not be of high quality when taken out of context). You may well find that applause by the participants arises naturally at the end of the music-making, reflecting their pleasure. If you have not yet experienced the uplifting phenomenon of collective synchronizing, I would encourage you to join an informal choir, drumming group or something similar – good things will happen!

We will now introduce the idea that children's curiosity *about* music is another way to make it irresistible for them, after which we will focus on teaching strategies that promote both joining in and curiosity.

What is curiosity and how does it help make music irresistible?

> ### SCENARIO A
>
> Imagine a deserted room containing a xylophone (instrument with wooden notes, played with beaters), a keyboard, a tambourine, a ukulele (small four-stringed guitar-like instrument), etc. If they were allowed into this room, children would explore the instruments, driven by their natural curiosity. What is the loudest sound that the tambourine can make? How many notes can they press at once on the keyboard? What does the note on each end of the xylophone sound like? How does the ukulele work?

Children love to find out *about* music and sounds. In the scenario above, the exploring would tend to be about testing the limits of the instruments to begin with, but quite soon it would be followed by more musical exploration, savouring the sounds themselves.

I remember a science adviser encouraging me to 'wow children with resources' and this advice works right across the curriculum, including primary music. Part of music's irresistibility is the wow factor of being able to handle, use and play a whole variety of sound-makers. 'Playing and exploring', where 'children investigate and experience things, and "have a go"', is one of the three characteristics of effective learning central to the Early Years Foundation Stage framework (Department for Education 2014, p. 9). It remains important through the primary years too. It is sometimes called 'discovery learning' or 'guided discovery' and it reflects children's natural curiosity: their desire to explore their world, to enquire about everything, to know and understand. It is important, therefore, to provide plenty of opportunities for

Figure 3.2 Have your pupils been to a live music event of any sort?

first-hand experience of sounds, sound-makers and music. How many of your pupils have been to a live music event of some sort? What was it? What did they make of it? Who did they go with? Can you organize live music experiences for your class? Who could play? Where? For what occasion?

As soon as they have acquired sufficient language, children start enquiring verbally about every possible thing, again driven by their curiosity. You will recognize this if you have ever spent time with a three- or four-year-old child wielding the word 'why'! Asking questions is another characteristic of effective learning throughout the primary phase, and most children have a seemingly insatiable appetite for facts and information. Children have a driving need to make sense of their worlds and they supplement first-hand experience with the 'second-hand' knowledge gained by asking questions to gain information from others. Their genuine questions are valuable and important, offering teachers golden opportunities to demonstrate ways of finding answers, which is a vital lifelong skill. Through asking and answering questions, children are accumulating *declarative* musical knowledge (i.e. knowledge *about* music that can be expressed in words) which should include knowledge about sounds, instruments, music, musicians and composers.

Later in the chapter there are numerous suggestions for harnessing children's curiosity, including detailed definitions of key musical terminology. As always, the emphasis should be on working in and with sound as much as possible, with visual and verbal material always in the service of the sonic.

How can teachers make primary music irresistible?

Effective teachers of primary music harness the irresistibility of 'joining *in*' and of 'finding out *about*' music. What pedagogic strategies can be used?

'Joining in' as a pedagogic approach

'Joining in' as a mechanism for learning has similarities with the strategy of 'immersion' in language teaching (Johnson and Swain 1997). More specifically, it can perhaps be viewed as an example of Rogoff's 'intent community participation' (Rogoff et al. 2003; Rogoff 2012) where children 'observe and listen with intent concentration and initiative, and their collaborative participation is expected when they are ready' (Rogoff et al. 2003, p. 176). Rogoff's ideas build on notions of 'situated learning' (Lave and Wenger 1991) which envisage newcomers to a situation engaging in 'legitimate peripheral participation', gradually becoming more expert until they can engage in it fully. Situated learning in turn grew out of thinking about 'apprenticeship' models of learning and social learning in general. For example, Bandura (1977a) said:

> Learning would be exceedingly laborious, not to mention hazardous, if people had to rely solely on the effects of their own actions to inform them what to do. Fortunately, most human behavior is learned observationally through modeling: from observing others one forms an idea of how new behaviors are performed, and on later occasions this coded information serves as a guide for action. (Bandura 1977a, p. 22)

As a practical subject, much of music is learnt by observing and imitating models of various kinds.

The apprenticeship model is at the root of Elliott and Silverman's proposed 'reflective musical practicum' (Elliott and Silverman 2015, p. 424) with its emphasis on making music education as 'real' as possible. They advocate working *in* music, involving 'thinking-in-action', that is, deploying and developing skills and understandings in the course of meaningful musical projects rather than learning *about* music as a step-by-step linear syllabus.

While these ideas are all relevant, none quite captures the particular irresistibility of the co-creation of musical sound that happens when a whole group of people joins in singing or playing together. There appears to be no definitive pedagogic term for this. Rather than invent one, I am going to continue to call it 'joining in', stipulating that it must include everyone in the group, making music in a synchronized fashion as a single 'unit' or collective. I strongly advocate its use as a pedagogic tool in primary music. The learning happens within each child constructively, as they first listen and watch, then gradually join in, with successively closer and closer approximations to what others are doing.

When using this approach the teacher (or someone – see below) needs to model how they wish to see the children joining in, but they do not have to be an exemplary musical model. In fact children appreciate seeing that their teacher is willing to have a go and to enjoy being part of the collective – the teacher is modelling learning characteristics and values as well as basic musical participation.

Teachers can instigate collective, synchronous music-making by encouraging everyone in the class together to:

- sing and/or move as they listen to a recorded song or piece of instrumental music
- chant (speak rhythmically, to a beat) – anything can be 'rapped' in this way: your own made-up words; or poems written for speaking aloud, such as those from Quentin Blake's book of poems for young children, 'All Join In' (Blake 1992); or something from the Sing Up resource bank such as 'Grandma Rap' or 'Who Stole the Cookies from the Cookie Jar?' (Sing Up 2016)
- sing a song
- tap, clap or stomp a rhythm pattern

- play a rhythmic pattern on any instrument
- clap, move or sing along – with permission – to music played by visiting musicians
- join in when a child leads a song, chant or rhythm

Joining in is a good way to familiarize children with new musical material and to give them time to practise and consolidate new learning. It is important to do plenty of it, to allow children to assimilate a solid sense of beat and rhythm and to develop their ability to sing in tune, all of which take time and experience.

It is also, by its very nature, a powerful and inclusive way of promoting class cohesion and community: 'Communal music-making is actively creating, rather than merely reflecting, that pleasing sense of unity' (McNeill 1995, quoted in Mithen 2006, p. 208). Similar benefits have also been reported in relation to dance: 'The matching of rhythmic behaviour between individuals (synchrony) increases cooperation' (Reddish, Fischer and Bulbulia 2013, abstract).

Figure 3.3 It feels good to join in with a synchronous musical activity

COLLECTIVE SYCHRONIZING

Recent research is beginning to shed more light on the mysterious and potent force of collective synchronizing – joining in – in both music and movement. It appears that it is an effective way of binding a group of people together and developing a deep sense of affiliation and trust. Such a 'collective' is well placed to accomplish 'joint action' – action so tightly coordinated that it is as if carried out by a single organism (Phillips-Silver and Keller 2012). 'Joint action' is what an expert team of people does in sport, or a restaurant kitchen, or a hospital operating theatre: each member of the team anticipates what is about to happen and acts in the common interest of the 'unit' or 'collective'.

If action is synchronized and rhythmic it is easier to coordinate, so it may be that dancing and making music collectively is a way that humans have evolved to develop and reinforce group identity and thereby 'joint action'. We seem to have an innate ability to 'entrain' rhythmic action to a pulse – in fact we can't help it (Phillips-Silver and Keller 2012). Have you ever realized that you were walking in step with music coming from an open window, for example?

The pleasure that musical joining in brings is known by jazz musicians as 'the groove'. Whatever the genre of music, joining in brings similar pleasure. At its height, individuals 'lose themselves' in co-creating music as part of a collective and it feels wonderful. Perhaps such activity has evolved specifically to feel good, to encourage humans to want to play their part in other collective actions.

Any song and/or action sequence to music can be the basis for joining in. Choose your own and the children's favourites and have some fun with them. Notice the pleasure that comes simply from singing and moving together – and the positive effect it can have on the group identity and 'fellowship' of your class. YouTube can be a good source of ideas. Sing Up (Sing Up 2016) is another online resource that many schools subscribe to as an excellent source of material. Each song comes with a full demonstration audio track to listen to, echo tracks where each line is presented and then your class copies it back to learn it, and backing-tracks with the music but not the voices, so you and your class can karaoke. There are also lyrics (words) for the songs for you to project on a screen (though if children learn a song or chant 'by ear' rather than 'by eye' this helps to develop their auditory memory, so consider keeping the lyrics out of sight). Sing Up includes useful teaching notes to support you as you use each piece. You can search for suitable material for children of different ages and on different topics. Some samples are also available on YouTube.

Pause for thought

Can you see your class joining in with one of these?

'Grandma Rap' (Key Stages 1 and 2)
https://www.youtube.com/watch?v=Yh-nwPZxSmY (This is a signed version that lets you hear the rap. If you are not signing, make up other suitable actions, including bigger movements in the middle section.)

'Hey Mr. Miller' (Key Stage 2)

https://www.youtube.com/watch?v=MKmj3VUkuUY (Again this is a signed version. You can see from the later part of the video how the song could be developed into a round, where different singers start at different times and it all fits together. However, you do not have to take it that far – it's a jazzy song anyway.)

'Raise My Voice' (Key Stage 2)

https://www.youtube.com/watch?v=szmKrOu0V4w

'Boom Chicka Boom' (Key Stages 1 and 2)

https://www.youtube.com/watch?v=3fjdEEl0GjQ (This version is not from Sing Up. It comes from America. As well as making up characters, verses could simply be 'one more time … lower' or 'one more time … quieter', etc.)

It is vital to make sure that every pupil can participate (Jellison 2006), since feelings of exclusion and exile could be strong if any child is inadvertently left out of what should be a collective activity. Take into account special educational needs and disabilities among your pupils and consider how to enable each child to access collective and synchronous musical experiences in an appropriate way. Seek guidance from those in school with responsibility and expertise as needed. Some suggestions are given here, but each circumstance needs individual consideration:

ENSURING INCLUSION

Possible issues:	Possible solutions:
An abundance of sound may induce anxiety	Give advance warning of the activity
	Keep the overall dynamic fairly low
	Use sound-reducing ear defenders
The activity may cause over-exuberance	Tactically ignore
	Shuffle children to engineer more conducive neighbours (but do this subtly!)
	Position adult near child
	General word to class about the line between 'enjoying' and 'being silly' and the consequences of crossing the line
Hearing difficulties	Ensure there is at least some synchronous movement that can be seen
Mobility difficulties	Choose synchronized movements that can be managed by everyone
	Focus on the timing of movements rather than their 'sameness'
	Find ways to amplify small movements, for example, using a torch beam, springy rod, magic wand – be inventive
	Ensure that child has a partner who physically interprets their limited movements
Vocal difficulties	Provide another means of making sound – investigate 'Bebot' app (Normalware 2008) for example, for its simplicity of use (see later in chapter)

Collective musical activities should be a staple component of the culture of your class community. Challenge yourself to establish this gradually and you will soon become more comfortable with including such activities in the regular routine of classroom practice, in music lessons or wherever they fit in the timetable. Can you all do something collective and synchronous while changing for a PE lesson? Tidying up? Celebrating a child's birthday? Straight after break? Just before home-time? As a class reward? Once you have established it in this way, you can also start to use collective synchronized work as one strategy to support the development and progression of musical skills. This is discussed in Chapter 5.

Harnessing children's curiosity: Some useful strategies

Some activities (like the first scenario in this chapter) work best with just a few children at a time. With a whole class, guided discovery should still be a key teaching strategy, but there is the option of managing it with more teacher control:

SCENARIO B

Children and teacher form a large circle. The teacher first establishes a 'stop' signal: a hand held in the air or some other clear visual signal, since sound signals have to compete with other sounds being made by the children. The children practise being still and quiet when they see the signal.

Then the teacher poses a question to stimulate exploration. 'What is the loudest sound you can make using just your hands?' After a short while, the stop signal is deployed. The children's findings can then be shared in various ways, for instance:

- All make a single hand-sound together after the teacher counts '1, 2, 3 ...'
- One child makes a single hand-sound when the teacher gestures to him or her
- 'Mexican Wave': each child makes a single hand-sound after their neighbour's sound

Now another question followed by similar activity. Here are some ideas:

'What is the quietest sound you can make using just your hands?'

'What is the shortest sound you can make?'

'Can you make a sound that goes on and on for as long as you want it to?'

'Can you make three/four/five sounds each louder than the last?'

Figure 3.4 Guided exploration of hand sounds

After such exploration, the findings should be put to a real musical purpose. For instance, children could work in pairs to develop rhythmic patterns of different hand sounds that could then be used to accompany another group of children singing a song. Or the whole class could create a short piece called 'Rainstorm' made from a 'collage' of hand sounds. See Chapter 4 for more on musical purposes.

Similar activities can be carried out with other sound-makers and instruments, such as:

- **untuned** (or unpitched) **instruments**

  Many typical classroom instruments are untuned, meaning that you cannot play a tune on them. Drums, tambourines, shakers and triangles are examples of untuned instruments.

Figure 3.5 A selection of untuned instruments

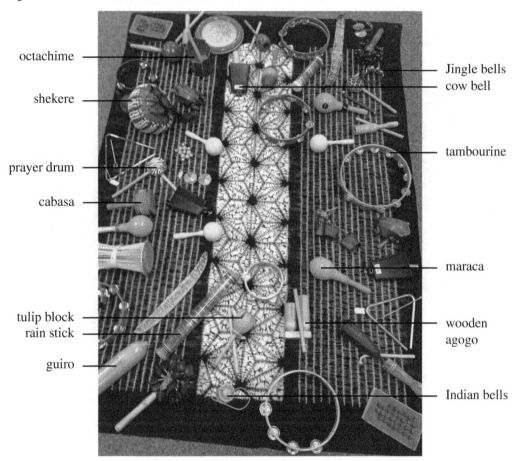

- **tuned** (or pitched) **instruments**

  You can play notes of different pitches on tuned instruments, so you can play tunes. Xylophones, metallophones, pianos, keyboards, steel pans and sets of hand bells are all tuned.

Figure 3.6 a & b A selection of tuned instruments – metallophones, xylophones and steel pans

- **body and voice**

  As well as a wide range of vocal and non-vocal mouth sounds, you can stamp, slide your foot, slap your thigh, pat your chest, clap, click your fingers, rub your hand on your sleeve ...

Figure 3.7 a, b & c More subtle ways of 'clapping' that make progressively quieter sounds

Figure 3.8 A long, quiet sound can be made by rubbing the hands over each other palm-to-palm

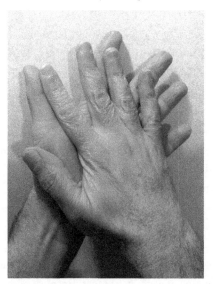

- **found sounds**

  Keep your ears open for all sorts of sounds around, such as rustling paper, a knife chopping onions, a dripping tap, footsteps, car sounds, machine sounds, a curtain swishing, a ball bouncing …

All of the examples of sound-makers given above are **acoustic**, meaning that some part physically moves – vibrates – to make the sound. Prove that a drum-head vibrates when struck, by scattering rice or salt on it!

- **digital/electric** sound-makers are also very useful for class music. These produce sound electronically, then use a speaker to convert the signal to an acoustic sound so that our ears can hear it. Useful sound-makers for primary music include

  ○ electric guitars and other electric instruments

  ○ programmes and apps, such as these simple-to-use apps for ipads:

    ▪ 'Singing Fingers' (Rosenbaum and Silver, http://singingfingers.com/, no date)

    ▪ 'Bebot' (Normalware 2008)

    ▪ 'LoopsequeKids' (Casual Underground, no date)

    ▪ 'Isle of Tune' (Happylander/Abstract Alien, no date)

    ▪ 'GarageBand' (Apple Inc. 2016).

Electronic recording devices are also very useful for recording interesting found sounds, that is, 'sampling', as well as for recording musical segments, with the possibility of looping and layering the sounds.

Pause for thought

Think about the resources available in a school you know, and the extent to which they invite children's curiosity:

Where are the musical instruments kept?

Are they easy to access and return?

Are they inviting?

Does it appear that they are valued?

Do the children have access to digital devices or computers with speakers, on which they could work sonically?

What are the logistical considerations?

It is essential that instruments are properly kept and displayed. One school I worked in had their instruments in the central corridor, displayed on shelves, well-lit and labelled with named photos of each instrument. Because of this, everyone understood that the instruments were important. Children were also able to fetch and return them effectively. Crucially, they looked fantastic – and tantalizing. Sometimes, as a reward, a child or a small group was allowed to use them independently at break time. Again, this communicates the value of music.

Figure 3.9 Store and display instruments thoughtfully

Figure 3.10 Teach children to use instruments with care and respect

Similarly, messages about valuing and caring for instruments can be conveyed when using them in whole-class work. Since this type of work is often done with children positioned in a large circle, an effective technique is to lay a colourful drape on the floor in the middle with the instruments for the lesson displayed on the drape. They are the centre of attention. However, they are also out of arm's reach, until the teacher invites children to come forward and choose one.

Another powerful way to 'wow' the children is to let them experience music being played live. Seize every opportunity. If your pupils are younger they will be in awe of the older children singing, dancing and playing in school assemblies. Older children love to see music performed by secondary school pupils. All ages find good live music compelling, whatever the genre (type of music). Look out for chances to invite performers into school or to visit venues locally. Widen children's musical horizons with live music wherever possible. Your job is not to know everything about it yourself, but to make sure your children have these opportunities. By all means also show children videos of live performances, though you should be aware that this is not the same as being involved in the unique musical occasion of a live event.

Your children may even be able to work in collaboration with other musicians. Orchestras and opera companies sometimes offer such opportunities to primary schools. Or get involved in an inter-school singing project led by experts.

An important strategy for the teacher is to make sure the correct terminology is used to talk about sounds and music, just as one would do in English, mathematics, etc. Here is a glossary of useful terminology for sounds. Refer to it frequently, so that you gradually teach yourself and become comfortable with the musical ideas.

USEFUL TERMINOLOGY WHEN TALKING ABOUT SOUNDS

(The seven <u>underlined</u> words are the 'inter-related dimensions of music' mentioned in the National Curriculum: see also Chapter 1.)

Describing single sounds:

<u>pitch</u> = How **high** or **low** a sound is. A mouse makes high-pitched sounds whereas a lion's growl has a low pitch. A single sound made of a single pitch is a musical **note.**

(In Western music, notes are given the seven letter names from A to G. If you think of a piano keyboard, it obviously has more than seven notes. So the same letter names are used over and over again, resulting in low Cs and high Cs, etc. A useful landmark on a piano is middle C: http://www.wikihow.com/Play-Middle-C-on-the-Piano)

<u>duration</u> = How **long** a sound lasts. A clap is a **short** sound whereas a hum lasts longer.

<u>dynamic</u> = How **loud** or **quiet** a sound is. (Probably better to use the word 'quiet' than 'soft' because 'soft' is related also to tactile experience and suggests a certain muffled type of sound as well as a certain dynamic.)

<u>timbre</u> (<u>pronounced 'tambr' as it is a French word)</u> = The quality, 'colour' or character of a sound. You could probably tell whether a trumpet or a violin was playing a tune even if you couldn't see the instruments, because of their different timbres. Descriptive words are used to describe the timbre of sounds, such as 'sharp', 'bright', 'dull', 'mellow', 'round', 'muffled' and any other everyday words that help to portray the sounds.

Describing two or more sounds:

<u>rhythm</u> = A **sequence** of sounds of particular **durations**. An example of a rhythm would be 'long – long – short-short – long'. Make the word 'long' last longer than the word 'short' when you say this aloud. Or model the rhythm using other words, like 'tea, tea, coffee, tea' or 'chair, chair, table, chair'. If you repeat the same sequence over and over you get a **rhythm pattern.** Try tapping out the rhythm above. Do the words help you to keep it in mind?

Think of a song you know. When you clap out the words, you are clapping the rhythm.

<u>melody</u> or **tune** = A sequence of musical notes of particular **pitches.** Think of a song you know. When you hum the song, you are humming its melody.

interval = How many notes apart in pitch two notes are. Count the lower-pitched of the two notes as '1' when describing intervals. As an example, the interval between middle C and the G above it is called a 'fifth', because if you count from C then C = 1, D = 2, E = 3, F = 4 and G = 5. At the beginning of the song 'Happy Birthday To You', the two notes of the word 'birthday' have an interval of a 'second'. The interval between middle C and the next C is an 'octave' which is a special musical word for an eight-note interval. In the third line of the birthday song, there is an octave jump in pitch between the words 'happy' and 'birthday'.

texture = How many sounds are happening at once. If just one sound is occurring at any moment, the texture is described as **thin**. If many sounds are happening simultaneously, the texture is **thick.** Is **silence** the ultimate thin texture?

harmony = The effect of putting together two or more notes of different pitches at the same time. If two people sing 'in harmony' this is what they are doing. One person sings one tune, the other sings a different tune at the same time. An easy way to start singing in harmony is to sing a **round**, like 'London's Burning' or 'Frere Jacques' (see Chapter 4).

chord = Clusters of two or more simultaneous notes are called chords.

A chord is named according to its most important note, using the note-names A, B, C, D, E, F and G. You will often see these written above the lyrics (words) of a song. The letter-name suggests a note or chord that would sound good at that point in the song. Children can play those notes on tuned instruments at suitable moments in the song and make short rhythms using those single pitches. Real and virtual guitars and ukuleles can play chords with the same names.

The most basic 'everyday' chords contain three notes: the root note (e.g. C), another note in an interval of a third above that (E) and another note a fifth above the root note (G). They are called major chords. So C, E and G make the chord of C major. The chord of F major would contain F, A and C. The chord of G major contains G, B and D.

If you get interested in chords, you can explore how to change these **major** chords to **minor**, or to add extra notes to the chords to give them different 'flavours'.

Describing complete pieces of music:

structure = The way that sounds of different dimensions and qualities are organized together into whole pieces. The structure may or may not contain rhythm patterns, melodies and harmonies including chords. The texture may vary from one part to another. There may be things that repeat within the structure. Whole sections of the structure may repeat, either as identical copies or with variations. Creating such a musical structure is called **composing** and the resulting structure can be called a **composition.**

The structure of a 'Rainstorm' might be a quiet beginning, increasing in dynamic and texture in the middle, with lower-pitched sounds then too, before quietening and thinning at the end. In contrast, many songs have a 'verse-chorus' structure built from a number of discrete sections, rather like a multi-decker sandwich.

beat = the regular **pulse** of much music. To understand how beat and rhythm are two different things, think of 'One potato, two potato, three potato, four'. The words give the rhythm but the foot-tapping beats are only at 'one … two … three … four'. Try it!

Some music is non-rhythmic and has no beat. Think for example of some atmospheric film music, or music for meditation, that just seems to float in time without any regular pulse.

tempo = How **slowly** or **fast** a piece of music goes. Sometimes this is expressed as a number of beats per minute.

metre or **measure** or **bar** = the 'beat-feel' or the 'count' of the music. A lot of music has 'feel' or a 'count' of four. The way to test it is to try counting along with the pulse of the music: 'One, two, three, four, one, two, three, four …'. If that fits, then the music is 'in a metre of four'. Sometimes this is described as 'having four beats in a bar' or as being a 'four-beat measure'.

Some music has a feel of three, as in a waltz. Try counting 'One, two, three' over and over to 'Happy Birthday to You', starting on the word 'Birth'. Other metres also exist. Try counting to Dave Brubeck's 'Take Five', for example – there is a clue in the title!

strong beat or **down beat** = Beat number one of the metre is the strong beat. It's the beat you want to nod your head to. Conductors of choirs and orchestras bring their stick down on that first beat.

Instruments and sounds can be included in short activities to help secure understanding of this terminology.

SUGGESTIONS

Hide a small object somewhere in a room. Instead of saying 'warmer, colder' to guide the child chosen to find the object, use **pitch**: the closer the child gets, the **higher** the hum made by the rest of the class. Or do it with **tempo**: the closer the child gets, the **faster** the clapping from the class. Or use **dynamics**: the closer the child, the **louder** the playing.

Hide a selection of sound-makers in a box. Ask the children to identify each one by listening to the sound it makes. Encourage children to use musical terminology by asking 'How did you know? Can you describe the sound?' Prompt for words relating to **pitch, timbre, dynamic** and **duration**.

Ask children to listen for the instruments when you play a short piece of recorded music. Then take suggestions. Give credit for reasoned answers about **timbre**, for example, 'I think there is a guitar because it sounds like someone is using their fingers to make sounds with strings' – even if in fact the sound came from a harp or a piano. If possible, arrange it so that you can replay the recording with video too, to see the instruments involved.

Clap the words of a well-known song. Can anyone guess the song? Remember to praise reasonable guesses which refer to **duration of notes** and **rhythm**, as they show musical discrimination. Clap the words together: this is quite a hard thing to do and takes practice.

With older children: play the first few notes of a piece of music – live or recorded. Can anyone guess the piece? How do they know? Again, give credit for good guesses that mention the **pitch** pattern of the **melody**. For instance, the first few notes of 'Twinkle Twinkle Little Star' are the same as 'Baa Baa Black Sheep'. Once the tune has been guessed, hum it through together.

Find opportunities for children to move to music, often. This is the best way to develop a feel for the **beat**. Ask them to tap their feet to the beat, or move in ways that might fit in with a current topic. Make up **rhythmic** moves and actions to go with songs as they are sung.

Try a 'Minute of Listening' (Sound and Music 2016) which is engaging for children in both Key Stages. The clips could inspire creative, cross-curricular work. Or find and play your own choice of mystery sound-clips to stimulate ideas and discussion. More rhythm and melody activity suggestions can be found in the next chapter.

Notice that in each of these activities, children are listening *for* certain dimensions of the sounds such as pitch, rhythm or timbre. It is excellent practice, in primary music, to prepare children to 'listen for' something in this way – Chapter 4 focuses on this in some detail.

There is no limit to how much learning can be driven by curiosity. With so much now available on the internet, resourceful and curious children in later Key Stage 2 could even manage to develop their own cover version of a favourite track by teaching themselves what they need to know. Chances are that they can find online:

- the lyrics for their chosen song
- an audio or video recording of the song
- perhaps a 'karaoke' backing-track version
- the names of the chords that will fit
- a guide on how to play those chords on a chosen instrument.

The teacher's role is to maintain a positive attitude and support children with their online searches. This self-driven approach to music learning is the inspiration behind an initiative called 'Musical Futures' which has been popular with music teachers in secondary schools for some time (*Musical Futures* 2015) and is based on work by Lucy Green on how rock musicians learn (Green 2008). 'Musical Bridges' is extending the approach into the later years of some primary schools, particularly as one way of easing the transition of children into secondary school.

Support children's curiosity by asking questions about their chosen music, such as:

How is this piece of music made?
What is the structure?
What instruments are used?
How is the sound produced on those instruments?
What are the main features of this music?
Are there repeats?
Are there contrasts?

In essence you are supporting children to deconstruct a piece of music to find out how it was made, just as you might deconstruct a product in a design and technology lesson.

Other questions could focus children on the effectiveness of the 'existing musical product'. For instance:

> How does that part of the music manage to make the listener feel happy/sad/calm/excited?

Harnessing children's curiosity is also an ideal way to enlarge their wider knowledge about music, musicians and composers. The National Curriculum specifies that in Key Stage 2 children should 'develop an understanding of the history of music'. This is a precursor to further work in secondary school and the emphasis in primary music should be on sparking children's interest rather than trying to cover everything comprehensively. Children might enjoy researching things like:

> When did music begin?
> What different kinds (genres) of music are there in the world?
> How did they start?
> Who are some of the most famous musicians from each genre?
> Who are some of the most highly regarded composers (inventors) of the music?
> What is the music for?
> Who takes part and why?
> What instruments are used?
> What is the music like?
> How does the music fit in with people's lives?

Classic FM (This is Global Ltd 2016) is one of many music radio stations with high-quality websites that can give you inspiration and information to support children's researches. Schools are also entitled to access 'Classical 100' (Associated Board of the Royal Schools of Music 2015). As its title implies, this is a website presenting one hundred selected pieces of classical music. There is information on each piece and it is possible to sort them by main instrument, mood, period or composer's nationality. You can also develop simple playlists. Ask children what they have noticed about the music on their video games and televisions, too: orchestras make a lot of their regular income by recording for these.

Quizzes, puzzles, challenges, missing information, competitions, card-swap games, memory games, online games, digital apps, 'If this is the answer what is the question?' activities and utilizing musical facts in other subjects can all be great ways of assimilating declarative musical knowledge. They can be prepared in advance, so teachers can gather and check the information for themselves without the pressure of being put on the spot for an instant answer. Keep in mind that this is knowledge *about* music, not a substitute for working *in* music. The knowledge should be related to practical musical activities.

Teachers and children can learn together in other ways too. For instance some schools project simple on-screen presentations with information about particular music, musicians, instruments and composers for people to view as they are settling down for school assemblies and listening to relevant music. So much the better if the presentation has been created by children in the first place.

Pause for thought

Could children use any of the following curious facts as a springboard for further work either in music lessons or elsewhere in the curriculum?

1   A famous orchestra, the London Symphony Orchestra, was booked on the *Titanic's* maiden voyage in 1912. The 100 players of the orchestra were switched on to a different ship just before the *Titanic* sailed.

2   Domenico Scarlatti was a man who composed many pieces for keyboard instruments. In 1739 he published a piece that people think was inspired by his cat, Pulcinella, walking over his keyboard from left to right.

3   Astronaut Yuri Gagarin was the first man to journey into outer space and the first human to make music there, by whistling.

Questioning is a central part of any teacher's expertise. For example:

What can you find out about that?
Why is it like that?
Who is that?
Who did that?
When was that?
How does that work?
How does that make a sound?
What else can you find out?
Where does that come from?
Why are those different from these?

The real stimulus to curiosity is to encourage children to ask their own questions. The teacher's prompts need to be questions-that-promote-questions:

What could you ask about that?
What's the first thing you want to find out about that?
What don't you know about that?
What do you think someone else might ask about that?

Explore different musical traditions such as jazz, blues, popular music, Western classical music, Indian classical music, folk music from different countries, dance music and film music. You do not need to be exhaustive in your exploration: it is more important to make a start and maintain children's enthusiasm for finding out more. Cross-curricular topics can be a good vehicle for exploring these types of questions. Children's own families and communities may be able to share at first-hand something of the genres of music important to their cultures and traditions, enriching everyone's experience. Start somewhere that interests you. Open children's ears to music that is new to them. Go on an adventure together to different places and times.

Summary

Children generally find music irresistible, unless something or someone has put them off. If you yourself have been put off music by some past experience, one of the most important things you can do is to make sure that attitude is not transmitted to your pupils. Instead, let their enthusiasm reignite yours.

Joining in with collective and synchronous musical activities such as chanting, singing, playing, moving and dancing is a deep-seated human urge with positive emotional and social outcomes. There are many ways of enabling such activities to happen, most of which do not require any particular expertise in performing on the part of the teacher but a willingness to model enthusiasm and participation. Such activities allow children to develop a sense of beat, rhythm and pitch, on which further musical development relies.

Harnessing children's curiosity about sounds, instruments, music, musicians and composers is a good way to support their learning of the more factual elements in the curriculum. As well as this declarative knowledge, curiosity can lead to increased understanding of how to select and produce sounds in different ways and how to think and talk about music. Teachers can help children develop a lifelong passion to find out more with the judicious use of questioning and by encouraging children to continue asking questions of their own.

Recommended reading

Associated Board of the Royal Schools of Music (2015). *Classical 100*. Available at: www.abrsm.org/classical100 (Accessed 14 July 2016).

Blake, Q. (1992). *All Join In*. London: Random House.

Dweck, C. (2016). *Mindset: The New Psychology of Success,* 2nd edn. New York: Ballantine Books.

Green, L. (2008). *Music, Informal Learning and the School: A New Classroom Pedagogy*. Aldershot: Ashgate.

Jellison, J. (2006). 'Including Everyone'. In McPherson, G. (ed.), *The Child as Musician: A Handbook of Musical Development*. Oxford: Oxford University Press, pp. 257–72.

MashupZone (2015). *Funny Babies Dancing — A Cute Baby Dancing Videos Compilation 2015*. Available at: https://www.youtube.com/watch?v=ZiV4KhvuQJw (Accessed 5 July 2016).

Mithen, S. J. (2006). *The Singing Neanderthals: The Origins of Music, Language, Mind and Body*. London: Phoenix.

Musical Futures (2015). Available at: https://www.musicalfutures.org/ (Accessed 10 July 2016).

Rogoff, B., Paradise, R., Arauz, R. M., Correa-Chávez, M. and Angelillo, C. (2003). 'Firsthand Learning Through Intent Participation'. *Annu. Rev. Psychol*. 54, pp. 175–203.

Sound and Music (2016). *Minute of Listening*. Available at: http://www.minuteoflistening.org/ (Accessed 3 July 2016).

This is Global Ltd (2016). *Classic FM*. Available at: www.classicfm.com (Accessed 3 July 2016).

uke3453 (2009). *I'm Yours (Ukulele)*. Available at: https://www.youtube.com/watch?v=ErMWX--UJZ4 (Accessed 5 July 2016).

ukroyalpriesthood (2012). *FEROmedia Presents Khaliyl Iloyi Rapping at 2years Old with Father Femi*. Available at: https://www.youtube.com/watch?v=tZh1_aaFqTQ (Accessed 5 July 2016).

Chapter 4
Music as a Practical Activity

Chapter objectives

- to explore the highly practical nature of primary music and how everyone can get involved – children and teachers! – irrespective of their level of 'technical' skills
- to become familiar with a range of good reasons and opportunities to make music
- to consider the different roles that children take as musicians and how their personal and interpersonal skills and capacities can be nurtured and developed
- to understand the part that talk should (and shouldn't) play in primary music

Introduction

This book takes such a 'hands-on' approach to music that you will find ideas for practical activities throughout. If the words 'music' and 'practical' in the same sentence make you start to tremble, hold tight! Practical musical work does not mean losing control of your class or your purpose. One of the recurring messages throughout this book is that you do *not* have to be a musical expert to facilitate children working practically. What you do need are these three things:

- good generic teaching skills
- the conviction that children are entitled to make music, just as they are entitled to speak and to move
- to follow up that conviction by providing children with
  - ○ *opportunities* to make music – playfully, incidentally, informally; and also more formally, with careful preparation, perhaps for an audience
  - ○ *capacity* to make music – through planned activities that gradually help develop and improve their musical *skills*.

In relation to the first bullet-point, Chapter 3 has already introduced several generic teaching skills: questioning, using correct terminology and instigating joining in. There are plenty more in this chapter and those that follow.

Concerning the second point, I think there are two powerful ways to convince yourself of the importance of music for children. One way is to observe them in action and see how much music means to them – whatever their ability. The other is to experience music-making for yourself, preferably in a group context. (There are suggestions in Chapter 2 for some groups you might try.) Once you have experienced what it feels like to be a musician, expressing yourself musically in even the most modest sense, you will understand 'from the inside' why practical music activities are so important. In fact, if you take just one piece of advice from this book, choose to engage in some group music-making. It can be a truly 'aha!' sensation, like flicking an internal switch, and any reluctance to teach music will turn into enthusiasm.

While the first two points above are both necessary, they will not translate into good music teaching without the third. As you can see from the sub-points above, primary music PCK (Shulman 1987) boils down to giving children the *opportunities* and the *capacity* to make music. The last chapter, and this one, will both help you develop your PCK relating to making *opportunities* for music. As to *capacity* for making music, there is such a range of musical skills to consider

Figure 4.1 Engaging in group music-making is a great way to understand 'from the inside' why music matters

that they fill three chapters of this book. Although they closely interrelate, they are presented and discussed as follows:

- This chapter: general musicianship skills – personal, interpersonal and communication skills
- Chapter 5: technical skills – singing, playing, listening, audiating (remembering and imagining sounds) and notating (representing music in some kind of visual format)
- Chapter 6: creative skills – exploring, experimenting, composing and improvising.

First, a reminder of why practical music is so important for children.

Why should music be a practical activity?

Perhaps the most obvious response to this question is: why would it not be? In most contexts around the world, music is and has always been a participatory activity, as mentioned in the previous chapter. Everyone joins in, young and old, regardless of 'ability', enjoying the sense of occasion and not worrying about musical imperfections.

Pause for thought

Can you think of an example of such 'everyone-joining-in' music?

In certain times and places however, particular genres of music have become more complex and specialized, evolving into forms of 'high art' that most people marvel at but few can produce. Now that we have such easy access to recordings of some of the world's best musicians, we ourselves can be left feeling musically small, inept and excluded. (See Chapter 3 too.)

Pause for thought

Can you think of an example of a world-renowned musician?

How do you know about them?

How are other people involved in their music?

This feeling of ineptitude, if you have it, needs to be acknowledged – and then put aside! As primary teachers our focus is on music for everyone, not for the few. Would teachers avoid teaching physical education if they were not Olympic champions? Or avoid teaching writing if they were not best-selling authors? The same argument applies to music.

The key to this is to remember what music *is*: a form of human expression and communication (see Chapter 1). All children can take part in musical expression at some level, just as they can all take part in physical or verbal expression. They have to work practically if they are to find sonic ways to express moods and feelings and to develop musical ideas as sound patterns or 'sonorous shapes' (Swanwick 2012, p. 2).

We should also bear in mind that if they experience enjoyable, practical music at school, some children will 'find their element' (Robinson and Aronica 2010) and want to make music a larger part of their lives over the long term. You never know: perhaps you have the name of a future world-class musician on your register. And if they do not have a musically rich home background, your music lessons could be their first inspiration!

Figure 4.2 All children can take part in musical expression at some level

Pause for thought

Find out about the early days of a now-famous writer, musician or sportsperson. Did they 'find their element' because of school, or despite it?

Practical work has long received unanimous endorsement from famed music educators. Émile Jaques-Dalcroze based his music teaching around whole-body movement work, while Zoltán Kodály employed a set of hand-signs for different notes (Benedict 2010). Carl Orff would quote the Chinese proverb: 'Tell me, I forget; show me, I remember; involve me, I understand' (Orffsite.com, no date).

General educational theories also hold that bodily actions are fundamental to learning (Piaget and Inhelder 1969; Bruner 1977). More fundamental still, a century ago Dewey posited his 'philosophy of action', arguing persuasively that the very nature of knowing was entirely bound up with interaction in an environment (Biesta and Burbules 2003). Recent neuropsychological research is beginning to uncover the mechanisms underlying the tight, reciprocal links between cognition, perception and action, leading to renewed interest in this 'embodiment' of cognition (Fischer and Zwaan 2008, p. 826).

Nowhere is 'embodied cognition' more true than in music. As Philpott (2001) puts it: 'The importance of the dynamic body is not only crucial to all learning (musical or otherwise), but is also wrapped up in the very nature of music itself as a medium for knowledge, expression and understanding' (p. 80). Moreover, as we saw in Chapter 3, music-making in a group context can have powerful positive emotional and social effects that depend on embodied, practical participation.

If all these arguments for practical music work are not sufficiently convincing, here are some more straightforward ones:

- the National Curriculum for Primary Music is full of requirements that can only be fulfilled if children work practically
- OFSTED thoroughly supports practical work in music (OFSTED 2012a)
- a promotional booklet encouraging schools to find ways to make music more practical has been published recently by a large consortium of music education organizations (Music Mark 2014)
- children *want* to work practically in music: they are motivated and engaged by it

Pause for thought

What would primary music be like if there were no practical activities at all?

What counts as a practical activity in primary music?

Pause for thought

Can you name some of the activities that different kinds of musicians 'typical' engage in? For example singers, players, producers, arrangers, composers and creators, DJs, directors and conductors.

Make a list of these 'musical activities'.

Musicians – of any age – demonstrate their 'musicianship' through the musical activities they engage in. By definition, only *practical* work in music will allow children the opportunities to develop their musical skills and capacities – their musicianship – through taking part in musical activities. Musicianship *cannot* develop passively.

It is worth reminding ourselves that playing an instrument with dexterity is not necessarily the same thing as being a musician. There are automatic pianos that can deliver complex pieces by Chopin and Joplin without a human being in sight. What is important, especially at the primary level, is *not* the degree of dexterity but the musical intent. OFSTED (2012b) agrees:

> 'Being musical' is much more than just the physical act of playing an instrument or participating in singing – it is about the quality of the response, the degree to which the pupil creates and plays music with appropriate accuracy, expression, feeling, sensitivity and sophistication.
>
> (OFSTED 2012b, p. 2)

Remember that this chapter is exploring the general nature and benefits of practical music. Chapter 5 focuses on how to teach more specific skills of singing, playing and listening, while Chapter 6 is devoted to how to support children's creative musical work.

How can you provide opportunities for practical musical work?

You will no doubt be acutely aware of how precious time is in school and how many demands all clamour to be met. Remember that music matters to children, even if other things can seem to matter more to school leaders. Please advocate for music (using this book to back you up!) so that children do receive their statutory entitlement to curricular (as well as extra-curricular) music. Try to find enough time to incorporate a balance of three kinds of opportunities:

1 – Informal, incidental moments

Analagous to everyday conversation, some of the most pleasurable opportunities arise when you include music as part and parcel of the daily life of your class. Like a shared joke or a favourite class story, these musical moments feel integrated and natural, instantly giving everyone a feeling of belonging (see Chapter 3). They are also a bit subversive as they sneak music into the children's day even when 'proper' music time is hard to find.

Try instigating some of these:

- Choose a popular piece of music to play at the end of the day for someone's birthday/because it's Friday/if the tidying-up went well/if behaviour was good … and everyone gets to sing and jig along with it, including you.

- Extend that idea by having a choice of three pieces of music on the go. The birthday child or child who is receiving a reward gets to choose which one.

- From time to time, consult your class and refresh the music choices.

- Develop a tidying-up song to the tune of 'London's Burning' or 'Frère Jacques' – get the children to invent suitable words and sing it as you end a session. After a time, older children can even sing it as a round while tidying up!

- Find a piece of music of suitable character that lasts a certain amount of time, such as three minutes. Play it as children are fetching what they need for the next session, preparing to go outside or changing for physical education. As they become familiar with the piece they will develop a sense of what three minutes feels like and will learn to be ready within that time.

- Adopt or create a simple welcome song. There are some 'hello' songs on the Sing Up website, for example (Sing Up 2016). You can find a good one on an OFSTED-commissioned YouTube video here: https://www.youtube.com/watch?v=eB6Hhyf16U4. Or experiment with changing the words to part of a simple song such as 'Twinkle Twinkle'. Or get the children to make one up. Could a child lead it?

- Use action songs as brain-breaks between activities. Could a child lead?

- With younger children, and those who have English as an additional language, if you sing all sorts of everyday instructions they are even more recognizable. Invent your own little tunes for 'come to the carpet now, please', 'let's have quiet', 'time to line up' or whatever you need. Keep the tune the same each time so that it becomes familiar. Or bypass language altogether and just 'dah-dah' the tunes, or use different instrumental sounds for different instructions. (See also the listening section in Chapter 5.)

- When you want to gather your class on the playground, try singing 'their' song – one you have learnt together beforehand. When they notice it, the children should join in as they walk towards you. The signal will soon spread and it is far more pleasant than a bell or a whistle.

- Can you and your class develop a repertoire (a 'known collection') of songs that are good for singing on a coach, or when walking somewhere as a class?

Pause for thought

Which one of these ideas will you try first?

Pause for thought

How could you adapt one of the ideas so it works for the age, experience and maturity of your class?

Pause for thought

Which personal and interpersonal skills can be developed through activities such as those mentioned above? In other words, how do such activities help to develop children's general musicianship? (There is more on this later in the chapter.)

---

2 – Class music lessons

Here is your golden opportunity to focus more systematically on challenging and extending the expressive and communicative musical skills of the children in your class. Do this by providing opportunities for them to 'use and apply' their singing and playing skills (see Chapter 5). For instance:

- Include music in your cross-curricular work.
  - ○ Find or invent relevant songs, using music to support learning in other subjects (Barnes 2012). Be inventive – what about a song to help children understand food chains in science, for example? You could use an existing tune but write new lyrics (words).
  - ○ Listen to relevant sounds, collect or re-create them and incorporate them into multimedia presentations. For example, in a geographical topic listen to the sounds of a rainforest or the sounds made by water at different stages of the water cycle. In a history project, look at a contemporary image of people at work and re-create the sounds that might have been heard in that scenario.
  - ○ Take ideas from across the curriculum into creative musical work (see Chapter 6).

● In music lessons themselves, as well as singing, playing and creating (see following chapters), devote practical time to improving children's skills in communicating musically.

○ Model, coach and facilitate effective individual practising (see below). The hardest thing of all is finding sufficient time for this activity: once children know a bit about *how* to practise, can they use some of their break time to do it?

○ Teach children how they can coach and support each other to practise effectively, too.

○ Then bring individuals and pairs together to make music as a group, focusing on the effectiveness of expression. (See below for support in how to do this.) In other words, avoid simply bashing through a piece in music lessons. Consider how to shape the piece. How can the beginning be most effective? Which is the most important moment in the music? Is there more than one? How can these key moments best be performed? How might the music best end? How can the whole piece of music be made to flow?

○ This group music-making can be with small groups or with the whole class as one big group. Involve the children in asking and answering questions about expression and communication like those just posed (Cremin 2015).

○ Using audio or video recording can help to focus everyone on the intent. It also serves as a celebration and a reminder of the music made together. Your class may well request repeated airings of their recorded music!

○ Putting the focus on the expressive intent in this way will also motivate children to improve their singing and playing skills (see Chapter 5).

○ The more children take ownership of this, the more they are 'being musicians' (e.g. Green 2008) rather than simply doing the teacher's bidding. Watch out for this because, as the teacher, there is a common tendency to take over all the decision-making oneself, effectively demoting the children to a set of sound-producing servants. Expect and encourage *them* to make many of the musical decisions. A good teaching strategy for this is to try speaking only in questions.

○ Sometimes, this group music-making should include rehearsing for specifically planned performances. (Again, see below for guidance.)

○ To help you to achieve all these things, it can be useful to check your planning to ensure that you have included a mix of individual, paired, small-group and whole-class work. Also ask yourself, 'Where are the communicative opportunities?' (See Chapter 8 for more on planning.)

○ OFSTED has produced a succinct and helpful guide for improving music lessons called 'Making More of Music' (OFSTED 2009b). They link everything to three clear principles:

- have one simple musical focus for a lesson that all the activities relate to (e.g. developing performance skills) – see Chapter 8 for more on this
- start and finish with sound
- help pupils to get better, by being aware of the next steps.

Pause for thought (same one again)

Which personal and interpersonal skills can be developed through activities such as those mentioned above? In other words, how do such activities help to develop children's general musicianship? (There is more on this later in the chapter.)

---

3 – Occasions where an audience is present

Look out for opportunities for children in your class to perform to others, as this provides another great reason for making music. Performances can range from hardly-rehearsed informal sharings of work-in-progress to well-rehearsed, polished and memorable events.

See below for how to prepare a performance. The audience could be:

- the rest of your class (e.g. the case study in Chapter 6)
- another class
- children in assembly
- families at a school event
- people at a local community centre
- invited visitors
- families at an inter-school event, where your class joins with others in a mass performance
- a 'virtual' audience, such as people accessing a school website where your performance is uploaded, or another school watching and listening live via webcam.

The performance could be a purely musical one, or the music could be a component of a play or a presentation or a celebratory event: the possibilities are numerous. Interestingly, you will often find that time is suddenly found for class music by the 'powers that be' when a public performance is in preparation, because such events are much appreciated by families and friends and are great public relations opportunities for the school. Use this to your advantage!

CASE STUDY A

Year 1 children learnt a traditional song called 'Oats and Beans and Barley Grow' and sang it to the Reception class. A few days later some senior citizens arrived in school, taking up their monthly invitation to come for a school dinner, so the Year 1 children sang for them too, making a useful link between farming and food.

CASE STUDY B

Classes from six schools were involved in learning and rehearsing the same set of sea-shanties including 'Haul Away Joe', 'Spanish Ladies' and 'Drunken Sailor', with occasional input and support from 'singing leaders' who were children from the local secondary school. The secondary school then invited the six classes to one of two performances of a home-grown musical sea-faring adventure. The children were able to join in with singing the key songs and had an opportunity to become somewhat familiar with their likely future secondary school.

CASE STUDY C

As part of a topic called 'It Could Never Happen Here!', the songs from a commercially written musical comedy about aliens were shared among all the classes in one primary school. Each class worked to bring their song to life, inventing costumes and actions. The Year 6 class provided the main actors and soloists for the musical, rehearsing largely independently during their lunch times. The whole musical was brought together as an end-of-year performance for families and friends.

CASE STUDY D

Key Stage 2 worked on a cross-curricular topic about the Second World War, focusing on life in the UK during wartime. They sang typical songs from the period such as 'We'll Meet Again' and 'Run Rabbit Run' during a re-enactment of evacuation to the country by steam train, complete with gas-masks and labels. Later, at the end of the topic, they decorated the Village Hall for VE Day. Family members were involved in providing food made from 'rationed' ingredients and joined the children in the celebrations, waving flags and doing the 'Hokey Cokey'.

CASE STUDY E

At a school's Summer Fayre a small group of Year 3 children, who had been working on creating different moods with sound, ran a stall called 'The Living Juke-Box'. They created a giant colourful cardboard 'juke-box' with a large fabric-screened sound-hole at the front, and they positioned themselves inside with a selection of instruments. Customers put 50p into one of three slots labelled 'happy music', 'scary music' and 'relaxing music' and were treated to a minute of suitable sounds, played live by the mystery performers.

CASE STUDY F

Year 4 children were inspired to get creative when they attended a local 'Inspiration Day' workshop run by music education students focusing on the BBC's 'Ten Pieces' (http://www.bbc.co.uk/programmes/b04lyj10). Over the following weeks they developed a short animated video of a futuristic craft visiting a number of fantasy locations. This project combined Computing, Design & Technology, English and Music, since the sound track was entirely composed by the children based on ideas from John Adams's 'Short Ride in a Fast Machine'.

Figure 4.3 A student-run workshop at the start of a creative musical project based on BBC's 'Ten Pieces'

Pause for thought (one last time)

Which personal and interpersonal skills can be developed through activities such as those mentioned above? In other words, how do such activities help to develop children's general musicianship? (There is more on this later in the chapter.)

You need to find a balance between the 'process' and the 'product' in primary music. As a student teacher said to me recently, 'Music is for life, not just for Christmas.' Nevertheless, having a real audience is a powerful motivator, and the thrill of being involved in a musical performance is unique. A well-rehearsed piece sung or played by a good-sized group of children is something very special for the audience too. The whole is more than the sum of the parts somehow, like when you stop noticing the pieces of a completed jigsaw and instead see the full picture. Unlike a picture though, a performance is transient, leaving audience members and performers alike with the glowing sense of 'I was there'.

Pause for thought

When there is no audience for a group's music, is there still musical communication?

Figure 4.4 Musical communication

How can you help children to develop their personal and interpersonal musical capacities?

Pause for thought

What personal skills and capacities do you think are particularly important for musicians?

What interpersonal skills and capacities do musicians need?

Create two lists, one for personal skills and the other for interpersonal skills. It would be worth revisiting your answers to the previous pause for thought (which was posed three times in all) to see what more you can add to your two lists.

Your lists probably illustrate the point that many of the personal and interpersonal skills that musicians use are valuable generic life skills. Have a look through your lists and highlight the items that could be thought of as generic. This once again reinforces the argument for the importance of music in the curriculum!

When I challenged myself to produce two lists, I came up with a number of ideas. You can find my lists at the end of this chapter. They might be interesting to compare with your two lists.

Pause for thought

How do your lists compare with mine (at the end of this chapter)?

If possible, discuss the lists with a colleague and perhaps draw up a 'master-list'.

What follows is some PCK that will help you to support children's development of these crucial aspects of musicianship, in particular the key activities of **practising, rehearsing, making music in a group** and **performing**. You can develop this PCK over time and with experience. You will not be able to do it all straight away. I suggest you revisit this section every now and then to choose a 'next step' for your own development as a great music teacher!

Effective individual practising (which works for you as well as your pupils)

1 Whatever music you want to sing/play, get to know the music yourself first. Listen to a recording or a live performance. Try playing or singing the music

through to get a sense of what it is like to produce it. Which parts are the hardest? Which parts are most enjoyable?

2 Break the music down into smaller, easier bits and practise each one separately:

PRACTISE SMALL SECTIONS BY:

- taking one small portion at a time
- taking just a few tricky notes at a time
- going more slowly
- going more quietly
- tapping out the rhythm only
- humming the tune – no words
- chanting the words – no tune
- playing an instrument with one hand only – not both – then the other hand

---

3 Repeat each small bit of the music until it can reliably be sung/played successfully, without tension. This repetition gradually allows internalization of the music and 'automation' of the skill involved.

4 Remember to practise making it sound good, look good and feel good. Imagine how your musical heroes would practise – emulate them!

5 Notice tricky bits. Analyse why they are tricky. Become aware of what the body is doing: is there another way? Become aware of the sound produced: is there another way? Experiment. Listen. Adjust.

6 It can help to get a second opinion on how to conquer the trickiest bits. Ask someone for feedback, try searching for a 'how-to' guide on the internet, try again while watching yourself in a mirror, or make a quick audio/video recording and analyse that, listening and watching closely.

7 Only then, begin to put the bits back together into progressively larger chunks, repeating the chunks to automate them, too.

8 Once the 'mechanics' have been mastered, enjoy playing whole sections, making them expressive and fluent.

9 Revisit what has been accomplished in one practice session, after a short break.

10 Continue to revisit the music frequently until it has been completely mastered and can be played or sung without difficulty.

11 Come back to it occasionally to remind yourself how to play or sing it, in other words to keep it 'in the repertoire' or 'in your set list'.

Figure 4.5 Listening is a most important musical skill

Making music with other people effectively

1 Listening is the most important skill to develop.

2 Get to know what the whole piece of music sounds like first, if you can.

3 Learn your own part really well (see <u>individual practising</u> above) so that you are comfortable with it and have some 'brain-space' left over to concentrate on the group work. If possible, sing or play along to the complete music, 'shadowing' your part.

4 When there is a pulse to the music, listen carefully so that your part keeps to the beat. You can 'listen' with your eyes too, becoming aware of the body language of the other musicians.

5 Get to know the sound cues that come just before any changes in the music, so you are ready to change.

6 As you sing/play, listen for the sound cues that signal you will need to start or stop or change what you are doing.

7 Also listen to how your sound blends with that of others. Adjust your dynamic level as needed.

8 If there is one person singing or playing a key solo part, the job of the group is to support and accompany them, allowing their sound to take 'centre stage'. If the soloist changes dynamics or tempo, the rest need to notice and follow suit.

Figure 4.6 Actions can help singing

9 The trick to keeping your part going, in the midst of everything that is going on in the music, is to have it very well internalized beforehand so you can split your attention between what you are doing and what the music as a whole is doing. The ultimate aim is to forget your own part, allowing it to take care of itself while you take care of the blend.

If you don't believe that the last point is possible, try this experiment with your class. Ask them to sing a song, concentrating on their singing. Now add some rhythmic actions to the song. Chances are that when the children concentrate on their actions as they sing the song again, the quality of singing will improve. Strange but true!

Effective group rehearsing (i.e. improving what they are singing or playing together)

1 If different members of the group are contributing different sounds to the 'ensemble', ensure that each person has had the chance to practise individually first (see above).

2   The procedure for rehearsing in a group is the same as for <u>individual practising</u> (above). Step 4 there is the most important!

3   If the group is small, decisions can be made consensually.

4   If the group is large, it helps to have a director. The next few points describe how directors can be most effective. You – and perhaps more experienced pupils too – can gradually learn to do these things by being aware of them and experimenting. There is further guidance in Chapter 5 in the section on 'improving the quality of singing'.

5   The director is to some extent the 'brains' of the group and the other members are the 'body'. The director follows the practice steps (above), paying attention to the sound produced by the group. The director ensures that tricky sections are taken apart and practised in easier bits, before being recombined. This might include asking some people to listen while others sing/play (see below). The director also needs to listen to how different sounds combine. This is the 'balance' of the music. If one part is too quiet or too loud, the director will need to suggest an adjustment.

6   Therefore, a prime job for the director is to listen and assess the music. (See Chapter 7.)

7   The director should cultivate clear body language and a simple set of agreed signals.

8   The director needs to take particular charge of the group's opening sounds. The group needs to know how fast to go, so count aloud at the desired tempo. Singers also need to know the pitch of their first note and the clearest way to communicate this is to *sing* your counting-aloud, at the song's starting pitch (and at the desired tempo). Practise this by singing 'one, two, three, four, twinkle, twinkle, little star', singing the numbers on the same note as the first 'twinkle'.

9   It is harder to start a song off silently, but it can be done, with an experienced director and group, as follows:

DIRECTING THE MUSIC TO START

- The director needs to 'hear the beginning of the music in his or her head' before starting.
- With singers, the starting note needs to be agreed upon, by asking everyone to hum the note (copying the first note played on an instrument).
- The director also needs to establish the pulse of the music before it starts (if there is one), by counting, clapping or – even better because it is silent! – nodding or moving rhythmically.
- Consider getting the group to move rhythmically too, to establish the beat. (Why not make this a part of the performance?)

- When everyone has a feel for the tempo (speed) in their bodies, the director should signal that the music is about to be started. (This can be done by holding up both hands in front of the body at about waist height, keeping them still, and catching each person's eye using a facial expression that means, 'Are you ready?')
- Clearly indicate the beat-before-the-start with an in-breath and a lifting movement of the hands (done in time to the beat), then make a precise downward 'go' signal on the next beat.
- Practise all this privately first!

The group's role is to follow directions. They need to keep their focus on making and listening to the music and to keep their eyes on the director. It is hard work so there will need to be breaks.

10 As the rehearsal proceeds it is good practice for the director to ask group members for their ideas about how to improve the music. Take care not to lose pace, though, or people in the group will lose focus.

11 The director needs to look after the needs of the group, being sensitive to how much stamina people have, when it's time to move on to something fresh or have a break, and how to keep everyone's spirits up. Directors need to be very positive and encouraging!

Figure 4.7 Following direction takes concentration

Effective performances

1   It is appropriate that the verb used is to *give* a performance to an audience. The needs of the audience are the most important factor, so the performers need to do whatever it takes to ensure that the audience has the intended experience.

2   An effective performance is a bit like those pavement artworks that, from a certain angle, look completely 3-D. The performers are parts of the artwork and the audience gets the desired effect if everything is arranged carefully in relation to them.

3   During final rehearsals it is a good idea for someone to stand and listen from wherever the audience will be, to find out how the music comes across.

4   You may need to alter the dynamics of the music, or the balance of sounds, so the audience gets the desired mix.

5   You may need to exaggerate certain sounds, such as over-pronouncing word endings, so that they can actually be heard by the audience.

6   Pay attention to visual aspects of your performance too:

VISUAL ASPECTS OF A MUSICAL PERFORMANCE

- consider the appearance of the performance area and the various objects that might be needed during the performance – do they all look their best?
- decide on the positioning of the performers and find a way to remember this, so everyone can take up their position smoothly in front of the audience
- cut down on extraneous goings-on which might distract audience attention – find a comfortable way to sit or stand and practise not fidgeting
- use facial expression to reinforce the meanings and messages in your music – practise this in advance by miming your music and concentrating on expression and on facing the audience where possible, looking just over the tops of their heads
- consider the way performers are dressed and presented
- consider the use of movement and action in the performance

---

7   Remember that a room full of people damps the sound, whereas an empty room allows the sound to ring and resonate more. Will this affect what the audience hears?

8   Pay attention to beginnings and endings. How will the performance get underway? It is a good idea to begin by performing a silence, with everyone stock-still and ready. Hold the silence at the end too, by 'freezing' as the last note fades.

9   How will you 'take applause'? Practise this.

10 Practise coping with nerves, by trying out your performance on a 'test audience' or in front of a video camera. Here are some of the common things that can happen – with suggestions that might help:

Figure 4.8 Practising not fidgeting

OVERCOMING 'NERVES'	
Possible issues:	**Possible solutions:**
there is a tendency to rush	practise breathing deeply and deliberately taking your time – what feels too slow will probably end up just right – think of how slowly good speech-makers speak
muscles tense	a few physical warm-up activities are useful
bodies want to curl up	practise open postures
people want to hide, somehow all ending up in a back corner	decide on positioning and mark spots on the floor with masking tape if it helps
people forget what they have learnt	learn the material well – practise giving clear cues – and be ready to offer subtle prompts and encouragements during the performance as needed
some people suffer a strong urge to 'spoil things'	treat this sympathetically, tactically ignoring nervous giggles and random weird behaviours, since focusing on them usually exacerbates the problem whereas with more experience of performance these tend to fade away consider positioning likely sufferers in 'sober' parts of the group coach performers to look at a point just above the audience's heads rather than
others 'freeze'	again, treat this sympathetically – consider positioning likely sufferers in the middle of a group

11 Deliberately practise making mistakes and pretending they never happened. Have fun with this! Get used to ignoring mistakes and carrying on regardless. Most of the time an audience will not even notice. It is important to get used to this, otherwise one little mistake can trigger nervous giggles or even tears – not what music should be about!

12 Judge how much to challenge performers. Some children relish the limelight while for others it is a torture. Never force anyone to perform solo. The larger the performing group, the safer individual children will feel. Get this balance right and your class will enjoy the exhilaration, joy and pride of being part of something very special indeed.

LEARNING 'BY EAR'

Note that all these activities may be done with or without written music in any form. I would counsel you to keep the use of written music to a minimum. Teach and learn words and music 'by ear' as much as possible. If written music is used, encourage everyone to learn it so well that after a while they can do without the paper. Reading, on top of all the other things that are happening moment by moment, adds extra complexity to the situation. It is no coincidence that most professional performers dispense with written music, or keep it only as an 'aide-memoire' if needed. Just like the professionals, you and the children will find you can concentrate much better on your individual and 'ensemble' music-making without paperwork in the way. It is a good idea to sing and play 'old favourites' once in a while, to refresh memories and to take pleasure in making music.

Here again is an important justification for music's place in the curriculum: the lifelong value of learning to commit things to memory and also to trust one's memory.

One tip for managing without printed lyrics (words) is to make sure you learn the first word of each section particularly well – the rest will follow. Use your favourite mnemonic tricks to make those first words memorable!

How does talk develop music as a practical activity?

At its heart, music is not a verbally mediated phenomenon, but a distinct medium of communication. There are times when words are irrelevant and even bothersome, like gnats spoiling the deep pleasure of being in a breathtaking landscape.

Often music lessons contain too many words and too little music (OFSTED 2012a). 'The special kind of non-verbal knowing-in-action ... required for expressive music-making is easily overwhelmed by the emphasis schooling tends to place on verbal knowledge' (Elliott and Silverman 2015, p. 412). You might well notice this if you browse YouTube for clips about music teaching: nearly all the teachers talk far too much.

I have found one exception: a video clip without too much talking. Some deft behaviour management can also be seen in this rather closely controlled lesson: https://www.youtube.com/watch?v=DwZJB883Z7A.

Pause for thought

What do you think children are learning, in the YouTube clip mentioned above?

OFSTED uses terms borrowed from second-language teaching to make the point that as much as possible we should 'immerse' children in the 'target language' of music. This is quite a helpful analogy. Put another way, we should encourage children to learn about music as active, developing musicians rather than as spectators. It is difficult to dispense with words entirely, but your aim should be to minimize them. Curtis, a second-year BEd student, expressed it well when he said we should aim for 'a silent voice, but a musical body'. What a great goal to have, for the teacher even more than the children!

Having said all this, there are several ways that talk is beneficial to practical music work.

Talking *about* music

In the last chapter, some basic musical terminology was introduced. Making use of such terminology allows children to talk *about* both existing music and their own practical music-making. It gives them the power to take a step out of the music itself to reflect on it from a distance, using the meta-language of words. They stop being 'in' the music and view it as an object, a thing to be critiqued. (Rosen [2016] makes a similar point about the importance of word-play in helping children 'objectify' English.)

Using musical terminology can help to focus attention on aspects of practical music-making that have gone unnoticed. For instance, talking about the timbre or texture of the music being worked on, and exploring what is meant by those terms, may open children's musical ears and minds to those dimensions and so add to their musical understanding.

Talk supports social interaction

A second way that talk supports practical music-making is as part of social interaction. Music lessons are an ideal context in which to help children improve their verbal social skills. Demonstrating and coaching the use of constructive and conditional language can work wonders for children's abilities to work in small groups successfully.

Conditional language, for suggestions:	Language of give-and-take:
Why don't we ...?	Thank you
What if ...?	Please
It might be ...	You go first
Maybe we could ...	My pleasure
Perhaps ...	Your turn
I'm not sure but ...	I'd rather ...
Should we try ...?	Let's ...
What about ...?	Let's share ...
Could I suggest ...?	Great idea!
	I'm not quite sure that ...
	Why not!
Children asking their own questions:	Giving feedback constructively:
How can we ...?	You sang/played that so well/ expressively/ smoothly .....
What can I ...?	
Where do I ...?	I can tell that you are really thinking about your breathing/ posture/ dynamics/ phrasing/ pitch/ body language/ facial expression/ diction/ timing ....
When does it ...?	
Why doesn't it ...?	
Why is it ...?	
Who can ...?	I liked the part where you ...
What if ... ?	To make that bit even more X, you could try Y...
Which one ...?	Have you thought of trying Z?
Can you help me with ...?	With a bit more practice of doing Z, you will make that part sound amazing!

> ## Pause for thought
>
> How, as the teacher, can you encourage your class to adopt these forms of words? Might it help to plan this when you are planning your music lesson?

Success in this area has another knock-on benefit. We gradually internalize the language that we use and it becomes part of how we think. So even when children are working individually, having this language will be helpful in terms of their resilience and resourcefulness. For instance, when a child is practising a tricky bit of playing, they can keep themselves positive, ask themselves questions to analyse the issue, and try self-suggested ideas. In other words, they can adopt 'possibility thinking' (Cremin, Burnard and Craft 2006). See Chapter 6 for more on this.

Words in music

Perhaps it is an obvious thing to say, but music and words often combine. A third use of talk to support practical music work is to focus on song **lyrics**. Exploring lyrics, lyric-writing and the use of language-chunks in music can all enhance children's understanding of the workings of both music and language.

There are several approaches to lyric-writing, for young musicians just as much as for professionals:

1 compose/choose the music first, then develop lyrics to fit
2 compose/choose the lyrics first, then develop music to fit
3 work on both simultaneously

Often music is used as a vehicle for delivering the more important lyrics. Elsewhere, the sounds of language are used as music, with the verbally mediated meaning less important than the sonic effects – much of the music by Bon Iver would perhaps fit

Figure 4.9 Lyrics written by a boy in Year 5

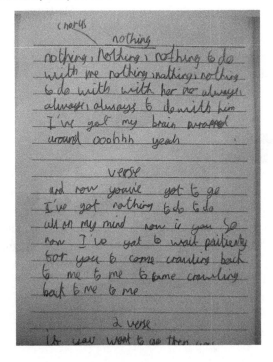

this description. Some composers combine lyrics and music in ways that complement each other or even merge into an inextricable whole. Björk is good at doing this, as were Flanders and Swann, Cole Porter, Benjamin Britten, Palestrina and many others, across a variety of genres. All of these approaches are worth exploring with your children.

Often lyrics are written with rhythm and rhyme in mind: most raps and songs have a rhythm and a rhyme-scheme of some kind. Through performing existing music, your class can explore and discover these schemes, then use them as 'templates' to compose lyrics on any topic that they like: the cross-curricular possibilities are endless.

There is no rule book that says you must have either rhythm or rhyme, however.

MUSIC MADE FROM WORDS

Here is an example you might like to try:

Teach children how to say, 'She sells sea-shells on the sea-shore. The shells she sells are sea-shells, I'm sure.' (Why not use this as a showcase to try out some of the strategies for practising and rehearsing outlined earlier in the chapter?)

When everyone can reliably say the words, develop them into a musical sound-scape. Set the scene – and the mood – with a real or imagined image of small waves breaking on a sandy shore. Direct the children to say the words quietly, slowly and calmly, over and over, at their own pace. Now explore the effect of whispering the words.

Shape this idea into a performable piece, by making decisions about texture and structure. How will it begin? How will it end? What signals will you make as director so that each child knows when to speak, when to whisper and when to stop? Can you shape the dynamics of the piece as it is performed, so that the overall sound effect is a little like waves on a shore?

Offer individual children the opportunity to direct, too.

Summary

Primary music should be a highly practical subject. This does not mean that teachers need to give in to chaos or be music experts. It is more important that they are good teachers who are truly convinced of the value of music for children. An ideal way to become convinced of the value of music is to join an adult group and 'get' the pleasure of being a musician personally.

Teachers need to squeeze opportunities for music into what is always a busy timetable. There are a number of ways in which time for music can be found and a whole range of reasons to make music, from the incidental and informal to the performance-oriented and polished.

To develop children's personal and interpersonal capacities as musicians, teachers need to provide opportunities for practising, group work, rehearsing and performing. The skills that children learn through such opportunities will have powerful beneficial effects across the curriculum and beyond.

While talking has an important role to play, the aim should be to communicate as much as possible in musical sound, the 'target language' of music lessons.

Personal skills and capacities of musicians include...	Interpersonal skills and capacities of musicians include...
Persistence, perseverance	Give-and-take – suggesting, accepting, asking
Resilience	Synchronizing
Self-discipline	Anticipating the actions of others
Self-awareness	Anticipating effect of own actions on others
Sense of responsibility for own actions	Ability to give feedback constructively
Letting go, trusting musical instincts	Leading
Concentration	Directing
Courage	Following
Ability to handle pride properly	Being supportive of the efforts of others
Drive to improve	Leaning on others
Ability to listen and notice	Turn-taking
Honest evaluation	Sharing
Honest self-evaluation	Cooperating
Resolving own difficulties	Blending in as part of an 'ensemble' (group)
Researching	Standing out
Ability to receive feedback well	Playing part reliably, taking responsibility
Anticipating what will happen	Communicating verbally
Coping with being in the spotlight	Resolving group difficulties
Coping with being in the shadows	Coaching
Valuing difference	Being coached
Practising, repeating, rehearsing alone	Communicating non-verbally
Managing a range of emotions	Practising, repeating, rehearsing in a group
Ability to make decisions quickly	Contributing to joint enterprise
Ability to make decisions slowly	Enjoying shared feeling of achievement
Coping with sudden unexpected events	
Enjoying feeling of personal achievement	

Recommended reading

Barnes, J. (2012). 'Integrity and autonomy for music in a creative and cross-curriculum'. In *Debates in music teaching*. Abingdon: Routledge.

Benedict, C. (2010). 'Methods and approaches'. In Abeles, H. and Custodero, L. (eds), *Critical Issues in Music Education : Contemporary Theory and Practice*. Oxford; New York: Oxford University Press, pp. 194–214.

Fischer, M. H. and Zwaan, R. A. (2008) 'Embodied language: A review of the role of the motor system in language comprehension'. *The Quarterly Journal of Experimental Psychology* 61(6), pp. 825–50. DOI: 10.1080/17470210701623605.

Music Mark (2014). Making the Most of Music in Your School. Available at: http://www.nottsmusichub.org.uk/site/files/2014/07/Making-the-most-of-music-in-your-school-Music-Mark-July-2014.pdf (Accessed 5 May 2017).

Philpott, C. (2001). 'The body and musical literacy'. In Philpott, C. and Plummeridge, C. (eds), *Issues in Music Teaching*. London: Routledge Falmer.

Chapter 5
Skills to Develop in Music

Chapter objectives

- To understand something of the nature of skill acquisition
- To present three pedagogic principles relevant to musical skill acquisition
- To outline how to support children's acquisition of:
  - listening skills
  - singing skills
  - playing skills
  - notating skills
- To signpost some relevant sources of further support

Introduction

While in Chapter 4 general musicianship skills were discussed, and Chapter 6 will focus on creative skills, this chapter looks at the more technical skills that allow children to listen, 'speak', read and write in music. After having explored curiosity in Chapter 3, this chapter focuses on another of the 'natural energies that sustain spontaneous learning … a desire for competence' (Bruner 1966 p. 127). If curiosity is a drive to acquire knowledge and understanding, the 'desire for competence' is a drive to acquire skills. Before looking at particular music skills, it is worth thinking about skill acquisition in general.

My two-year-old grandson demonstrates this natural desire to master skills during almost every minute of his waking day, in everything from spreading butter to jumping off steps, posting shapes, climbing ladders, using crayons, building towers and talking. Austin, Renwick and McPherson (2006) describe how young children tend to approach all their skill-learning in this way, intrinsically motivated to develop skills wherever they find a suitable challenge.

Figure 5.1 Young child developing physical skill on climbing frame

Older children and adults often also find skill acquisition and mastery fulfilling. Computer games, for example, appeal for this reason as they motivate players to move through progressively more difficult levels of skill. The motivation is intrinsic, stemming from the activity itself rather than any external reward – so much so that families often have to limit the amount of time children spend playing computer games. Csikszentmihalyi (1999) has studied such engrossing, 'autotelic' experiences (that are a reward in themselves) and the way people get 'in the zone' or 'in flow' when totally immersed in what they are doing: it feels very good and time seems to fly by.

Pause for thought

Have you experienced being 'in flow'?

Figure 5.2 Child 'in flow' playing a steel pan

An important criterion for this enjoyable 'flow' is that the level of challenge must be appropriately related to a person's current level of skill. If there is a mismatch, either boredom or anxiety are the inevitable outcomes and the activity ceases to be intrinsically rewarding. Because boredom and anxiety are unpleasant emotions, the net results are disengagement, a poorer self-image and reduced likelihood of tackling future challenges.

Pause for thought

Can you remember a time when you were asked to do something that was far too easy or far too hard? Perhaps you can also remember the negative emotions that resulted from this, which can be intensely uncomfortable.

One reason why a challenge may be inappropriate is that it is not set by the learner but imposed on them. This can happen if a teacher sets an inappropriate target, perhaps under pressure to have their pupils working at some norm-referenced level (i.e. comparing each pupil with others rather than allowing each pupil's skills to develop in relation to their own previous achievements). Inappropriate challenge can also arise due to a child's desire to conform to perceived peer expectations. However, if peer pressure and teacher anxiety are prevented from warping the learning environment, then children are able to set their own challenges very sensibly, as they have been doing since birth. An effective strategy for teachers, therefore, is to allow children to do this. For a good example of the strategy in practice, read the description of the physical education lesson towards the end of Chapter 2.

When considering how the 'desire for competence' might operate in the context of children's acquisition of technical skills in music, it is helpful to bear three principles in mind.

1   Make sure that the *level of challenge* is just right, so that it is motivating, not demotivating. To achieve this, consider letting children set their own challenges within your lesson framework. This principle is a powerful way to ensure every child can be included.

2   Allow time for skill-learning and more time to *use and apply* the skills in purposeful musical contexts (see Chapter 4). Developing the listening and expressive skills discussed in this chapter (and the creative skills in Chapter 6) should be enjoyable, but ultimately the purpose is to engage in meaningful musical activities (Daubney and Mackrill 2015, p. 250). In practice, skill-learning and skill-using are often closely interwoven within a single music activity.

3   Remember that 'being musical' is not equivalent to 'being a proficient performer': it is a much wider concept. *Singing and playing skills aren't everything*. The rest of the primary music curriculum does not have to wait until children have acquired any particular proficiency. Their singing, listening, ensemble (group) work, performing, selecting, creating and composing skills will all develop over time if they are engaged in worthwhile musical activities. As for playing, there is not enough time in curricular music lessons for children to become highly skilled on technically difficult instruments (see Chapter 2), but there are ways around this that enable children to produce musical sounds: see the 'playing skills' section later in this chapter.

One more point. I do not advocate focusing on musical skills in isolation. The three main aspects of the music curriculum – skills, knowledge and purposes – go hand in hand (see page 20) and you will find that all these skills develop over time if children are engaged in plenty of purposeful and practical musical work. See Chapter 8 for more on planning.

What are listening skills?

Listening and **audiating** ('hearing in your head') are discussed in this section. They are both aspects of auditory ability – the ability to detect and discern, remember and recall, imagine and distinguish sounds, melodies, rhythms and music.

Listening

There is a big difference between hearing and listening. You cannot help hearing, but you choose to listen. Listening is a deliberate, active process, done for a reason.

ACTIVE LISTENING

Try this for yourself: listen to the place you are in right now. What is the quietest sound you are able to hear, when you listen carefully? Does it help if you shut your eyes, or fix them on one object, while you listen? Do you notice how your effort and attention are channelled into listening? What happens to your body?

The National Curriculum says that children should be taught to 'listen with concentration and understanding' (Key Stage 1) and 'with attention to detail' (Key Stage 2).

Figure 5.3 Children listening to a wind-chime

Pause for thought

What does it mean to listen with concentration, understanding and attention to detail?

Write a short explanatory paragraph. Revisit it later and see whether you want to amend it in the light of what you have been learning about primary music.

A key teaching strategy for supporting children's listening-skill development is to be aware of the importance of listening for a *purpose*: think of it simply as the *listening-for* strategy.

Concentrated listening-for

Active, focused listening-for is hard work and the skill of concentrating on sound takes time to develop and master. Keep listening-for times very short to begin with, so that the challenge is not too great. The best listening-for activities lead straight into other active musical work. For example, having listened to some music that begins very quietly and gradually builds in texture and dynamic, such as 'Bydlo – the Ox Cart' from Mussorgsky's 'Pictures at an Exhibition' (lucpebo 2012), children could apply that idea to their singing, playing or creative work.

Many of the activities suggested in Chapter 3 for assimilating musical terminology have a listening-for focus. Here are some further ideas. When you try them, notice what children are asked to listen *for* and how they *respond* to the listening (see below).

SCENARIO A

Listening for quietness.

'Before we begin to sing/play, we need a good silence. Can we make it so quiet in here that we can hear the traffic outside/the children next door/the hum of the projector fan?'

(This works much better than asking children to quieten down or to stop making any sound. The quality of the silence achieved can be profound!)

SCENARIO B

Listening for pitch: the 'Please Stand Up' game (Lougheed 1997)

- With children seated, sing the phrase 'please stand up' using the same little rising tune as the first three syllables of 'Frère Jacques'. (This simple tune consists of three notes, each a step higher in pitch. It doesn't matter if you use a high or a low voice, as long as the shape of the tune is like that.) Gesture to the children to stand as you sing the instruction.

- Next, sing the phrase 'now sit down' in a little descending tune (the same as 'Three Blind Mice': each note is one step lower in pitch). The children sit.
- Sing each of these once more and invite the children to stand and sit again.
- Now sing the rising tune but without the words (use 'dah dah dah' or similar). At least one child will stand up: praise that and gesture to everyone to stand.
- Sing the descending tune without the words: the children will sit.

Now the children have realized that the tunes alone carry the instructions. (You can use them at any time during the school day!) Try inventing more as you feel ready. For example:

- When children are seated, sing 'stay sitting down' all on the same low note. Later you can omit the words but keep their rhythm 'dah da da dah' on that one note.
- When either standing or sitting, try 'hands in the air', 'put your pencils down' or 'come to the carpet now please' – make up your own little tune for each one. Always keep your tunes the same shape so they can be recognized by that alone.

Some soldiers use similar listening-for skills to interpret and respond to the variety of bugle calls that direct their activities (e.g. lirbugler 2012). For example the first tune of the day, called 'Reveille', is played to wake them.

SCENARIO C

Listening for the <u>beat</u>.
   Ask children to respond physically to the beat of music in some way. For instance:

- tapping a foot
- clapping with one finger on the palm of the other hand (so that it does not mask the sound of the music for others)
- patting a leg with a hand
- swaying
- nodding
- moving the whole body – perhaps in a pre-arranged way that can be synchronized with the movements of others – it looks and feels fantastic
- travelling (moving from place to place) in a rhythmic manner – in a circle?

Figure 5.4 Boys tapping sticks to the beat while listening to music

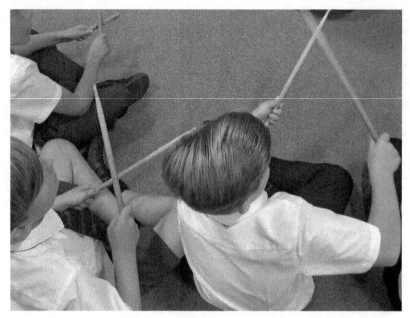

SCENARIO D

Listening for a <u>mixture of things</u>.
    When listening to music, or sounds, holistic questions such as these can be helpful:

- What do you notice?
- What can you hear?
- What else?
- What else?
- What else? (The more you ask this, the more you will get from the children – even if you would not be able to answer the question yourself!)
- Are there any big changes in the music?
- What is it like? How could you describe it to someone who has not heard it?
- How does it make you feel?
- What is the mood/atmosphere of the music, do you think?
- What can you imagine?

The questions above focus on the music as a whole. Depending on your reason for asking children to listen, you might also want to ask children, especially in Key Stage 2 to go into more analytic detail, with questions such as:

- What instruments do you think are playing?
- Why do you think that?
- Is the tempo fast or slow here?

- Is the dynamic loud or quiet in this part?
- Is the texture thick or thin at the beginning?
- Are high- or low-pitched notes being played here?
- Are most of the notes there long or short?
- Can you hear the same rhythmic phrase (small group of notes) being repeated? Put up your hand when you hear it again. Can you tap out the rhythm?
- Can you hear a tune at this point? If I stop the music, can you hum that tune?
- Then what happens?
- Describe how the music begins/ends.
- Why do you think the composer chose to make this part sound this way?
- Would you add/remove/alter anything here? If so, why? If not, why not?

All the questions above will help children to develop their musical listening. None of them ask for a trite response ('I liked it', 'it was nice'): all require thoughtful attention to detail.

Pause for thought

Apart from verbal responses to listening, how else are the children responding in the four scenarios above?

Figure 5.5 Talking about music just experienced

Responding to listening

When planning a listening activity, consider carefully *how* – in what mode – children will be asked to respond. Whichever mode of response is used, remember that children may know more than they can 'prove' through their responses, because each mode presents challenges in itself. To illustrate this, imagine that you are asked to talk about your favourite band … in Fijian. Unless you are a Fijian speaker, you will probably have much more that you want to say than you can actually put into words.

The ideal way to respond to music is *musically* or at least *sonically*. Some of the responses in Scenarios C and D are musical ones because they involve children making musical sounds. I consider that the response in Scenario A is also musical, since the silence is being produced in the course of music-making. Think of ways to encourage children to respond to questions musically or sonically by demonstrating what they mean using sound, copying or inventing rhythms, tunes and musical ideas.

Physical responses to music are also to be encouraged. Many writers have highlighted the close association between music and movement (Philpott 2001; Mithen 2006). Encourage children to express their ideas about atmosphere and mood through movement. Rhythm is a common feature of music: could children invent patterns of movement that synchronize with the music? Younger children have a particular need to involve themselves physically. For this reason, Scenarios B and C are likely to be the most appropriate for them.

Responses in *visual* media can be fascinating. Some music conjures up visual imagery which can be depicted in a visual medium such as a drawing or painting. It is important that children do not feel there is one single correct answer: whatever they imagine is correct, because it was prompted by the music. If you struggle with this idea, think of dreams. There is no such thing as a 'wrong' dream: you dream what you dream and it is the right dream for you. Listen, for example, to some or all of the piece 'Aquarium' from *Carnival of the Animals* by French composer Camille Saint-Saëns (e.g. Barton 2016) but do not reveal the title to your pupils. Let children respond to the music by drawing. Later, share their images as the music is replayed. Use musical terminology to discuss the choices they made – if you feel any words are needed. Make the point about there being no such thing as a wrong answer, before revealing the title Saint-Saëns gave his piece and considering how the idea of an aquarium connects with the sonic qualities of the music, just as the children's ideas do.

Much music is not meant to be about specific 'visuals', being purely an aural world of sound qualities and juxtapositions, melodies, rhythms, harmonies, patterns and structures, to be savoured for themselves, for the emotions they often evoke and for the responses they may invite. You could experiment with more abstract responses in visual media, using colours, shapes and textures.

Verbal responses both depend upon and develop children's use of useful terminology (see Chapter 3). Bear this in mind when inviting verbal responses to music. It can be a good strategy for building vocabulary. Younger children, and those with less well-developed linguistic capacities, will find a verbal response more

Figure 5.6 An exhibition of visual responses to music (photograph by Kip Pratt)

challenging than a physical one so be aware of the demands you are placing on them. Similar caution is needed when considering *written* responses to music, as this mode poses an additional challenge.

Whatever the mode of response, remember that the purpose is to deepen and refine the children's listening.

'Background' listening

As well as short, focused, intense listening-for activities, include more relaxed 'half-listening' opportunities throughout the school week. Experiment with what kinds of music might support quiet working times, more energetic tidying-up times, etc. It is important that children's lives are as musically rich as possible, to allow them to develop their tacit awareness of beat, rhythm and melody and also to expand their musical horizons. This simple exposure to music is a vital part of primary music in the same way that exposure to language is vital for children's linguistic development.

Audiation

Gordon (1999) is credited with establishing the word 'audiation' for auditory imagination. As he puts it, 'audiation is to music what thought is to language' (p.

42). In verbal language, we communicate inner *thoughts* via audible *speech*. In music, we communicate our inner *audiation* via audible *music-making*. In Chapter 1 it was suggested that you might be able to 'hear' the 'Happy Birthday' song in your head. That is an aspect of audiation, or musical imagining. With enough listening experience, one can bring remembered melodies and rhythms to mind and even manipulate them mentally. For example, try audiating 'Happy Birthday' but change the last note. This is auditory imagination at work.

Audiation is implied in the National Curriculum as a skill to develop so that by Key Stage 2 children can 'recall sounds with increasing aural memory'. The skill of audiation will develop if attention is paid to good active listening in primary music. Some specific audiation challenges are suggested here:

---

1 Play Kim's Game with sounds

Hide four (or fewer, or more) sound-makers behind a screen or in a deep box where you can play them without the children seeing them. Ask the children to listen-for four different sounds as you play each one, naming the sound-makers silently in their heads. Then play three of the sounds again: which one was missing?

2 Silent Singing

This is often done with 'Heads, Shoulders, Knees and Toes' and the idea can be used with many songs. Sing the song over and over, each time leaving out more of the words. The words have to be audiated ('sung' in one's head) in order to keep the rest of the song intact. Actions help.

3 Silent Singing – advanced

Could the class sing a round that they are very familiar with (such as 'Frère Jacques') leaving out some of the words, without it falling apart?

4 Dodgy Karaoke

Sing a familiar song (in a group or, if anyone is brave enough, solo) to a backing-track from Sing Up (2016), YouTube or elsewhere. Once underway, someone turns down the backing-track for a short while – but the singing must keep going. Will it fit with the backing-track when that is turned up again?

5 Shy Copy-Cats

Sing, say or play a short section of a song, chant or rhythm. Children 'think it back' in their heads, keeping in time (and maybe using actions to help), before actually copying it back in sound. (In the next section, copying-back is discussed as an effective teaching strategy for developing singing and playing skills.)

Remember that although listening and audiating have been discussed in isolation here, the best context for developing these skills is within a lesson that includes a variety of musical activities.

What are singing skills?

It may sound obvious that primary teachers need to consider both the quantity and the quality of children's singing. But the quality cannot improve without plentiful opportunities just to sing, so it is fundamentally important to make sure that children sing, often. This does not mean that the teacher has to be an opera star, just that he or she gets singing happening.

The National Curriculum states that pupils should learn to 'use their voices expressively and creatively by singing songs and speaking chants and rhymes' in Key Stage 1 and should 'sing musically ... with increasing accuracy, fluency, control and expression' in Key Stage 2. Children are also expected to develop the ability to reproduce sounds from aural memory, in other words to sing songs that they have learnt and remembered 'by ear'. (Recalling a song is part of audiation, as we have seen, but the added skill here is that the remembered song can be expressed in sound.)

One might think that the development of singing would be similar to that of speech, with a long period of listening before beginning to produce words (Gordon 1999). However, it has been shown that this is not the way singing begins. Very young babies are already engaging vocally in musical 'dialogues' with their caregivers (Mithen 2006; Malloch and Trevarthen 2010) and experimenting with using their voices, whereas it takes at least a year before the most basic speech begins to emerge. Joining in was discussed in Chapter 3 and it appears that no one is too young or too unskilled to begin: it is human nature. Virtually everyone can sing.

Getting singing happening – often

The emphasis on inclusive participation should continue into primary school singing. Welch (2006) points out that in musical cultures which are effective at fostering the development of singing, 'opportunities [for children] to engage in vocal play and exploration, to share in singing games with peers and "experts", as well as to improvise and compose their own songs are essential features' (p. 325). Equally, it is important to honour children's 'right to silence': they need plenty of opportunities to listen and internalize as well as to explore their own vocalizing in private. They will join in when they are ready. The focus is on exploring and gradually mastering vocal possibilities in a playful way rather than to meet any externally imposed standard, which echoes the earlier remarks about levels of challenge.

Children need their 'singing hours' just as pilots need their flying hours. This principle is true of skill acquisition generally: there is no shortcut to spending time repeating, practising and refining any skill. This being the case, how can less experienced teachers get singing happening?

Figure 5.7 Children should have frequent opportunities to sing

The obvious way is for children to learn existing songs. There needs to be a *model* of the song to learn from and ideally this will be a live singer. Hedden (2012) says there is evidence that the best models of songs are sung by children because their voices most closely match the learners' voices, and it can be a good strategy to ask pupils to demonstrate songs to their classmates. Take care with issues of self-esteem if you adopt this strategy, though. The singer must be comfortable about singing in front of their peers. Equally, no one should feel that the singer is 'the best' or the only valued singer in the class. Perhaps different children could model different short sections of a song. Use this strategy frequently in a matter-of-fact way and it will become normal classroom practice, accepted by all.

Pupils appreciate their teacher singing, too, as this models a positive attitude to challenge and conveys the important message that 'we all sing here'. It is useful to develop a small set of songs that you as the teacher know well. See Chapter 8 for a list of suggestions.

If there is no live singer available, audio or video recordings can be used. Sing Up (2016) is a valuable source of recorded songs chosen to fit the vocal ranges of children at different stages in their singing development (see below).

Children are expert imitators and will attempt to reproduce exactly what they hear, so at least one of the models should be of good singing quality. (What counts as 'good quality' is discussed below.) If a teacher does not feel their own singing is a good model I suggest using a mixture of recorded versions, pupils modelling short extracts and the teacher singing at least some parts themselves as a powerful model of 'having a go'. (See Chapter 8 for ideas if you wish to develop your own singing.)

Another way to get singing happening is for children to invent new songs, or new lyrics for familiar tunes. This also lends itself to cross-curricular work and can be a good way to increase children's 'singing hours'. (For more on creative work, see Chapter 6.)

Improving the quality of singing

As well as singing purely for enjoyment and 'singing hours', to consolidate and automate the skills involved, there should be occasions when the *quality* of children's singing is considered and worked on, to develop singing proficiency. What 'good-quality singing' is depends upon the age and experience of the children. Take their first attempt as a baseline and make sure that the final outcome is a clear improvement on this. It is useful to record the first attempt for later comparison. Children also love to see and hear for themselves how they have improved.

All teachers can make significant improvements to children's singing, even if they do not feel they can sing well themselves, by focusing on the aspects described in the following sections. Select which ones, and to what extent, on the basis of children's ages and experience as singers. Visit each teaching point quite briefly: if you labour a point children will become too focused on it, potentially distorting the overall result. Avoid singling out individual singers for comment, though you could ask a different group to sing each verse of a song to allow you to focus discreetly on a few voices at a time.

The key is to listen carefully. Zoom in on parts of songs that could be improved, rather than always singing the whole song. As you become more experienced and confident, aim for a repeating cycle of bursts of singing (while you listen-for one of the aspects below) interspersed with brief breaks in which you say three things as succinctly as possible:

- something you noticed that you liked
- something you noticed that you think can be improved
- a suggestion for *how* to improve it

Then immediately put the suggestion into practice, listening again ready to make your next three points. Keep all your comments positive and constructive.

EXAMPLE

'You are managing your breathing very well now, making one breath last for the whole first line of the song. Let's try and make the words a bit clearer. Notice how your lips help to make the "p" and "b" sounds in these words, as you whisper the line to me.'

This cycle of improvement will quickly make a difference. It is how musicians practise to improve and how they rehearse for a performance (see Chapter 4). Don't be afraid to repeat the improved section to consolidate the learning. The long-term aim is to encourage children to listen-for aspects of quality in their own singing, perhaps using recordings or perhaps listening to half the class singing, and to hear what needs improving for themselves.

Posture

Precede a focus on posture with some gentle physical 'wake and shake' activities. Here is a good basic posture for singing, though often you will want children to include actions and movements with their singing.

- Ideally singers should stand.
- Feet should be flat on the floor, about as far apart as the front legs of a chair. Try rocking slightly on the feet, so that the heels, then the toes, lift off the ground a little. End with heels and toes taking an equal load.
- Knees should be loose, not locked back: without lifting heels off the ground and keeping the body straight and eyes forward, bend the knees a little, repeatedly, to feel a slight 'bounce' in the standing position. End with knees just fractionally bent.
- Hips should not stick forward or back, but be in line with the body.
- (If seated, try to arrange it so that feet are flat on the floor and upper legs are parallel to the floor.)
- Backs should be straight.
- Arms should be fairly straight and loose, like the arms of a string puppet. Try hunching shoulders then letting them flop again, with arms passively hanging. Think of the hands as heavy.
- Shoulders should be comfortable and relaxed, not hunched forward or upward.
- Backs of necks should be long.

Figure 5.8 Good singing posture

- Chins should be low, though not tucked in. Imagine balancing a beanbag on the top of the head, for the correct angle.

- The highest point of the head should be the crown (near the back), not the forehead. It can be helpful to imagine a 'magic thread' from the crown to the ceiling keeping the body tall. Or use a 'nodding dog' analogy so the neck is kept relaxed and mobile.

- Having taught children these postural elements, they can be summarized as 'standing tall' (or 'sitting tall') or 'standing ready to sing'. Resist the phrase 'chins up' as this posture is a hindrance to vocalizing.

Breathing

First, singers need to become aware of themselves breathing. Briefly discuss what breathing is and how it works. When they are standing ready to sing, ask children simply to breathe, slowly. Now add a challenge of breathing without letting the shoulders rise. One way to achieve this is to imagine being in a shop window facing out and to breathe with no change in shoulder profile so window-shoppers do not guess you are a living mannequin. The breathing movement is now happening mostly in the stomach region. To make the point about how effective this 'belly breathing' is, it can be exaggerated by asking children to lean forward with their hands on the back of a chair or a tabletop, bending a little and imagining they have just run a marathon. As they breathe in, they should let their tummies expand.

To take a good breath in, stand tall and breathe in slowly using the belly breathing followed by a lifting of the ribs and opening of the shoulders (chest breathing). Breathe out slowly too. (Too much deep breathing is so effective it can make people feel giddy.)

When singing, in-breaths need to happen quite quickly, whereas out-breaths need to be paced and controlled. Try these short exercises (but do not dwell long on breathing in any individual singing session):

- Imagine you are holding a candle in front of you with one hand. Take a good breath in, then breathe out slowly so that the imaginary flame flickers gently but does not go out.

- Take a good breath in, then quietly count aloud (or say the alphabet) for as long as possible on a single out-breath. Try again and see if you can beat your first attempt.

Figure 5.9 Decide where to take in-breaths when singing a song

- Take a good breath in, then hiss or hum on one out-breath for as long as possible.

When working to improve a song, consider where the best places are to take a breath. Practice using a hand-signal (scooping upward) that means 'breathe in now' and then make a quick pointing motion to indicate when to begin singing (see Chapter 4). Use these signals consistently so that children learn what they mean and follow them. Sing just the part that should be sung on that single breath and reflect on how it went. Gradually these **phrases** can be combined into the whole song.

Voice

The vocal chords vibrate to make the voice sound. You can feel the vibration as a buzzing sensation in your fingers if you touch your throat as you speak: compare the feeling of whispering 'hello' with saying 'hello' out loud (voiced).

Children's voices span a wide pitch range from high wails to low growls. However, it takes time to develop the skill of controlling the voice to produce particular notes, and this seems to happen first within the middle range (the 'speaking range') of the voice. The exact range varies a little from child to child and gradually expands with practice. As a rough guide, children are usually comfortable with songs that make use of middle C (hear it https://www.youtube.com/watch?v=LgjgAAkhLs8 and find it on the piano http://www.wikihow.com/Play-Middle-C-on-the-Piano) and the 5 or 6 notes above that in pitch. Many children will be able to manage 2 or 3 notes below middle C and perhaps 8 notes above.

> To get a sense of this range of notes, consider 'Twinkle Twinkle Little Star'. It makes use of just 6 different notes. If middle C is used as the first note, then the first two lines are: C C G G A A G, F F E E D D C. (These are white notes to the right of middle C on a keyboard. The note A is to the right of note G.)
>
> Contrast this with 'Baa Baa Black Sheep' which begins with the same first 4 notes, but then keeps rising in pitch: C C G G ABC'A C (where C' is another higher-pitched C that is 8 notes to the right of middle C on a keyboard). So this song uses a range of 8 notes in total, an octave from C to C'.

Fortunately, many well-known songs keep within a manageable range. Books and online sources of songs for children usually take children's vocal ranges into account. However, it is important to advise children not to strain their voices by singing too high or too low. Also, avoid singing too loudly or in a 'singing whisper' as neither of these are good for the voice. It is important to *warm up* the voice, focusing on it and what it can do, before using it in singing activities.

WARMING UP THE VOICE

Short playful vocal activities are good as warm-ups. For example, play or hum a low-ish note (middle C would work well) and then ask (or gesture) children to take a good breath in, then slowly sing the numbers 1 to 8 starting on the low note and going up one note with each number. Repeat, but this time sing number 4 with a sad face, number 6 with a smile, number 7 with an excited happy face and number 8 with 'jazz hands'. Facial expression affects the quality of the vocal sound.

'Boom Chikka Boom' is another good warm-up which explores vocal quality (Sing Up 2016). Or try chanting any rhyme with a voice like a giant, a witch, or a favourite book or film character who has a notable voice or accent. Make a noise like a police siren and take the high part higher and the low part lower on each 'nee naw'.

Ask children to provide vocal sound-effects as you tell a made-up story about starting your car on a frosty morning (footsteps crunching on frozen puddles as you walk to the car, scraping frost off the windscreen, starter motor going for ages, engine finally starting, revving the engine to warm it, a radio jingle as you wait for all the windows to defrost, etc). Any story will do as long as it includes high and low vocal sounds: what about a trip to the zoo, helping a babysitter or a ghost story? Could your class make up a warm-up story or activity themselves?

The voice is the source of the tune (melody) of any song. It works by making notes of different pitches. Listen-for pitch carefully as children sing a line of a song. Is each syllable sung in the right pitch or does the tune sound wrong? Focus on a part where the children are not singing the tune correctly. Listen together to a live or recorded model, or sing yourself if you can model the correct tune, then try to copy it back more accurately without bothering with words – just use 'lah' or 'dah' or 'boo'!. How does it sound now?

If it still does not sound right, listen to the model again and describe what the tune does. Does it go up in pitch steps? Down in steps? Does it suddenly jump to a higher or lower pitch? For instance in 'Row, Row, Row Your Boat' the pitch stays on the same low note for 'row, row, row' then goes up in steps for 'your boat'. There are more small steps down and up in the next line, then a sudden jump to a high pitch for the first 'merrily'. Follow the model tune physically, raising and lowering one hand – or the whole body – as the pitch rises and falls (see Figure 5.10). Now try singing or 'lah'ing the tune again, slowly, with more awareness of its 'pitch contour'. How does it sound now?

Having mastered the tune, consider the tone of the children's voices. Try singing the song 'like Gandalf' or 'like Gollum' – which one sounds better? Sing with a relaxed voice rather than a tight one. A bright, alert, smiling, 'high cheeks' expression tends to produce the best vocal tone.

Figure 5.10 Teacher and children making hand gestures for high pitch

Diction

While the vocal chords produce the voice, the mouth shapes the sounds of the words. Work on clear diction (pronouncing words clearly). Warm up with some tongue-twisters and nonsense rhymes that work with the lips, tongue, teeth and mouth-shape, like 'Peter Piper' or 'She Sells Sea-Shells'. Or take some tricky words from a song and turn them into patterns like 'caterpillarcaterpillarcaterpillar'. The Sing Up website also has good warm-ups for diction, such as 'Warm Up and Stomp' (Sing Up 2016).

Notice the tendency for final consonants of words to be lost during singing and experiment with exaggerating them for clarity. Chant them first, before singing them. Then try whispering them, or mouthing them totally silently. Can another child recognize which part of the song is being silently mouthed?

Actions and movements

As well as being enjoyable to do, moving while singing has significant benefits. Actions can help singers to remember their words. If they are simple, movements can also improve the quality of the singing because, paradoxically, they take attention away from the singing leading to a more relaxed approach. However, if actions are complex and demanding, the singing will suffer because there is too much to think about at once. In this context, consider splitting the class in half with one group singing and another moving. Later the groups could swap roles and eventually children will have practised enough to be able to manage everything at once.

Armed with the information just given and a constructive approach, non-specialist teachers are perfectly able to teach songs to children.

HOW TO TEACH A NEW SONG

1 Preparing

- Know the song off by heart yourself. Practise in the shower, the car, the kitchen. Children will appreciate the fact that you know your way around the song, even if you might not be confident enough to sing it (but do sing at least sometimes if you possibly can).

- Consider which parts of a song are likely to be the most difficult to learn (for example because the tune jumps around in pitch, or the words are delivered rapidly). Sometimes it is helpful to isolate those parts to teach them separately first.

- To work out what note to start on, the easiest thing is to use a published version meant for children (in a book or online, e.g. from Sing Up). If you have to make the decision yourself, identify where in the song the highest and lowest pitch comes. Is the first note close to the highest, the lowest or somewhere in the middle? Remembering children's vocal ranges, pick a reasonable starting note and see if the song feels comfortable for the class. (For example, 'Happy Birthday to You' starts on the lowest note in the whole tune, so consider starting it on middle C. Otherwise, the middle part of the song may go too high for many singers.)

- Where are the best places to breathe, still keeping the meaning?

- Consider actions or other body movements.

2 Teaching

- When you first introduce the song to children, sing it (or let them hear it) right through intact, with dynamics and actions, so they know what it is that they are going to be learning. The complete song should be heard as often as possible, perhaps 'in the background' while changing clothes, tidying up or waiting for lunch. This repetition allows the whole song to become familiar. Children may spontaneously begin to sing along. This is fine, but ask that they do it quietly so the model can still be clearly heard by others.

- Teach the lyrics on their own, chanted (spoken rhythmically not sung), bit by bit using the copy-cat technique (known as 'call and response'). Make hand gestures to signal 'my turn – your turn' so you don't have to speak. (As a rule, resist sharing lyrics in visual form as this detracts from the aural/sonic nature of music. Specific children may need visual aids for reasons of inclusion, but teach the rest of the class aurally to promote their auditory capacities.)

- Teach the melody on its own (no lyrics, just the tune). The teacher – or another 'model' – sings/hums/'lahs'/plays the tune with no lyrics, bit by bit, and the children copy it back. Remember to start on a note with a sensible pitch (see above).
- Then start to put the words to the correct tune, a short section at a time. The teacher – or another model – sings one line of the song, or one section, or one tricky phrase, and the children copy back. (If the model is a recording from Sing Up, you can choose the echo track version which is designed to allow for copying-back each line of a song i.e. 'my turn, your turn' again.)
- Consider incorporating the Shy Copy-Cats idea (from earlier in this chapter).
- LISTEN to the children when they sing back to you. Learn to notice things that do not sound quite right, and go over them again. Try to think why they are difficult bits and share your ideas with the children. (Refer to the aspects mentioned in the sections above.) Feel free to deconstruct a tricky section and take it one tiny bit at a time, then build it back up again, slowly.
- To extend this important listening, ask half the class to sing a section and half to listen-for something specific (dynamics? diction? breathing? tune?). Ask the listeners to comment and then sing again in response to the comments. Later, swap roles.
- Can children find the key words or key moments of a song? Discuss and explore how to make them most effective.
- Always ask for children's evaluations and suggestions.
- Experiment with different dynamics, for different lines or verses. Use the dynamics to enhance the meaning.
- Consider shaping a song by inviting groups of children to sing different sections and contrasting that with whole-class sections.
- Revisit learnt songs often at first, to consolidate the learning.
- Always give positive, constructive, reinforcing feedback. Never resort to blame or humiliation as you can scar a singer for life with one unguarded comment.

Taking singing further

The level of challenge can be increased when children are ready, by choosing trickier songs and by having a group of children singing a different part to a song. A common and effective way into this part-singing is by using a **round** (such as 'Frère Jacques'). If everyone sings the song at the same time this is **unison** singing, but if one group starts after another, the singing is **in canon**. Such part-singing demands good audiation skills in order to keep one's own tune going even when others are singing something different. At the same time the common beat needs to be felt by all singers. It is important that each singer is totally familiar with their part before putting the parts together. Try practising a round in a chant first to get the beat and rhythm, before adding the tune. It may help to play a steady beat with a drum or foot-tap to begin with, then gently wean the singers off this audible beat.

What are playing skills?

The National Curriculum states that children in Key Stage 1 should learn to 'play tuned and untuned musical instruments musically', which I interpret as playing with musical intent, rather than purely to discover what sounds they can make. In Key Stage 2 they should also play with increasing 'confidence … accuracy, fluency, control and expression'.

As discussed in Chapter 2, generalist teachers are not expected to play or teach technically difficult instruments. Chapter 3 introduced the kinds of classroom instruments that are easy to play and very useful in primary curriculum music lessons. Here is some more PCK that will help you to make effective use of such classroom instruments.

Any instrument where something (a hand, a stick, or a part of the instrument) strikes against something else to produce a sound is a **percussion** instrument. Drums, cymbals, bells, gongs, xylophones and steel pans are all percussion instruments. Shakers and bells are also percussion instruments, since small parts of the instruments strike other parts to make the sounds. Pianos are also percussion instruments – look inside one!

Among the variety of sounds that children will discover, there are two general types of percussive sound: **resonant** (where the striking part bounces off the instrument and the sound rings out before it fades) and **damped** (where the struck surface is pressed and held so the sound is momentary and flat).

Untuned percussion instruments suitable for classroom work include

- drums of different shapes and sizes
- tambours (hand-held drums)
- tambourines (wooden ring with jingling metal discs)
- shakers
- rattles
- guiros (hollow wooden instruments with serrated surfaces which give a rasping sound when scraped)
- cabasas (several loops of linked steel balls around a textured metal cylinder)
- shekeres (networks of beads fitted over hollow gourds)
- individual bells
- sleigh bells/jingle bells

- Indian bells (pairs of tiny cymbal-shaped bells on cords played by pinching the cord just behind each bell and tapping the cymbal *edges* together)
- wood blocks (hollow and struck with beaters)
- pairs of claves (hardwood sticks, one struck with the other)
- rainsticks (hollow partitioned tubes containing small beads)
- triangles (metal, hung from a cord and struck with a metal beater)

You may also have access to:

- boomwhackers (plastic pipes of different lengths)
- sound shapes (flat plastic shapes that can be played like hand-held drums)
- djembe drums (tulip-shaped floor-standing drums held between the knees and tilted slightly forward)
- octachime (also called a stirring drum – a ring of wooden 'tongues' of different lengths played by stirring a beater around inside the ring)
- domino rattle (a set of domino-shaped wooden panels on a leather strap)
- castanets (attached to the palm of the hand, or on a stick)
- prayer drum (small drum on a stick with beads attached on strings, that strike the drum-heads when the stick is rolled between flat-pressed palms)

Figure 5.11 Untuned percussion instruments – see Chapter 3 too

Untuned percussion instruments are particularly useful in **rhythmic** work. For instance:

- With the children, develop repeating rhythm patterns. Spend time playing these, over and over, so that they are rock solid, fitting to the pulse – the beat – of the pattern.

- Consider supplying an audible pulse/beat, such as a steady drumbeat, to support this.

- It can help if words or phrases are chosen that match the desired rhythms. James Blades, a famous English percussionist, was known for saying, 'If you can say it, you can play it.'

- Try clapping 'cheese on toast' over and over, in its natural rhythm. What about 'brown bread and butter' or 'cornflakes covered in ice-cold milk'?

- Words related to any theme can be used, allowing cross-curricular links.

- Experiment with which instruments to use for which rhythm.

- In Key Stage 2 children are expected to develop the ability to 'reproduce sounds from aural memory'. So, can a child play the rhythm pattern from something they remember? For instance, can they play the pattern of the words 'Baa Baa Black Sheep Have You Any Wool?' (long, long, long, long, short-short-short-short long)

A simple rhythm pattern played over and over is a useful way to accompany live singing or recorded music.

Rhythm patterns also sound wonderful as stand-alone music if you layer two or more simple rhythm patterns on top of each other (i.e. play them simultaneously), with all the players sticking to a common beat or pulse. Consider how to turn this idea into a complete piece of music:

- Could one pattern start off alone, with a second pattern joining in later?

- Could there be moments during the piece where one pattern is heard by itself and other moments when everyone is playing?

- Will the piece end with everyone playing or will each pattern stop at a different time?

- Will there be any changes of dynamic through the piece?

- Will any changes be sudden or gradual?

Tuned percussion instruments suitable for classroom work include

- xylophones (wooden bars for notes)
- metallophones (metal bars for notes)
- set of chime bars (like a metallophone but each note-bar separated out into an individual instrument)

- steel pans (based on original oil-drum instruments, with notes produced by hitting flattened panels of metal)
- pianos
- set of tuned bells (handbells, hand-chimes or bell-plates)

Other tuned instruments you might have access to:

- wind instruments (e.g. whistles, recorders, ocarinas)
- stringed instruments (e.g. ukuleles, guitars)
- digital instruments (e.g. keyboards, software and app-based instruments – see Chapter 3 for some examples). Suitable software allows children to bypass a lack of technical proficiency and still express themselves musically. It is worth investing in some small rechargeable speakers to do the children's music justice.

Figure 5.12 Tuned instruments – xylophone, metallophone and keyboard

Tuned instruments lend themselves to work involving **pitch**.

- Can children make up a simple tune? Can you? Can children teach others their tunes?
- Given the expectation for children in Key Stage 2 to learn to 'reproduce sounds from aural memory', can a child pick out a remembered tune on a xylophone or keyboard?

EXAMPLE

Try picking out the first phrase of 'Happy' by Pharrell Williams (PharrellWilliamsVEVO 2014) on a tuned instrument, starting with the note A. (Williams himself sings it lower than this, starting on F, but if you begin on A you will not need any sharps or flats!)

Bet you can also find the little in-between tune that follows it, also starting on A. Why not use this little **riff** to accompany singers as they sing the whole of William's first verse (the section of the song before he starts to sing 'Because I'm happy').

Tuned instruments can also be used to play simple repeating patterns, for example on just one or two notes, to accompany songs and tunes, that is, to **harmonize** with the tunes:

- Often the final note of a song is a good note to choose as a starting point for inventing harmonies.

Make up a rhythmic pattern all on note A to harmonize with 'Happy', which finishes on note A. You could use some high As and some low As.

- Experiment with adding another note (maybe the fifth note above the song's final note, counting that as the first).

Make a rhythm pattern with these two notes and repeat it while the melody is sung or played. For 'Happy', use A and E. Any A, any E – they all fit!

- A repeating pattern of notes like this is called an **ostinato**, the Italian word for 'obstinate', that is, persistent!

Accompany the first line of the chorus of 'Happy' ('Clap along if you feel like a room without a roof') with a long F, E, E and A sequence. Maybe make each note last by playing it as a **roll** with two beaters alternating rapidly. This sequence works for each line of the chorus. Try adding the fifth note above each of these notes, too (see Chapter 3).

Incorporate some of these ideas into activities with genuine musical purpose (see chapters 4 and 6).

> Develop the 'Happy' work by adding some rhythm patterns too. Shape it into a performance and share it in a school assembly.

BASIC PLAYING TECHNIQUES WITH PERCUSSION INSTRUMENTS

drums

- Many drums are designed to be played with the hands. Discourage children from using sticks unless they can convince you that they need them to produce a particular sound.
- Consider leaving drums out of some lessons entirely: they are not always appropriate to the activity. Or include them but insist on quiet sounds only: this is perfectly possible.
- Explore how to achieve resonant and damped sounds. Also experiment with tilting the drums so that their openings are not covered: how does that affect the sound?
- With drums that are not hand-held, encourage children to use two hands in their playing.

xylophones, metallophones

Having allowed children to explore how these instruments make sounds when the note-bars are struck with beaters, the teacher can ask some questions to guide improvements to the sound quality, such as:

- What happens to the sound if you use a different kind of beater? (Beaters are made with harder or softer ends, which produce brasher/more muffled sounds.)
- What happens to the sound if you tap a different part of the note-bar? (The middle of each note-bar is the part to strike for the most resonant note.)
- What happens to the sound if you let the beater bounce? If you press the beater down?
- How could you play a sound of long duration? (A single beater-tap will produce a fairly short-lived note so experiment with using two beaters playing in quick succession to produce a roll: if this is done sensitively the effect can be close to a single sustained note.)
- How could you play your tune more quickly and easily? (Use two beaters instead of one: develop the skill of playing with both hands.)

a few words about beaters and drumsticks

- Using a stick or beater end-on to a drum-head (the playing surface of a drum) is likely to pierce the drum, so avoid this. Like hands, sticks are used almost parallel to the drum-head (if used at all).

- Beaters and sticks have developed to make the control of sounds more precise. Imagine playing a drum by bouncing a ball on it. You could control the ball better, without stopping the bounce, if you had a thin rod sticking out from it. This is what a beater or drum-stick is, in essence. A good technique is to hold the stick lightly between the thumb-tip and the base of your curled index finger, palm down, in such a way that you are not gripping the stick but allowing the end to bounce freely on the drum-head. Experiment with how far down the stick your hand should be: you are aiming to have your thumb and finger at the balance point. The other fingers curl loosely around the stick and also help to give control of the bounce. See Figure 5.13 for a good, relaxed stick grip and Figure 8.4 for an imperfect grip.

Figure 5.13 Relaxed stick grip

What are notation skills?

Listening, singing, playing, creating and sharing are by far the most important skills to develop in primary music. After all, music is sonic and many, perhaps most, musicians around the world do not read or write music at all and have no need to do so. In any case, 'students cannot learn to read what they have not moved to, responded to, sung to, improvized to, and audiated' (Conway 2003 p28). Nevertheless, the National Curriculum states that by the end of Key Stage 2 children should be able to 'use and understand staff and other notations'. (Staff notation is the classical Western notation involving a **staff** or **stave** of 5 horizontal lines on which notes are positioned. It is just one of many ways of notating music.) So children need at least to be introduced to the idea that you can 'catch' aspects of music as marks on paper and interpret the marks back into sound.

There are many ways of doing this and the best ways are often those invented by children themselves. Ask children how they might represent their music on paper so that they can play it again another day. This gives a musical purpose for using notation. Such a visual representation of music is called a **graphic score**.

Another strategy is to show notation, incidentally and without comment, along with lyrics from time to time, just as you would expose children to books and text before they ever begin to read words. (For example, Sing Up has staff notation **scores** you can project with the lyrics.)

From time to time, include some notation activities into music sessions as part and parcel of the practical work going on. Some ideas are given here, which if used in the order suggested will also lead to an understanding of staff notation. The two dimensions of music that are most often notated are **rhythm** and **pitch**, while **dynamics** are often indicated too.

Duration and rhythm

Rhythm patterns can be represented (notated) as visual patterns where each item represents a sound of a certain duration. Children should be encouraged to represent their rhythm patterns in ways they understand, to establish a connection between sound and symbol. Gradually encourage children to notate their ideas so that they read from left to right, like words on a page.

Pause for thought

How could you play or say this rhythm?

A useful way of notating rhythms is in a grid where each cell (box) represents one beat of music.

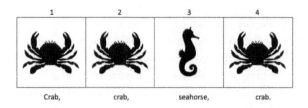

Crab,   crab,   seahorse,   crab.

Pictures, shapes or symbols can be used in **rhythm grids**. Different ones could represent different types of sound. They represent whatever sounds the children want them to represent.

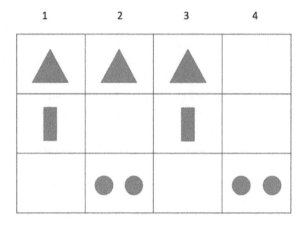

Three different shapes are seen in this grid, so three different kinds of sounds are needed. It is up to the players to choose what sounds each shape represents. Perhaps a triangle represents a clap, a rectangle means a stamp and a circle represents a single rub of the hands. Or perhaps each shape's sound will be made by a different instrument, or with a different vocal sound.

In this grid, there are four cells in a row, so the rhythm is in a metre of 4 (see Chapter 3). Count slowly and steadily 'one, two, three, four, one, two, three, four, one, two, three, four …' as you read the grid from left to right, over and over. The count is the beat. Try clapping where you see a triangle (i.e. on beats one, two and three). Beat four is silent: take a rest from clapping. It can help to make a physical movement to fill the silence, for example turning your two palms upwards in time to the beat. Repeat that top row several times more. 'Clap, clap, clap, rest, clap, clap, clap, rest', etc.

Once the top row has been mastered, try the middle row, counting the beat aloud and stamping on the first and third beat, then repeating the row. 'Stamp, rest, stamp, rest', etc. The bottom row is a little more challenging. There is silence during the first beat, two hand-rubs in the second, silence in the third and two more hand-rubs in the fourth. 'Rest, rub-rub, rest, rub-rub', etc. Each 'rub' only lasts for half of a beat: a shorter sound-duration. Experiment with playing each of the grid patterns while keeping the beat silently in your head (with no audible counting).

Rhythm grid notation is very versatile. Here are some possible activities:

RHYTHM GRID IDEAS

- Ask children to fill in blank grids for themselves, inventing the symbols.
- Challenge children to interpret the grids, ensuring that a steady beat underpins all their attempts. It helps if someone counts a steady beat aloud. (Later, when everyone has internalized the rhythms, the count can be done silently, though it is good if everyone moves to the beat to ensure synchronization.)
- Play the rhythms on different instruments (or body percussion) from those originally chosen.
- Turn the grid upside down and play it. How does the pattern change? What about turning the grid sideways?
- Each player in a group plays a different single row of the grid repeatedly. Put them together so that all the rows are played simultaneously. How does it sound?
- All players in a group play the whole grid row by row, then repeat from the top.
- As above, but each player starts to play when the last player starts the second row. (This is playing the grid as a **round**: see earlier section on singing.)
- Incorporate some silent beats (empty cells of the grid). Take a **rest** from making sound on these beats.
- Play the grid at a faster or slower tempo.
- Use smaller versions of the symbols to represent quieter sounds.
- Swap grids with another group and interpret each other's notations.
- Combine two grids to make a longer piece of music.
- Mix and match rows from different grids.
- Invent grids of different sizes.

Once children are used to these ideas – from later Key Stage 1 onwards if they have had plenty of experience – they can gradually be introduced to the way that sound durations are represented in **staff notation**:

The one-beat notes are called **crotchets**. The joined-up notes, worth half a beat each, are called **quavers**.

After this kind of familiarization with the note symbols, children can start to read rhythms such as:

Other useful note-values are **minims** (which look like crotchets but with white blobs and last for two beats) and **semiquavers** (which are very short notes, a quarter-beat long and joined with two bars). Silences are notated using **rests**. A one-beat rest looks like a seagull flying on its side.

ACTIVITIES TO TRY WITH STAFF NOTATION OF RHYTHM

- Can you write this rhythm? (Clap a rhythm.)
- Can you name this song/tune from its written rhythm only? For example:

- 'Lotto' with rhythms: leader plays the rhythm and players see if they have a match written on a card
- Could the idea be extended to 'Bingo'?

Remember that games and puzzles can be helpful for practising a skill in isolation, but they are not music. Give children musical reasons to read and write rhythms, for example writing down their own compositions.

There are an increasing number of free online resources and apps that can support children as they learn to read, write and play rhythm patterns written in staff notation. For example, explore apps such as 'Woodchuck Rhythm' (Wood 2013) and 'Rhythm Cat' (Melody Cats, no date). Layton Music (no date) provides a set of rhythm flashcards and ideas for activities.

With some basic knowledge of how to read note durations in staff notation, children can begin to work out the rhythms of songs by looking at the scores available on the Sing Up (2016) website, for example. If they are involved in first-access instrumental tuition (see Chapter 2), this will usually involve some written music too.

Pitch and melody

As with duration, early visual representations (notations) of pitch should be informal and preferably invented by the children. The convention is for time to be represented from left to right on a page in music notation, whereas pitch uses the high-low axis. This is not an easy thing for anyone to understand at first. Before attempting to notate pitch, therefore, children need to associate high-pitched notes with 'up' and low-pitched notes with 'down'. A xylophone propped up on its wider end can be a good demonstration: as a beater plays notes that are physically higher up, the pitch will also be higher. (If pianos were orientated this way our lives as teachers would be much easier!)

A good way to attend to the highs and lows of pitch is to 'follow' them with the whole body. Ask the class to make low, crouched body shapes as you play the lowest-pitched xylophone note (the longest one on the instrument). Now ask them to make high, tall shapes as you play the highest-pitched note. Choose a middle note and ask for middle-height body shapes from the children. Can the children proceed to make the appropriate body shapes for high/middle/low notes without looking at the xylophone?

Ask half the class to sing 'Row, Row, Row Your Boat' slowly while the other half starts off crouched low (because the tune begins at a low pitch). The moving children should match the pitch of the tune with the height of their bodies, standing tallest on the first 'Merrily'. Swap groups. Eventually children can sing and move at the same time.

One arm, held out flat with the palm of the hand downwards, can also be used to follow the pitch of a tune, whether sung by the same person, classmates or a recorded voice. Try the xylophone activity above but with arms, not whole bodies, to demonstrate higher and lower pitches.

Having related high-low pitch with high-low physical position – which takes time and will need much revisiting – children are ready to understand visual representations (notations) of pitch. Lines and dots on paper can represent sounds: the higher on the paper they are located, the higher the pitch of their sounds. When that idea is combined with reading left to right, all the ingredients are in place. Here is a police 'nee naw' siren sound:

Pause for thought

What might these lines sound like? Use a free-flow voice that rises and falls with each line as you follow it from left to right:

Children can be encouraged to sing the horizon, a roofline or even a mathematical line-graph by singing an 'aah' or 'ooh' or 'mmm' that changes in pitch as they follow the line up and down from left to right.

PLAY THE 'WHAT DID YOU SAY?' GAME (Lougheed 1997)

Display a number of rectangles, each containing the word 'what' three times, in different positions. For example:

what w		what
h		
a		
t what	what what	

One person 'sings' a rectangle, reading from left to right and using a high-pitched voice for letters and words near the top, low-pitched near the bottom, and so on. Can listening children guess which rectangle it is?

Having established a general sense of high and low, you can begin to introduce individual pitched sounds. Choose two notes to play on a xylophone or piano, one higher, one lower. Draw two lines, one higher, one lower. Reading from left to right, play along to this music:

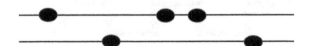

The final stage of developing understanding of how pitch is represented in staff notation is to see how specific notes (C, D, E, etc,) take their exact places on the high-low axis. Start with a single horizontal line, the G line. The symbol on the left is called the **treble clef** and it has evolved from a fancy capital G wrapped around this line to label it as the G line. Any note sitting on this G line has the pitch of the G above middle C, always, whatever the instrument.

If a note is positioned in the space just above the G line, it is one note higher in pitch, that is, A. The note in the space just below is F.

   Can children play this tune?

Note that some pitches are notated with blobs on lines and others with blobs in spaces. Staff notation uses five lines.

Pause for thought

Can you spot which one is the G line here?

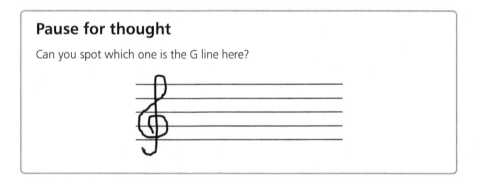

The tune above looks like this now:

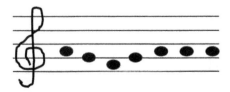

Again, at this point there are online and other activities that can help children to consolidate the names of notes in each position on the staff (or stave). One example is 'Noteworks' (DoReMiworld, no date). Always remember that acquiring skill

Figure 5.14 Learning to read staff notation

through such isolated practice activities is only a means to a musical end: find ways to use and apply the skills musically by providing genuine reasons for children to *need* to read and to write simple music.

Children can eventually combine their understanding of how to notate both pitch and duration. For instance:

Dynamics

In staff notation, dynamics are represented with abbreviated Italian words beside the music. To allow for gradual changes in dynamic, two symbols are also used.

NOTATING DYNAMICS (write these under the staff)

f = forte (loud)

p = piano (quiet)

ff = fortissimo (very loud)

pp = pianissimo (very quiet)

mf = mezzo forte (loud-ish)

mp = mezzo piano (quiet-ish)

< = crescendo (get louder – stretch this sign out to make it as long as you need it to be)

> = decrescendo *or* diminuendo (get quieter – again, the sign can be stretched)

subito = suddenly (so, for example, you might read *subito piano*)

What skills should I start with?

The skills that directly involve sound take precedence over those relating to its notation. Singing is the single most important skill for primary children to develop. It provides an ideal way for children to internalize the 'feel' for beat, rhythm and pitch. Singing also draws on the other fundamental skills of listening and audiating. Link singing with rhythmic movements and/or simple sounds played on body percussion or classroom instruments and you will have made a very good start in supporting children's acquisition of musical skills.

For further support with how to teach singing, contact your school music coordinator or your area's Music Education Hub and ask what advice, support, training and opportunities are available locally.

Summary

In this chapter we have looked at how to teach the skills of listening, 'speaking', reading and writing in music. None of this is beyond the non-specialist primary school teacher.

Remember that the first principle of skill acquisition is to have an appropriate level of challenge. This is true for teachers as well as children. Include time to repeat and consolidate new learning.

Pause for thought

Which part of this chapter do you think would make a realistic first challenge for you as you develop your skills as a teacher of primary music?

The second principle is that skills should not be taught too much in isolation. Instead, focus first on your main musical intentions for a lesson or sequence of lessons, and then build in short opportunities to develop relevant skills in support of those overall musical intentions. For example, spend five minutes of the lesson working on an aspect of singing quality, notation, listening or how to use beaters effectively, followed by an opportunity to apply that new learning in a practical, musical way that links to your main lesson objective.

Pause for thought

How could you include an audiation activity within a lesson which is mainly about a song from another country?

Pause for thought

How could you include a notation activity within a lesson which is mainly about a song from another country?

Finally, the last principle is a reminder that music is about much more than just technical proficiency on instruments so look for ways to compensate for (as well as help develop) current levels of skill. For instance, you could use a regular beat from a sound-producing app like the Smart Drums of GarageBand (Apple Inc. 2016) as children play simple rhythm patterns, helping them to learn the skill of playing in time with the steady pulse. As the teacher you can also find ways to support (or compensate for) your own skill levels so that your pupils can access their full musical entitlement.

Recommended reading

Apple Inc. (2016). *Garageband*. Available at: http://www.apple.com/uk/mac/garageband/ (Accessed 31 July 2016).

Austin, J., Renwick, J. and McPherson, G. (2006). 'Developing Motivation'. In McPherson, G. (ed.), *The Child as Musician: A Handbook of Musical Development*. Oxford: Oxford University Press, 11 pp. 213–38.

Barton, P. (2016). 'Aquarium' from *Carnival of the Animals* by Camille Saint-Saëns. Available at: https://www.youtube.com/watch?v=_sN3Xmnd5cs (Accessed 19 July 2016).

Csikszentmihalyi, M. (1999). 'If We Are So Rich, Why Aren't We Happy?'. *American Psychologist*, 54(10) pp. 821–7.

DoReMiworld (no date). *NoteWorks*. Available at: http://www.doremiworld.com/ (Accessed 31 July 2016).

Gordon, E. (1999). 'All About Audiation and Music Aptitudes'. *Music Educators Journal*, 86(2) pp. 41–4.

Layton Music (no date). *Games and Resources*. Available at: https://laytonmusic.wordpress.com/2007/12/19/rhythm-flashcards/ (Accessed 31 July 2016).

lirbugler (2012). *British Army Routine Bugle Calls Part 2*. Available at: https://www.youtube.com/watch?v=1UkW9aEP4fI (Accessed 12 December 2016).

lucpebo (2012). *Mussorgsky/ Pictures at an exhibition – Bydlo – Karajan*. Available at: https://www.youtube.com/watch?v=vOvIbfaUjIw. (Accessed 12 December 2016).

Malloch, S. and Trevarthen, C. eds. (2010). *Communicative Musicality: Exploring the Basis of Human Companionship*. Oxford: Oxford University Press.

Melody Cats (no date). *Rhythm Cat*. Available at: http://melodycats.com/rhythm-cat/ (Accessed 31 July 2016).

PharrellWilliamsVEVO (2014). *Happy*. Available at: https://www.youtube.com/watch?v=ZbZSe6N_BXs (Accessed: 21 July 2016).

Welch, G. F. (2006). 'Singing and vocal development'. In McPherson, G. E. (ed.), *The Child as Musician: A Handbook of Musical Development*. Oxford: Oxford University Press.

Wood, Marion (2013). *Woodchuck Rhythm* [ipad app]. Available at: http://woodchuck-rhythm.moonfruit.com/ipad-app/4575573291 (Downloaded 31 July 2016).

Chapter 6
Children's Ideas – Promoting Creativity

Chapter objectives

- to outline what we might mean by creativity in primary curriculum music
- to understand why musical creativity is important for children
- to explain how non-specialist teachers can support children's creative work in music, by deploying:
  - thoughtful planning
  - appropriate teaching approaches
- to illustrate these ideas through an extended case study
- to understand what improvisation is, in music

What is creativity in primary music?

Pause for thought

Can children be creative?

How do you know?

What is your definition of creativity?

In 2001, Bloom's 1956 *Taxonomy of Educational Objectives* was revised (Krathwohl 2002). One major change was to move 'create' to the top of the hierarchy of cognitive processes because of its complexity. Yet Barrett (2012) discerned creativity in very young children's adaptations and extensions of musical material. Creativity is a central characteristic of effective learning as defined in the Statutory Framework for the Early Years Foundation Stage (2014). So what is creativity and how might it manifest itself in primary music?

Creativity combines the skills, knowledge and curiosity we have explored in earlier chapters and adds another essential ingredient: 'the core element of imagination – imagining what might be' (Craft 2010, p. 293). This often involves making connections between ideas (Cremin 2015) and it is no coincidence that in revising Bloom's *Taxonomy* the new term 'create' subsumed and replaced the previous term 'synthesis'. Moreover, creativity takes imagination one step further. It is 'applied imagination' (Robinson 2001, p. 142), turning 'what might be' into something new and real.

OFSTED (2010) distilled a definition of creative learning from surveys of a large number of schools, characterizing it as:

- questioning and challenging
- making connections and seeing relationships
- envisaging what might be
- exploring ideas, keeping options open
- reflecting critically on ideas, actions and outcomes

Two fundamental points need to be made about creativity in children.

The first is that people can be creative even though they are not highly skilled or knowledgeable. Children are often the most creative people, as a personal example illustrates:

SCENARIO A:

Breakfasts were interesting when my children were small. While I had my usual toast and marmalade, they loved experimenting with food. My daughter's favourite breakfast for a while was shredded wheat with tomato ketchup, while my son had a thing for chocolate-flavoured puffed rice with grated parmesan cheese.

They did not acquire these ideas from me! They invented new breakfasts for themselves. Perhaps what I did contribute was a positive attitude: 'Try it and see.' It is important for teachers to cultivate this attitude in their music classrooms too: a culture of encouraging what Craft (2010) terms 'possibility thinking'.

Being able to produce sounds using *skills* of playing, singing or using digital technology is one attribute of musicianship. Being *knowledgeable* about music is another attribute. Being *creative* with sound is a third, separate attribute. People can have one, two or all three attributes of musicianship, to varying and independent degrees. Here is another personal example.

SCENARIO B:

I had been playing the cello for many years when my daughter, as a teenager, began learning the violin. As I played in concerts reproducing other people's music, my daughter developed her own simple violin parts to accompany her friend's original songs and they played at open mic evenings. This opened my eyes to the possibility of 'using what you have', showing that you don't have to wait till you're a virtuoso to start being creative.

The second important point concerns what we mean by creating 'something new'. Children are being creative when they invent something that is new in their experience, even though it might not be a world exclusive. When they invent a signature breakfast, a rhythm pattern or a tune, they are exhibiting creativity. Tafuri (2006), investigating creative musical work with children, puts it like this: 'A creative act produces something novel and meaningful for its creator' (p. 151). It is what Craft (2001) describes as 'little-c creativity' and it contrasts with Big-C creativity which produces new-to-the-whole-world ideas and inventions.

The current National Curriculum for Music (Department for Education 2013) clearly alludes to the Big-C aspect of musical creativity when it states that children should 'listen with discrimination to the best in the musical canon', that is, the best music that has ever been created. This ties in with an overarching aim of the entire National Curriculum in England to 'engender an appreciation of human creativity'.

BIG-C MUSICAL CREATIONS SOUND GREAT …

Most children and adults alike hear Big-C musical creations on a daily basis through digital media and it is easy to think 'I can't possibly compete with that.' Banish that thought, which is about the creative *product*: our focus as primary teachers is on supporting the creative *process*.

Happily, there is also plenty of focus on little-c creativity within the current music curriculum. It states that music education should inspire children to 'increase their … creativity' and one of its aims is for all children to learn to 'create and compose music on their own and with others'. It also outlines more specific requirements. In Key Stage 1, children should be taught to 'use their voices creatively' and to 'experiment with, create, select and combine sounds using the inter-related dimensions of music'. In Key Stage 2 they should build on this and 'improvise and compose music for a range of purposes using the interrelated dimensions of music', showing an 'understanding of musical composition, organizing and manipulating ideas within musical structures'.

Figure 6.1 A child exploring ideas on a metallophone

Our job is to nurture children's capacities to be musically creative, leaning on whatever musical skills and knowledge they have acquired so far. Who knows: perhaps we are nurturing a future Big-C creative genius. More importantly, we can certainly nurture a positive and confident attitude to creativity in all our pupils and help them to develop their creative capacities as described by OFSTED (2010). The next section discusses the importance of this.

Why should children be creative?

In Craft's (2010) survey of the generic arguments for encouraging children's creativity, four main reasons are discussed. Each of them is relevant to musical creativity.

First is the need to react to change: creativity is 'necessary as a response to rapid social, technological, economic and environmental change' (Craft 2010, p. 290). Although musical creativity might not lead directly to innovative ways to save the planet, music is important in people's social and emotional lives and creative musical solutions may well have a positive part to play in the future. Yip Harburg, composer of 'Over the Rainbow', is quoted as saying, 'Words make you think a thought. Music makes you feel a feeling. A song makes you feel a thought' (The Yip Harburg Foundation, no date). This power of music to combine the cognitive with the emotional gives it tremendous influence which could be used to support wise and sustainable reaction to change. More fundamental is the fact that music is part of what makes life worth living and as our lives change we will want new music to go with new circumstances.

Second, there are links between the national economy and creativity. This is certainly true for music. UK Music (2014) reports that the music industry's growth has been outstripping that of other economic sectors. 111,000 people are employed in music-related jobs with over half of these involved with creating new material. UK Music quotes the Secretary of State for Culture, Media and Sport: 'The UK accounts for less than one per cent of the global population, yet one in every eight albums sold anywhere in the world is by a British artist. … In six of the past seven years, the biggest-selling album worldwide has been by a British artist. And we're second only to US in terms of music exports' (UK Music 2014, p. 3).

Craft (2010) worries that the economic argument for creativity might be harmful: 'Framing creativity enhancement as primarily or even entirely an economic imperative promulgates a high-consumption approach that is environmentally, culturally, and spiritually blind' (p. 306). Her concern extends to the third reason too: that creativity has the potential to support cultural cohesion (National Advisory Committee on Creative and Cultural Education 1999). Craft points out that 'just any creativity will not do; rather it is *wise* creativity that is needed in the classroom' (Craft 2010, p. 304). This goes for musical creativity: depending on the intent of the creators, it can promote cultural cohesion or division. However, music does have enormous positive potential to overcome barriers of language and circumstance, allowing people to communicate in a 'language' far deeper than words.

Figure 6.2 Music offers genuine opportunities for children to have agency over their learning

The final reason is related to concepts of empowerment and 'agency', 'the extent to which individuals have the freedom to take control of their actions' (Carlile and Jordan 2012). It is well documented that empowerment, motivation, engagement and deep learning go hand in hand and this is a strong reason for promoting children's creativity across the curriculum. Creative work taps into current levels of knowledge and skill and fuels the desire to learn more, thereby driving further learning.

Primary music has had a mixed history in terms of allowing children agency over their learning (Paynter 2002) and many children have not had any chance to be musically creative in school. Green (2008) has recently had a major influence on the pedagogical approach in many secondary music classrooms. Now the approach is often akin to the kinds of informal music learning practices engaged in by pop and rock musicians who are completely self-driven. Her ideas allow for considerable creativity and have a great deal to offer primary music too.

Being creative is one of the fundamental ways of being a musician, whether that involves improvising, composing, arranging, interpreting or producing. Failing to support children's creative work in music would be like teaching reading but not writing, or teaching art without making any pictures.

> Music may have a role in school life socially but, if it is to be a valuable curriculum subject, what is done in the classroom must reach out to every pupil; that is to say, it must exploit natural human musicality. How, then, is this inherent musicality manifest? Not, I think, in the first instance by listening to music, nor even by learning from someone else how to play on an instrument, but by making up music. Across the ages most of the world's music has been made up – invented and performed – by musically untutored people. There are still people like that in every culture, and they are still making music. It may be that most of us have come to think of music as something to be listened to – in the same way that we think of paintings as objects to be looked at – yet, in essence, both music and paintings are what human beings make: it is the act of making that justifies the art.
>
> (Paynter 2002, p. 219)

How can teachers promote children's creativity?

There are, unfortunately, teachers who deliberately avoid allowing children to work creatively. I can clearly remember the stock phrase used by the teacher I had when I was nine years old, explaining why we could never do any such thing: 'There will be pan-de-monium!' There are other teachers who think they are supporting children's creative work when in fact they are the only ones being creative and the pupils just do as they are told. School productions can be like this!

Yet it is not difficult to allow children scope to be musically creative and the class need not descend into pandemonium. The key point is that children themselves need to have opportunities to use their imaginations, to explore ideas and envisage what might be (OFSTED 2010). They need to have agency over 'the transition from "what is" to "what might be"' (Craft 2010, pp. 294–5). If the children are not making the creative decisions, they are the human equivalents of 'cute' dogs barking 'Happy Birthday' on YouTube.

The aim of this section is to discuss and illustrate how children's creativity can be nurtured in primary music, even by cautious teachers. Two useful aspects of PCK are:

- to plan thoughtfully and
- to use appropriate teaching approaches

These are discussed below. There is also a detailed case study illustrating the way that careful planning and good pedagogical decisions enable the teacher to maintain control of the class while at the same time giving children licence and support to do creative musical work.

Thoughtful planning

A lesson that promotes children's creativity needs to be as well planned as any other. Children do not like the idea of classroom chaos any more than teachers do. Equally, they want to know what is expected of them and what the purpose of their work is.

How much scope will you allow for children to be creative?

It can give teachers confidence to know that allowing scope for children's creativity in a lesson does not have to be an all-or-nothing decision. Sometimes you might plan very brief opportunities for children to flex their creative muscles. At the other extreme, a creative project might span several lessons. This is true for every subject. In a maths warm-up activity, for example, you might ask children to invent interesting number statements that equate with 25. They will then be 'making connections and seeing relationships' (OFSTED 2010). In a music lesson, you might ask children to watch a short silent video clip and make suggestions about the kind of music that would go well with it, thereby 'envisaging what might be' (OFSTED 2010).

As well as considering how much time you want to plan into your lessons for children to work creatively and which aspect/s of their creative learning you want to promote, you might also want to plan in some musical parameters or constraints. For example, if children have been challenged to invent short tunes, you could limit the palette of note pitches they are allowed to include. If they are focusing on beat and rhythm, challenge them to invent rhythm patterns that have a mix of short and long sounds. More experienced children could be challenged to make their pattern fit to pre-recorded music of some kind. Choose musical parameters that complement your current musical focus. There is another example of this in the case study presented later in this chapter.

While they could appear constricting at first glance, such constraints do actually help the creative process. Watson (2011) quotes Stravinsky on this:

> In art as in everything else, one can build only upon a resisting foundation: whatever constantly gives way to pressure, constantly renders movement impossible. My freedom thus consists in my moving about within the narrow frame that I have assigned myself ... I shall go even further: my freedom will be so much the greater and more meaningful the more narrowly I limit my field of action.
>
> (Stravinsky 1970, quoted in Watson 2011, p. 37)

Pause for thought

Have you ever noticed this phenomenon of constraints making you more creative? Here's an illustration for you to try. Which of the following challenges do you think you could respond to more easily?

A: Invent a story.

B: Invent a story not more than five minutes in the telling, which involves a dustbin and a mouse.

What will the children be creating?

Children can undertake a variety of musical ventures, large and small. Here are four:

1 inventing sounds
2 inventing small musical ideas, by putting a few sounds together
3 creating new versions of existing music
4 creating new compositions (pieces of music), which might be on a small scale or a larger one

Some of these musical ventures can be accomplished in a short time, whereas others take longer. Older and creatively more experienced children will, on the whole, be better equipped to undertake the more involved ventures. Remember that we are talking about little-c creativity: the outcomes of their creative activities will be new for the children, even if the world has heard them all before. Also note that the important thing is for the children, rather than the teacher, to be the ones asking 'What if ...?' and making the musical decisions.

The following table gives just one example of each venture (but there are many, many ways to launch each one):

1 inventing sounds	Children sit in a circle, each with a small percussion instrument.
	'I'll give you two minutes to explore your instrument. Can you find three different ways to make a sound with it?'
	'Can you make a different/quiet/quick sound?'
	'Can you make an even quieter/quicker sound?'
	'Can you make a peaceful/excited/weird sound?'
	'What is the longest-lasting sound you can make?'
	etc.
	'Let's make a Mexican Wave of our quickest/loudest sounds, starting here and travelling around the circle back to here. Each person play your sound just once'.
	'Which was the quickest/loudest sound that time?'
	'Now pass your instrument to the person on your left'.
	etc.
2 inventing small musical ideas, by putting a few sounds together	Children are in a circle; one tambour (small hand-drum) is in front of the teacher.
	'Let's get a steady clap going to give us a beat.' Everyone claps at about heart-beat speed.
	'Now sing with me [to the tune of *London Bridge is Falling Down*]:
	Pass the tambour, pass it round,
	Pass it round, pass it round,
	Pass the tambour, pass it round,
	Now you play!'
	As the group sings the song, the tambour is passed from hand to hand. Whichever child holds the tambour at the end of the song plays whatever they like on it, while everyone else keeps clapping a steady pulse. When the child has finished, they hold the tambour high. This is the signal for the song to begin again.
3 creating new versions of existing music	Once children are familiar with a song, they can start to customize it. Depending on the current learning focus, children might:
	• make up new verses
	• vary the tempo (speed)
	• decide how many children should sing each section
	• experiment with dynamics, expression, gesture and movement
	• invent a second tune that fits with part of the song
	• use percussion instruments to invent rhythm patterns to go with the song
	• find out what the most important notes and chords are in the song accompaniment and experiment with them (see Chapter 3).
4 creating new compositions	[see case study below for an example of this]

Figure 6.3 Waiting for the Mexican wave to arrive

Pause for thought

What age-group of children do you imagine taking part in each of the examples above?

Pause for thought

Can you think of different ways to inspire similar creative venturing for younger or older children?

When and where is the inventing going to happen?

For the most part, children's creative musical activity is likely to happen separately from activities focusing on performing. In the first venture in the table above, for instance, there are moments to invent, followed by moments to perform.

However, in the second venture described above, the child with the tambour in each round of the song was invited to invent a pattern of sounds immediately, without any private practice or preparation. This is improvisation and it is good practice to build in small opportunities for children to create 'in real time' in this way. As another example, the traditional song 'Aiken Drum' (Sing Up 2016 or https://www.youtube.com/watch?v=KcC4_km61aU – an American version) lends itself to enjoyable improvisation: children suggest what foodstuff each part of Aiken Drum's body is made of, as the song is sung. There is a further note about improvisation at the end of this chapter.

Creative work can be planned as all or part of a music lesson. It can also be encouraged by setting up a music area with enticing sound-makers and some inspirational prompts, or by finding sounds outdoors, perhaps while on a visit or as part of a Forest School session.

Quest or Exploration?

They say necessity is the mother of invention, and people often demonstrate creativity in the *quest* to solve a particular problem. In primary music a useful format for creative work is to give children some kind of musical 'problem', as will be illustrated later in this section. Such a format makes the purpose of the learning clear and also provides a means of assessing children's learning through reflecting on their problem-solving quests.

Creativity can also occur in an open-ended *exploratory* context, from inspiration rather than necessity. Rather than setting up an end-point to aim for, creative work might instead be inspired by a stimulating starting point. This could be as simple as the chance to explore a new instrument to savour the sounds that can be made. (See Chapter 3, too.) Often a good stimulus comes from something the children are doing in another curricular area, or in the wider life of the school.

Possible starting points or stimuli for musical explorations:

- an unfamiliar musical instrument or sound-maker, such as a new ipad app or strange instrument donated to the school
- a picture – perhaps an image from work in another curriculum area
- an artefact – again, cross-curricular links can be made
- an experience, such as a journey or an occasion
- a silent film – choose a short clip and turn the sound down
- a feeling – link music with personal, social and health education
- an atmosphere or mood
- something from a story – a character, an event, a setting
- an existing piece of music – make up verses, instrumental breaks, accompaniments
- an instrument – take a beater for a walk on a xylophone
- a social situation, such as welcoming guests or saying goodbye to someone
- an environment
- an issue, perhaps arising in another curricular area – a problem with litter, empathy with people in distress, a protest, a different perspective
- a repeating pattern – on a curtain, on a piece of clothing, on a wall

- a found sound – walking across pebbles, opening a bottle of fizzy drink, a creaky floorboard
- a piece of music by a specific famous musician or composer – the BBC recently showcased 'Ten Pieces' that make excellent starting points for creative work
- using ideas from learning about the musical characteristics of a particular genre (type) of music such as blues, jazz, baroque, folk, pop ...
- a random rule – only quiet sounds allowed, only long sounds allowed, only three of each

Whether it is a quest or an exploration, the purpose of the activity needs to be carefully planned and facilitated by the teacher and clear to the children. The purpose may be to develop generic creative learning skills (see OFSTED's list earlier in the chapter) or to deepen musical understanding, or both.

Do you want to focus on a particular phase of the 'creative process'?

It can be useful to think of creative work as a process – though often not a tidy or linear one – loosely consisting of a sequence of phases. These phases have been described in a variety of ways (Carlile and Jordan 2012; Hennessy 2015) and are not exclusive to music: in design and technology, gymnastics, writing and many other curricular areas a very similar process can be conceived.

PHASES OF THE CREATIVE PROCESS

- clarifying the purpose
- generating ideas
- selecting, manipulating and combining ideas
- refining and testing creations
- sharing the outcomes

CLARIFYING THE PURPOSE

Ensure that children understand the challenge or brief or starting point, including constraints. This early phase is crucial to ensuring that what follows is both manageable and musically valuable. So it is important that the teacher establishes a crystal-clear purpose, whether framed as a quest or an exploration (see above).

GENERATING IDEAS

This phase is about exploring musically, doodling in sound, inventing small musical ideas and also imagining overall impressions and effects. All ideas are good ideas at this stage of musical 'brainstorming' (Jesson 2012, discussing Osborn in the 1950s). Unusual and unlikely ideas are welcome: the more the merrier. There should be no criticism whatsoever of individual contributions. In the earlier table, the first two examples focused solely on this phase.

SELECTING, MANIPULATING AND COMBINING IDEAS

Children will probably now have some tentative ideas about the overall shape and feel of 'what might be' as a whole, plus a variety of fragments of invented musical material. These are the sketch plans and building blocks for composing (making, building) a piece of music. This phase is where the composing (building) happens. Many creative decisions need to be made. How many different musical fragments will be used? Which ones? How many times will each one be used? When? Will they be altered, manipulated or transformed? How will the different building blocks be arranged into an overall structure? (The analogy of making a collage is helpful: see below.)

REFINING AND TESTING CREATIONS

This phase may alternate with the previous one several times while draft compositions are played and perhaps recorded, listened to and considered. Everyone should understand that the first play-through is part of the process, not its end. Large and small changes will probably then be made, shaping and adjusting the new creation so that it fulfils the brief and meets all the agreed success criteria.

SHARING THE OUTCOMES

How will the composers know when their composition is finished? Will the new creations be shared and celebrated in some way?

You may decide to engage the children in just one part of this process, or to allow more time and let children undertake an entire creative project. The first two ventures mentioned in the table earlier are concerned with the initial phases only, whereas the last two span the whole process.

Pause for thought

How are you creative? Perhaps you like inventing different sauces for pasta, or doing some interior decoration.

Would you say that your creative process includes phases like those described in the diagram above?

Appropriate teaching approaches

As can be seen from the description of the creative process, children need different kinds of guidance and different degrees of autonomy at different points in their creative ventures. This means that teachers need to adopt different approaches at different times (Qualifications and Curriculum Authority 2004; Jesson 2012).

CLARIFYING THE PURPOSE

The success of the initial clarification phase depends on the teacher having clarity to begin with. You need to be clear what musical learning lies at the heart of your idea. What parameters will you impose to help ensure that the learning actually happens? Will there be a tangible outcome of some sort and if so how will it be shared? This helps children 'find relevance in their work either through practical application or by making emotional and personal connections' (Cremin 2015, p. 36). Teaching approaches at this time are likely to include

- explaining
- instructing
- using questions to check understanding
- (larger projects) developing, with children, a set of success criteria as a guide to keep referring to throughout the process
- modelling enthusiasm

GENERATING IDEAS

To encourage a free flow of ideas in the generative second phase, the teaching approaches need to change. Jesson (2012, p. 18) discusses how important it is for the teacher to model relevant characteristics such as:

- modelling the willingness to take a risk
- modelling enjoyment in experimentation
- modelling playfulness
- modelling an openness to new ideas
- modelling the ability to live with uncertainty

Children also need time and autonomy to generate their own ideas (Cremin 2015). Robson (2014) found that with young children there was 'less evidence of using new knowledge, speculation or analysis in activities initiated or led by adults in comparison to those where they were absent' (p. 131). Consider:

- standing back, leaving alone, allowing time
- discreetly monitoring the social well-being of children
- asking open, supportive questions that re-focus children to the aims of their creative venture without giving leading suggestions (i.e. the questions you ask should prompt questions, rather than answers, from the children: 'What's the next thing to think about?' 'What are you wondering?')
- modelling speculation ('What if …?' 'How could we … as if …?')

- coaching children in the art of brainstorming musical ideas, by:
  - ○ modelling and praising quantity rather than quality at this stage
  - ○ withholding and discouraging any judgemental comments about ideas
  - ○ welcoming unusual ideas
  - ○ congratulating children for ensuring that all of their peers are involved and included

SELECTING, MANIPULATING AND COMBINING IDEAS

As the second phase grows into the third, it might be useful to consider a visual analogy. To make a collage, an artist needs a generous collection of fragments and scraps of material from which to select those that are used in constructing the artwork. As the collage develops, perhaps some identical fragments are used. Perhaps some are delicately patterned while others are brightly coloured. Perhaps there is space between some of them, while others overlap. The artist sometimes works 'from the bottom up', focusing in on tiny details, folding, trimming, positioning, layering, repositioning, fixing. At other times the artist stands back and views the whole emerging picture, working 'from the top down' by making judgements about texture, space, composition and overall effect.

There are strong parallels between this and the development of a musical composition. Children will select, use and combine their fragmentary musical ideas in a 'bottom-up' approach while from time to time also considering the overall shape and structure of their music from a 'top-down' viewpoint. The main teaching approach here is:

- facilitating children's making activities by:
  - ○ ensuring adequate resourcing (time, space to work, sound-makers, personal and social skills)
  - ○ encouraging persistence, resourcefulness and flexibility
  - ○ asking questions that support children's own creative speculations (see below)

It is all too easy to take back the agency of the process unintentionally by asking questions that stifle children's own ideas. Webster (2012) considers how to support creative work sensitively 'without squelching the creative spirit of the young composer' (p. 95). Teacher intervention can be positive if it is playful and exploratory but not at all critical, leaving the children to be the judges of their own work and to make their own creative decisions.

How can teachers form effective facilitative questions? Research on 'possibility thinking' (Craft et al. 2013) reminds us that our role is to support children's imaginative work, so that they move from 'what is' to 'what might be'. Teachers should model and encourage the use of questions built around 'What if?' and 'As if'. Jesson (2012) offers further examples of the kinds of question-stems that can be useful: giving a creative twist to the usual 'question-words' she suggests 'What if?' 'Why not?' 'When could?' 'How can?' 'Where should?' and 'Who might?'

The focus of facilitative questions could revolve around the musical dimensions of pitch, timbre, texture, etc. When considering the overall shape and effect of a piece, the five 'foundational correlates' identified by Kaschub and Smith (2009) can also be extremely useful. They are:

- sound/silence
- motion/stasis
- unity/variety
- tension/release
- stability/instability

(Kaschub and Smith 2009, pp. 15–19)

EXAMPLES OF FACILITATIVE QUESTIONS

Can you play your idea to me?

Which idea are you going to use to begin your piece? How could you introduce it? (suddenly/quietly/slowly at first/etc.)

When could you use that idea?

I can hear that you are using different pitches/playing the last note loudly/keeping together/etc. How can you take that idea even further/do that even more?

Are you happy with this part? (If the answer is 'no': 'What don't you like about it?' and then, based on the child's response: 'How could you make it more/less XXX?')

What if you played that more slowly/backwards/on the xylophone/etc.?

What mood do you want your music to have? How could you change this part so it sounds more XXX (mood)? Try some different ways and choose your favourite.

How do you want your listeners to feel at the beginning/in the middle/at the end?

Have you thought about repeating that part?

Are you going to make that change suddenly, or gradually?

Could you keep something going steadily while the other bit changes? Who might do that?

Silence is a powerful part of music. Are you going to build in some silence? Where?

Do you think you have enough different ideas in your music now?

Note that these questions open up children's musical thinking rather than closing it down. Try to avoid 'Why don't you …?' because you are taking back agency over the creative process. Also note that the questions are not loaded with the teacher's value judgements, but do encourage the children to evaluate. Try to avoid questions like 'How could you play that better?'

REFINING AND TESTING CREATIONS

As the making activity phases into refining and improving, there may be requests from children for help with practical skills or musical understanding. A teacher may also want to develop children's capacities to give and receive feedback constructively. So an appropriate teaching strategy in this phase is:

- coaching, while taking care to ensure that agency over the creative process remains with the children, for example:
  - how to produce a desired sound
  - how to use a recording device
  - how to communicate with peers wordlessly when playing live
  - how to check back with the project success criteria
  - how to make a suggestion for improvement in a positive way
  - how to accept suggestions

SHARING THE OUTCOMES

Finally, the teacher needs to ensure that the children appreciate what they have learnt and achieved through undertaking their creative ventures, by:

- setting up a suitable reflection opportunity/activity that highlights the process rather than the outcome
- drawing children's attention back to the success criteria and the original brief
- giving positive feedback and praise in recognition that the brief has been fulfilled
- demonstrating how the children's efforts are valued, for instance by describing some things that happened along the way through which individual children learnt and applied something new
- ensuring a real audience for the newly composed music

Case Study

An extended example is offered here to show how creative work can be effectively managed and to encourage teachers to develop their confidence to work in this way. It illustrates the whole creative process.

Pause for thought

As you read through the following section, can you identify the various phases of the creative process?

CASE STUDY:

In October, after starting with sound by singing a song about the seasons, a class of Year 3 children are set a challenge: they will be working in groups to compose short pieces of music reflecting one of three autumnal scenarios:

- 'Falling Leaves'
- 'Halloween'
- 'Bonfire Night'

The children are told that they can choose which of the three scenarios they are going to focus on but that they must keep their choice a secret from their peers. Later in the lesson, their compositions will be shared and their classmates will be invited to guess which scenario they had in mind.

The three scenarios have been chosen by the teacher as having potentially very different moods and patterns of activity. The somewhat game-like format helps to make the purpose of the lesson clear to the children. It also sets up the basis of a listening-for activity later on in the process (see Chapter 4 for more on listening-for). It is a widely adaptable format: for a different time of year, or to link with another subject or theme, a different set of contrasting scenarios could be suggested. The number of scenarios is another variable the teacher can consider.

Clear parameters now need to be set so that the children and the teacher share expectations and are comfortable with them. The most important parameters are musical ones. Depending on the children's current learning needs in terms of their musical understanding and skills, the teacher can limit musical options or stipulate certain musical features to be included in the compositions.

The teacher wants to focus on dynamics. She knows that the children can reliably recognize and produce loud and quiet sounds. She now wishes to focus on how the dynamics might change as a piece of music is played. She adds two musical parameters related to dynamics (and suitable for the challenge). Whichever scenario is chosen, each piece of music must:

- Include silence at least once
- Include quiet playing at least once

These are musical parameters, directly related to the National Curriculum. They help to keep a focus on what is happening dynamically in the children's musical creations. Although it would be possible to set a composition challenge without such parameters and still fulfil some of the curriculum requirements, it would be a missed opportunity. In addition, as mentioned earlier, constraints actually encourage the generation of ideas.

Pause for thought

What else could you limit, to narrow down the children's options even further and get them focusing on mood and dynamics?

It is good practice at this point to help children develop a clear set of success criteria based on the brief given, including the musical parameters.

The teacher asks the children to summarize the challenge they have been given and she scribes a set of success criteria that looks something like this:

- Have we composed a piece of music called 'Falling Leaves'/'Halloween'/ 'Bonfire Night'?
- Can our classmates guess what our music is called?
- Have we used silence in our music?
- Is some of our music very quiet?

Figure 6.4 The teacher has limited the choice of sound-makers available

As well as musical parameters, practical guidelines are needed such as how long the piece of music should last (e.g. about one minute) and which sound-makers children can use. (Body percussion? Voice? Instruments? Digital sources? Found sounds? See chapters 3 and 5.) Possibly the teacher will add 'rules' about how many sound sources are allowed for each composition, who is to fetch them, and so on. These parameters are part of the teacher's classroom management expertise and help to ensure a conducive learning environment.

There are two particularly important practical decisions to consider.

One is the decision about how to *group* the children. Typically, this type of creative activity takes place in small groups. Whatever grouping is planned, it is a good strategy to hold back the information from the children until all the other instructions are clearly understood, because once children know who they are working with they will think about little else for a while!

> When all the 'rules of the game' have been clearly understood, the teacher explains that the children will be working in groups of three or four people. The first job of the group will be to choose a scenario and to begin talking about musical possibilities. No group is to start making musical sounds until invited to do so. She reminds the class that she particularly respects those who are willing and able to work with any of their classmates. She asks those who don't mind who they work with to approach her, then invites the class to form themselves into groups and sit down to talk together when they have done so.

The result of this tactic is that those children who very much want to work with certain classmates can choose to do so while others, including those who find it hard to assert themselves or to be accepted by their peers, gravitate towards the teacher who can judiciously form the remaining groups with no loss of self-esteem in any quarter. Because the group formation comes last in the list of instructions, children can start discussing musical ideas straight away.

The other important decision concerns *location*. Where can each of the groups work, when there are likely to be seven or eight groups all needing to hear their own sound-making and all needing supervision and support from the teacher? There are several pragmatic ways to deal with this problem:

- keep the whole class in one space and insist that all sounds are made quietly during the inventing stage
- allow certain groups to work in other spaces with less intensive supervision from the teacher if they are reliably self-disciplined enough to do so, but build in checks
- split the activity so that not all the groups are making sounds at the same time

The teacher completes the setting up of groups and allows a few minutes for them to settle and to talk about first ideas. She then asks half the class to pause at this point and directs them to spend time individually exploring GarageBand (Apple Inc. 2016) on ipads wearing headphones. This leaves half the class to continue their creative work, making everything more manageable.

The teacher visits each remaining group briefly to check whether they have managed to agree on a scenario. She asks them to discuss the instruments they think they would like to use and to fetch them when they are ready. She explains that a **musical fragment** is a musical idea made of a small number of sounds. She asks them to start creating a collection of separate musical fragments, keeping their chosen scenario in mind.

Figure 6.5 Exploring instruments and beginning to invent small musical ideas

She returns to each group a little later and asks them to play some of their musical fragments. She models uncritical acceptance and a positive attitude to unusual ideas. She tells the children that they can change their instruments if they want to, reminds them about voice and body percussion options, and asks them to continue collecting musical fragments that might come in useful for their composition later.

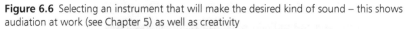

Figure 6.6 Selecting an instrument that will make the desired kind of sound – this shows audiation at work (see Chapter 5) as well as creativity

In a third brief intervention the teacher asks each group to think about the overall mood and structure of the piece they would like to create for their chosen scenario. She invites them to choose some of their musical fragments to begin to build their piece. She reminds each group about the success criteria, asking 'Where do you think silence might work well, in your music? Will there be sounds before the silence? After? What might they be like? Which of your great musical fragments do you think might be useful? Do they need changing at all? What other sounds might help? Why not try some different ways and talk about them together?'

Between visits from the teacher, each group has plenty of time to work autonomously. When the teacher does visit each group to facilitate its work, she can focus her questions on the musical dimension of dynamics in particular, because this is built in to the success criteria. She knows that silence and quiet playing are harder to control than loud playing. She also knows that slow transitions between different dynamics are harder to control than sudden changes so she can ask questions like 'Is it going to get louder suddenly, or bit by bit, gradually?'

She also thinks of the overall effect, which is dependent on the scenario chosen. 'How will you create the calm of the beautiful forest/excitement of bonfire night/ suspense of Halloween? What kinds of sounds could help? Will you repeat any musical fragments? How do you want your audience to feel? What will help them to guess which scenario you have chosen? How will your music begin? How will it end?' etc.

As the teacher works with each group it is possible to tune in to the contributions of individual children, which helps the teacher assess their level of musical understanding and skill (see next chapter).

The teacher continues to visit the composing groups in turn. They are encouraged to make final decisions about the structure of their piece and its musical ingredients. It is time to play it through with the audience in mind, making alterations as desired and working through issues to do with playing together. Do they need extra players to help them? How will they communicate non-verbally to start their piece, cue different sounds, control the dynamic changes together, finish?

Soon after this the teacher checks on how rehearsal is going, gives a five-minute time limit and invites the other half of the class to get ready to listen.

Before each group performs their music, the teacher coaches the listeners in their role. They are to try and guess which scenario the composers had in mind, and to think about why the music fits that title. When each piece finishes the audience is first to applaud and then to indicate if they have a reasoned guess to share. The teacher reminds everyone that a moment of silence is important before and again after the piece is played. She chooses one group to play their piece first, counselling them not to begin 'until you can hear the sound of the cars in the distance'. Immediately, there is silence in the room.

She makes audio recordings of each piece as work in progress, to help the children remember their ideas in the next lesson. (This is also useful for the purposes of assessment – see next chapter.)

Notice the way the teacher achieves a working silence using a listening-for activity. Depending on the room, children could listen for a projector fan humming, birdsong outside, a clock ticking – the effect is powerful.

When classmates listen to each piece, it is important to stress that their guess is not as important as their musical reasoning. The teacher models and encourages respectful giving and receiving of feedback.

The teacher asks those who have performed to discuss briefly how they will modify their composition to take the audience's ideas into account. Now, the other half of the class have their turn as composers, while the first batch of composers take their turn with the ipads.

By the end of the lesson every group has played their draft composition to their classmates for feedback and the teacher has a recording of each.

Figure 6.7 The first play-through with the class listening

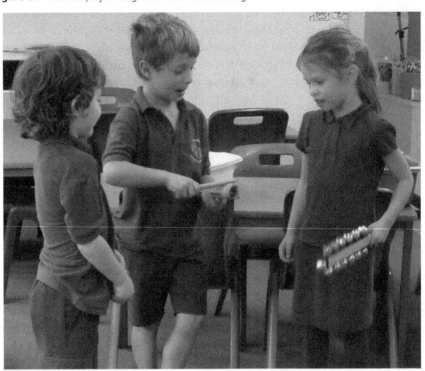

Figure 6.8 The class listens intently, knowing what they are listening for

Figure 6.9 After applauding, the listeners will be asked to talk in musical terms about what they have heard

This initial sharing is part-way through the creative process and there will be more time for the composers to reflect on their peers' feedback and refine their ideas, in the following lesson.

Notice the musical work being done by the audience as well as the composer-players. Peer assessment is an effective teaching strategy as the opinions of classmates are very salient for children. The teacher can coach and support the use of musical terminology through which everyone learns by listening. This stage is another good opportunity for the teacher to make assessments about children's musical understanding (see next chapter).

In the following lesson, the teacher explains that the pieces are going to be linked into one overall composition called 'Autumn'. She discusses with the class what sequence they would like and whether they need to add anything more. Each group has the chance to refine their piece in the light of their earlier play-through.

Eventually a complete performance of 'Autumn' is recorded and the children watch and listen to the playback, making final comments. Later, the class plays their piece in a school assembly, to riotous acclaim. Again, the audience is given some hints about what to listen out for, so the musical learning spreads even further.

When children are clear about the purpose and the parameters, and confident that their work will be treated with respect and sensitivity by their peers and their teacher, they find creative work immensely motivating. If you do not feel completely confident to support creative work yet, I urge you to give it a try anyway. Start with something small and have fun! Success will breed more confidence in your own abilities (Bandura 1977b, p. 194). As one of my students put it, 'Just take the risk!'

Improvisation: Creating and performing at the same time

Sometimes in music, a new idea is sounded out 'on the spot' during a performance. This is known as improvisation and is a feature of many genres (types) of music. In jazz, for example, it is common for each musician to be given time to 'solo' while the rest of the group play an accompaniment. West African drumming typically features a lead drummer who improvises freely while other musicians keep up the steady, complex rhythmic patterns of the music. This improvisation often becomes a dialogue between the lead drummer and a dancer, with each performer responding to the contributions of the other. Pop, rock and gospel singers often improvise melodically (invent new tunes) when singing so that each performance is unique.

In all these examples, the improviser is a highly skilled and knowledgeable musician and they lean on their experience for ideas. However, their ability to improvise is an additional and distinct aspect of their musicianship. Not all musicians have developed this ability. Many excellent players of classical music, for instance, would struggle to improvise.

It is quite possible to develop the ability to improvise without large amounts of musical knowledge or skill. Just as speaking, singing and playing skills are acquired slowly from small beginnings, so the ability to make spontaneous musical utterances can be learnt by people of any age. In my opinion it is an important facet of our musical work and we should include it from the earliest stages, so that children learn to 'speak music' and find it natural and comfortable to do so.

It can be hugely rewarding too. There is a *frisson* about improvising, daring to ignore the fearful voice inside one's head (What if I can't make a sound?), letting go of verbal thinking and instead trusting in one's musical self, then elation in having 'spoken'. As the character Tarek says in the film *The Visitor* (2007), 'OK. Now Walter, I know you're a very smart man but with the drum you have to remember not to think.'

Don't worry about making mistakes. A mistake is not wrong, but interesting. Repeat it, hear it and use it as the inspiration for the next idea. Use easy-to-play instruments, or voices.

Here are some ways into improvising:

For pairs of children:

- two xylophones facing each other – have a musical 'conversation'
- two instruments (any) – one child plays a simple musical pattern over and over again (this is called an ostinato from the Italian 'obstinate' – see Chapter 5) – the other plays whatever they like – then swap roles

For a whole class:

- set up a simple musical pattern that repeats (ostinato) with the whole class – one or more children play what they like over the top of that
- one child is in charge of who plays, using two outstretched arms to represent a spotlight beam – anyone 'in the spotlight' plays for as long as the 'light' shines on them – the beam can change in speed, width, track – combine this with setting parameters on the kinds of sounds that children can play 'in the spotlight'
- gaps in songs and rhythms – everyone sings/plays but leaves a gap at a certain point (perhaps for four beats – count and feel them) and one or more children play/sing something in that gap

Figure 6.10 A child improvising on a cajón during a short gap in a piece of music being played by his class

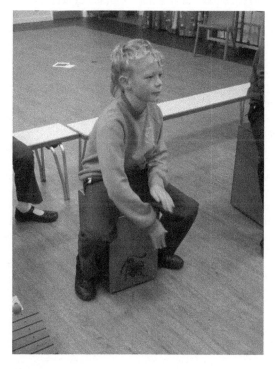

Summary

Creativity in primary music is little-c creativity that involves envisaging what might be, exploring ideas, keeping options open, questioning, making connections and reflecting on ideas and outcomes. It is an important dimension of being musical and has generic benefits too.

Children can be offered brief or extended opportunities to work creatively. With thoughtful planning and the use of different teaching strategies, non-specialist teachers can support children's creative work in music very effectively.

Recommended reading

BBC (2016). *Ten Pieces: Teaching Resources for Educators Working with 7–11 Year Olds*. Available at: http://www.bbc.co.uk/programmes/articles/3xWSYQhHfM9dZYfmRmTwVqN/teaching-resources-for-educators-working-with-7-11-year-olds (Accessed 31 December 2016).

Carlile, O. and Jordan, A. (2012). *Approaches to Creativity: A Guide for Teachers*. Maidenhead: Open University Press.

Craft, A. (2001). 'Little c Creativity'. In *Creativity in Education,* edited by Craft, A., Jeffrey, B. and Leibling, M. London: Continuum. pp. 45–61.

Craft, A., Cremin, T., Burnard, P., Dragovic, T. and Chappell, K. (2013). 'Possibility Thinking: Culminative Studies of an Evidence-Based Concept Driving Creativity?'. *Education 3–13*(5), pp. 538–56.

Cremin, T. (2015). 'Creative teachers and creative teaching'. In Wilson, A. (ed.) *Creativity in Primary Education,* 3rd edn. Exeter: Learning Matters, pp. 33–44.

Hennessy, S. (2015). 'Creativity in the music curriculum'. In Wilson, A. (ed.) *Creativity in Primary Education*. London: Sage, pp. 219–33.

Jesson, J. (2012). *Developing Creativity in the Primary School*. Maidenhead: McGraw-Hill Open University Press.

Kaschub, M. and Smith, J. (2009). *Minds on Music: Composition for Creative and Critical Thinking*. Lanham, Maryland: Rowman & Littlefield Education.

National Advisory Committee on Creative and Cultural Education [NACCCE] (1999). *All Our Futures: Creativity, Culture and Education*. London: Department for Education and Employment. Available at: http://www.readyunlimited.com/wp-content/uploads/2013/02/all-our-futures1.pdf (Accessed 5 May 2017).

Office for Standards in Education, Children's Services and Skills (2010). *Learning: Creative Approaches that Raise Standards*. Manchester: Crown copyright. Available at: http://www.creativitycultureeducation.org/wp-content/uploads/learning-creative-approaches-that-raise-standards-250.pdf (Accessed 21 May 2016).

Qualifications and Curriculum Authority (2004). *Creativity: Find It, Promote It*. London: QCA Publications. Available at: https://www.literacyshed.com/uploads/1/2/5/7/12572836/1847211003.pdf (Accessed 20 May 2016).

Robinson, K. (2001). *Out of Our Minds: Learning to be Creative*. Oxford: Capstone.

Watson, S. (2011). *Using Technology to Unlock Musical Creativity*. Oxford: Oxford University Press.

Chapter 7
Assessing Children in Music

Chapter objectives

- to establish the principles of effective assessment in primary music
- to consider the reasons for assessing in primary music
- to explore how to assess in primary music
- to see how the current National Curriculum relates to effective assessment in primary music

Introduction

Pause for thought

What is your definition of assessment?

What are the essential ingredients of any assessment?

To assess is to make a considered judgement or evaluation of something. Any assessment needs an assessor who has access to relevant evidence. The assessor also needs a frame of reference as a guide when making judgements. The comedian Eddie Izzard illustrated this when talking about choosing fruit in a supermarket:

> Do you do that squeezy squeezy thing on fruit? Where you go in and go, 'Oh, squeezy, oh!' It's a test squeezy thing that you've seen French chefs do on television – 'Oh, squeezy, oh.' But – I have no frame of reference. I'm going, 'Oh ... Is that good? Um, I'm squeezing about this much, is that good squeezy?' That's an expert thing, isn't it? Definite Article (1996)

Being an effective assessor is 'an expert thing' and this expertise is something that can be developed over time. Good primary teachers are experts in assessment because it is fundamental to helping children learn. This chapter explores why assessment is such an important aspect of good primary music teaching and will help less experienced teachers to develop assessment expertise.

One important point is worth noting at the outset. Some teachers fear that they will not be able to make relevant judgements in primary music, because they do not consider themselves to be knowledgeable about music as a subject. However, the focus of all our assessments is the children's musical *learning and development*. We are not assessing the quality of their musical *output* per se, though it constitutes some of our best evidence. Therefore all primary teachers, as experts in children's learning, have the potential to assess effectively in music lessons.

What does assessment look like in primary music?

In the context of primary music, assessment is not about doing tests. It is not about lining up a class of children and asking each child in turn to sing to a 'judge', nor is it measuring their music against some absolute standard. Rather, effective assessment in primary music is integrated within musical teaching and learning activities.

This book is underpinned by a praxial philosophy of music education (Elliott and Silverman 2015) with children's musicality as the central focus. Assessment in primary music is therefore concerned with what is *happening*, the quality of the musicianship demonstrated in what is happening, and the musical understanding that can be deduced from the outcomes of the children's activities. Sometimes individual children are the focus; at other times a broad judgement is made about a group or a whole class of children.

Praxial musical assessments also need to be conducted in ways that preserve and nurture each child's positive self-image as a musician. Too many people spend their entire lives excluded from any possibility of 'being musical' simply as a result of one thoughtless comment or action by someone making a musical judgement. An important principle of effective primary music assessment therefore is that the assessor should be an incorrigible optimist, sharing his or her 'growth mindset' (Dweck 2016). The phrase 'not yet' is often useful.

The assessment of children's musicality takes place on three main timescales, which can be described as *real time, short term* and *long term*. First and foremost, teachers need to be engaged in assessment as they are teaching, as an integral part of every lesson:

> Assessment is part of day-to-day teaching … and, over time, teachers become highly skilled in noticing details, in recognising the slightest improvement in a child's work or in sensing a reduced effort in the completion of a task.

> (Murphy 2013, p. 141)

Figure 7.1 Assessment is part and parcel of classroom practice

A teacher cannot teach children in music without assessing them frequently. You will be doing this, even if you are not fully aware of it. In order to support children's development as singers, players, composers and listeners, a teacher makes numerous almost instantaneous judgements in the course of a single lesson. Each individual assessment guides the teacher as to the best action to take next, whether that be a verbal or musical intervention, a suggestion, a question to promote further thought, or perhaps a step back to allow more uninterrupted time. There is further discussion of how to develop such real-time assessment expertise later in the chapter. The main point here is that most primary music assessment is embedded in the minute-by-minute unfolding of musical lessons. Here are two examples of such real-time assessment:

SCENARIO A

A class of Year 4 children is singing 'Row, Row, Row Your Boat' in **unison** (all together). After they have sung the song through once, the teacher chants (speaks in rhythm) the last line, making the word 'but' short and crisp. She repeats the rhythmic chant, gesturing towards herself, then gestures towards the class to invite them to copy the line back. Indicating herself again, she sings the last line with a clearly articulated 'but', then gestures for the class to repeat the line.

SCENARIO B

A different class is working on 'Row, Row, Row Your Boat'. Once the children have sung the song through, their teacher sings the third line to them, to the words 'diddly, diddly, diddly, diddly'. He also holds one hand high, palm downwards, and lowers it step by step with each 'diddly'. He then repeats the first 'diddly' once more, making the high hand-sign again and exaggerating the duration (length) of the last syllable. He gets the class to sing that one word, making high signs and sustaining their notes for a while. Then they all sing 'diddly, diddly, diddly, diddly' with the hand gestures.

Pause for thought

What rapid assessment did each teacher make about how well their class sang the song?

How do you know?

These two scenarios demonstrate that effective teaching depends upon real-time assessment. The current needs of the children are assessed by the teacher and straight away a strategy is used that will improve the children's singing. This point will be developed in the next section.

The second assessment timescale occurs on a lesson-to-lesson basis and forms part of the short-term lesson planning cycle. After each lesson, a teacher gathers and reviews the evidence of children's musical learning. (Later in the chapter this activity will be discussed in more detail, with suggestions to support the process.) As a result of assessing the learning of the class over the course of a whole lesson, the teacher is in a position to plan the next lesson in a way that will more accurately address the children's musical needs. Brief records or annotated samples of work may also be kept, to capture the assessments of children's musical learning.

Finally, there is the long-term assessment timescale. Children's musical development takes time. 'Being musical' is multifaceted and involves a wide variety of skills, knowledge, understanding and characteristics that do not necessarily develop in a steady or linear fashion. The level of musicianship a child demonstrates also depends on context: it might be easier to keep a steady beat as part of a group than when playing solo, for example. For all these reasons, it is helpful to review children's musical development over a longer timescale to appreciate change and progress.

The current National Curriculum states that 'by the end of each key stage, pupils are expected to know, apply and understand the matters, skills and processes specified in the relevant programme of study'. Periodically, therefore, it is important to examine children's musicality in relation to National Curriculum descriptions to get a sense of whether, by the end of the key stage, the 'expectations' are likely to be met. This long-term assessment timescale again relates to planning processes: in this case the medium-term and long-term planning activities typically undertaken in half-termly, termly and yearly cycles.

> ## Pause for thought
> What is the difference between assessment and record-keeping?

> ## Pause for thought
> What records might be useful in relation to the three different assessment timescales?

It is important to notice the differences between assessment and record-keeping. As we have seen, assessment is a process of making judgements. Only a select few of teachers' many judgements will ever be recorded. How to select and record assessments depends on their purpose, as will be discussed in the next section. Just as there are assessments that are never recorded, there can also be records that are not assessments. In primary music these often consist of audio or video recordings of children performing and annotations of observations made during lessons. In themselves these are simply pieces of musical evidence. Such evidence, if considered in relation to a frame of reference, can support assessment. It is useful to keep selected samples over the long term, perhaps in a 'portfolio of evidence', to inform assessments of gradual musical development.

Why should children be assessed?

In this chapter the definition of 'assessment' has deliberately been limited to the process of making a judgement on the basis of some evidence and in the light of some frame of reference. This distinguishes the *process* of assessment itself from the *purpose* to which it might be put. In the literature, a variety of terminology is used in relation to assessment and there is often an implication that 'assessment' also includes the purpose, that is, the use that is made of the judgements.

> ## Pause for thought
> How many reasons can you identify for assessing children's musical learning? Make a list.
>
> Which of your reasons are directly linked to children's continued learning? Annotate the list.

The single most important reason to assess children's musicality is to be better able to support their further learning.

There is now a strong body of theoretical and empirical work that suggests that integrating assessment with instruction may well have unprecedented power to increase student engagement and to improve learning outcomes.

(Wiliam 2011, p. 13)

(N.B. The term 'instruction' in this quotation is an American usage, roughly equivalent to the British use of the word 'teaching'.)

In discussing the terminology around this developmental use of assessment, Wiliam (2011) explains that 'assessment for learning' is generally the term given to the *intention* to use assessment outcomes to benefit learning by adapting teaching and learning activities in the light of the judgements made. If those adapted activities *do* in fact support further learning, then one can say that the assessment has indeed had a 'formative' function: this is often termed *formative assessment*.

In the two scenarios outlined earlier, for example, both teachers were intentionally assessing the children's singing in real time, in order to decide on their next teaching activities, so they were carrying out 'assessment for learning'. The scenarios do not state whether the children's singing improved as a result of the subsequent teaching but if it did, the teachers had succeeded in using their assessments formatively.

Both teachers made use of their assessments immediately. This close, real-time coupling of assessment and teaching has long been a component of effective music teachers' expertise or PCK. Swanwick (1997) sums it up concisely: 'The first question is surely "to what extent is this evidence of musical understanding?" The next question is "how might I best respond?"' (p. 209).

Assessments made over the longer term can also function formatively if they are used to guide decisions about how best to support further learning. It may be that weeks or months pass before formative use is made of assessment information. For example, teachers in a school might judge that children's singing could be better overall, perhaps using a recent performance at an inter-school singing project as their frame of reference. The improvement of singing might then become an element of the whole-school improvement plan, with all staff involved in making decisions about how to plan and teach singing more effectively over the following twelve-month period.

Pause for thought

Which of your listed items from the previous pause for thought concerned 'assessment for learning'?

What other reasons did you list in the previous pause for thought?

As well as using assessments formatively, assessment information can be used to 'paint a picture' of a child's musicality at a particular moment in time. This use of assessment information is 'summative' – it sums up the current position.

Figure 7.2 Skills and knowledge grid for long-term tracking of musical learning

Key Stage 1 is in **bold text**. Key Stage 2 is in plain text. NAME: **Demonstrates the following musical engagement / skills / behaviours:**	**Knows & uses musical dimensions: pitch, duration (incl. pulse, rhythm), tempo, dynamics, timbre, texture (incl silence), structure** [you may wish to expand this one column to seven: one per dimension]	**Knows 'inside out' and 'outside in' some specific pieces of music**	Knows about some famous performers and composers	Knows something about the history of different genres	Knows something about the purposes of music
Enjoyment of musical activity and confidence in making & responding to music					
Increasing mastery (accuracy, fluency, control, confidence, **expression**) of • **Singing** • **Using voice in other ways** • **Untuned instruments** • **Tuned instruments** • Digital sound-makers					
Perseverance • *Developing ability to sustain rehearsal.... With ongoing assessment and improvement... including recording and playback*					
Performing alone or in a group • In an ensemble • Taking a solo part • Holding a part against others • Directing / following direction • Awareness of audience					
Responding in non-verbal media – art, design, physical movement, music, dance...					
Remembering & reproducing ... in increasing detail					
Listening / experiencing with concentration, understanding and discrimination (reviewing, evaluating, appreciating)					
Speaking and listening using musical terminology					
Reading • Graphic scores • Rhythm notations; Pitch notations • Staff notation					
Writing • Graphic scores • Rhythm notations; Pitch notations • Staff notation					
Searching & Exploring for an increasingly wide range of **sounds made by** • **Voice** • **Body** • **Instruments** • **Digital technology** • **Found sounds/acoustic sources**					
Creating • **Choosing sounds** • **Organising sounds** • Developing work over time .... Composing ... including use of software • Making real-time decisions .... improvising					

Summative assessments are helpful when sharing information about a child's musicality with other people such as parents and carers, other teachers involved in music, the school's music leader or coordinator, other school leaders, the child's next teacher and, eventually, the receiving secondary school. Sometimes the information is simply received. It is to be hoped that at other times it is used formatively, as the starting point for planning further musical education.

Another important summative use of assessment information is to track change over time. A manageable system of recording teacher assessments is needed and schools have a variety of such systems. One suggestion is to keep a succinct, cumulative long-term record for each child based on the skills and knowledge described in the National Curriculum for Music, as in Figure 7.2.

On a few occasions each year, very brief dated notes can be added into the cells of the grid, which will expand over the course of Key Stages 1 and 2 to reflect each child's developing musical understanding. Links could also be made to audio and/or video recordings exemplifying the learning.

It is also useful to make summative assessments before and after planned musical learning activities to gauge their effect. Once again, this can happen over various timescales. In the singing scenarios described earlier, if the children are asked to sing the song again after working on particular aspects, the teachers can compare the 'before-and-after' singing, using the evidence summatively to ascertain whether their teaching has made an immediate difference. In the medium term, 'before-and-after' assessments can be made at either end of a unit of work for the same purpose. With whole-school improvement projects, such as the development of teachers' abilities to teach singing, it is good practice to conduct 'before-and-after' assessments to measure the impact of the initiatives undertaken.

Finally, a simple long-term record such as the 'skills and knowledge grid' in Figure 7.2 can show up areas of the curriculum that have been neglected, allowing teachers to plan to include them in future units of work.

How can children be assessed?

Having discussed the principles and purposes of assessment in primary music, it is time to focus on some practicalities. Always bearing in mind that what is being assessed is children's musical learning and development (rather than their musical output per se), the *evidence*, a suitable *frame of reference* and the *assessor* can be considered in turn.

Evidence needed for making assessments of children's musicality

An issue for all teachers, and particularly for new or inexperienced teachers, is that there are so many things to think about at once. Typically, in the early stages of a teacher's career, the act of teaching tends to be thought of as 'teacher in the spotlight'. Teachers naturally focus on their own performance, making sure they plan diligently, give clear instructions, remember to ask their key questions, ensure the correct use of spoken language, model impeccable manners, explain things using the target vocabulary, keep to time … the list goes on.

All these teacherly activities demand the teacher's intense concentration and enable information (in a wide sense of the term) to flow from the teacher to the class. But, important as all these aspects of teaching are, they only constitute part of the picture. If teaching was solely about 'giving out' in this way, a single teacher could be live-streamed to all schools, to teach every child in the country.

However, that live-streamed teacher would not know anything about the children in a particular class. Were they enjoying the lesson? Were they engaged? All of them? Was it too easy or too hard? Did they need more time? What did they learn? Were they actually there at all? Early-career teachers sometimes realize that they, too, have been so focused on their own performance that they have no idea about how the children fared.

Lack of space precludes a discussion of learning theories at this point but the important idea is that the children should be the centres of attention, not the teacher. Learning, of all kinds, is an active process that depends on each learner, so the focus needs to be on what the children are doing.

Effective teachers know this and do much more than just 'giving out'. They are also 'taking in' all the time, by attending to the children. As a new teacher gains experience, the 'giving out' activities gradually start to get easier and become semi-automatic aspects of professional expertise. The teacher's anxiety level also tends to drop over time, as the role becomes more comfortable and familiar. Now the teacher is cognitively and affectively able to 'take in' information from children by 'noticing details' (Murphy 2013). This is important, because a better definition of 'teaching' would be 'maximizing children's learning'. As we have seen, real-time assessment, used formatively, is a fundamental part of this.

This 'taking in' skill is fundamental to good primary music teaching – and good teaching in general – and should be deliberately developed. Teachers need to be continuously receptive in this way. In addition, it can be useful to plan some key 'taking in' moments in a lesson. Organize specific opportunities to elicit evidence of learning, through making time for children to 'show what they know' – share what they have been working on and demonstrate what they can do. (See later in this chapter and also Chapter 8 for support with planning in this way.) In the singing scenarios earlier, the teachers did not sing along to begin with, but listened. For evidence of secure learning, select activities in which children work musically with a greater degree of independence, or apply their musical learning in a new context. Perkins and Blythe (1994) call these challenging activities 'performances of understanding'.

In music, useful evidence can take several forms (Fautley 2010). The best evidence is *musical evidence*, that is, the evidence you gain by observing children's behaviours as musicians and listening to the music they make. OFSTED (2009b) stresses that effective primary music teaching includes 'giving constant attention to

Figure 7.3 A 'performance of understanding' by two children as they fill a box with instruments that they think make metallic sounds

the quality of pupils' musical responses' (p. 3). It takes time and effort to learn how to do this deliberate, concentrated noticing of musical evidence but it is a crucial skill to develop. It can be helpful to adopt the habit of asking oneself, 'What did I notice? What else? What did I see? What did I hear? What was surprising, or unexpected? What musical understanding is implied?'

To underline the importance of gathering *musical* evidence, consider the analogy of assessing a child's cycling proficiency. The evidence of the child's skill comes through observing them actually riding a bike and noticing how well they balance, steer and brake. Evidence of understanding can also be gathered by noticing the choices and decisions that the child makes. Why did they avoid riding over the cobblestones? Why did they stand up on the pedals as they freewheeled over a bump? Why did they slow down before making a tight turn on a wet road? These are not choices based on declarative knowledge but on purely physical 'knowing'. In addition, there is evidence of cognitive input or 'road-sense', such as keeping to the left, or slowing down at a zebra crossing.

Pause for thought

What are the musical equivalents of cycling skills, physical 'knowing' and 'road-sense'?

There are things that can be understood musically that do not translate into words, just as a cyclist understands things physically. The analogy with cycling ends there, because cycling is not usually considered an expressive medium. However the point about being able to know or understand things non-verbally remains. Music exists because it is sometimes the best – or the only – way to know, understand and communicate. As Eisner (2005) puts it, 'Not everything can be "said" with anything' (p. 153).

> One who has not experienced the unique contributions of the arts to human understanding is in no position to understand the variety of ways in which humans come to know.
>
>   (Eisner 2005, p. 65; See also page 9 in this book's introduction.)

In summary, musical evidence is needed in order to assess musical skills and musical understanding.

It can be useful to make audio or video recordings during music lessons, so that more time and attention can be given after the lesson to considering the musical evidence. This can be a valuable way of developing the all-important 'taking in' skill – the ability to notice musical evidence – away from the demands of the lesson itself. Both summative and formative use can be made of assessments based on recorded musical evidence. The playing-back of a recording can also be done immediately, during a lesson, as a highly effective real-time technique for assessing musical evidence and using the assessment formatively right away (see later section on assessors).

Pause for thought

In the earlier singing scenarios, would it be useful if the teachers recorded the initial singing?

If so, in what way?

When might the recording be played back?

Who might find it useful?

Children's *verbalizations* are another source of evidence. The more carefully a teacher crafts the questions asked of children, the better the quality of verbal evidence elicited (see Chapter 6). Another good opportunity to gather verbal evidence is during small-group work when children are interacting as musicians. Note that this type of evidence bears only an indirect relationship to a child's musicality, as it depends on each child's facility with spoken language. Returning to the cycling analogy, if children are asked about their proficiency on a bike, one may be very articulate while another may find it hard to say what they can do on their bike. Yet the second child might be a better rider.

Evidence can also be found when children are expressing themselves in other 'modes', including *movement, drawing and writing*. Once again, however, caution must be exercised when considering this indirect evidence, because underlying musicality may be masked by difficulties with the mode of expression. Would a child's drawing of their cycling necessarily mirror their actual prowess on a bike?

CASE STUDY

A group of student teachers from the Plymouth Institute of Education were investigating the ability of children in a Year 1 class to feel the steady pulse in some rhythmic music. They played various pieces of music and invited the children to move in a different way to each piece – jumping, walking, crawling and swaying. The students watched for physical evidence that the children were feeling the beat of the music, by looking for steady rhythmic movements. They discovered that children's beat awareness seemed to vary and they realized this was because some movements were more difficult than others, so that children's 'performance of understanding' of the beat varied – but not their underlying understanding.

Pause for thought

In the following scenario, what evidence might the teacher be able to gather about the child's musicality?

SCENARIO C

A child has recently joined a class having moved to England from Turkey speaking very little English. He is part of a group of four children who are developing a piece of music together in response to a short video of a bird in flight.

Frames of reference to support assessment judgements

Once evidence of musical learning has been obtained, whether through brief real-time 'noticing' or more considered gathering, the next question, as Izzard would say, is, 'Is that good?' (Definite Article 1996) There are essentially two frames of reference that are important in helping to answer the question. One is to do with the child, the other is to do with the music curriculum.

The first frame of reference is a teacher's accumulated knowledge of each child's prior learning and development. When assessing evidence of a child's musical learning, ask yourself, 'Is this good, for this child, given what I already know about their musicality?' In other words, a comparison is being made between new evidence and older evidence. This helps when deciding on the best way to respond to a child in primary music, to challenge them appropriately.

The second frame of reference is the current National Curriculum for Music. This is a broad, succinct description of children's 'expected' musical knowledge and prowess at the *end* of each Key Stage. It is important to bear in mind that it outlines a number of major musical learning goals to be achieved gradually over a timescale of years.

The fact that the National Curriculum is limited to end-of-key stage descriptions has its advantages when thinking about assessment. Although progress in children's musicality is clearly expected when viewed long term, as seen by comparing the Key Stage 1 and Key Stage 2 descriptions, there is no assumption that musical development will be linear, steady or evenly spread in the short term or medium term (Hammerton 2014).

The 'openness' of the current National Curriculum frees teachers and schools to plan and teach primary music in ways that take best advantage of opportunities, interests and inspirations. An engaging, challenging and varied spread of musical experiences and activities will, over time, enable children to develop all aspects of their musicality and musicianship. There is no rigid sequence that must be followed, as long as the end-of-key-stage curriculum descriptions are kept in mind 'in the background'.

However, the current National Curriculum is not sufficiently detailed to be a helpful frame of reference for the assessment of children's musicality in the shorter term and, in any case, it would be unfair to use it directly as a 'measure' during the first years of a Key Stage, as it only summarizes expected achievement at the end of Years 2 and 6. There is a need for more detailed guidance. Different schools will address this issue in different ways and the local Music Education Hub (see Chapter 2) can also be contacted for advice. Here, three possible long-term frameworks are briefly examined, as examples.

The first example, by Daubney and Fautley (no date), is designed as a complete assessment framework for primary music (see Figure 7.4 for an extract from this framework). It spans everything in the current National Curriculum and also includes some elements not explicitly mentioned there, such as responding to music and communicating thoughts and feelings through different modes of expression. It contains four sets of suggested assessment criteria to guide teachers' judgements about the evidence they have noticed and collected. Daubney and Fautley are careful to avoid any sense of strict linear progress. Instead they suggest four sets of criteria that seem apt together, for different periods of a child's time at primary school, reflecting their holistic musical development. They label these 'Stages A, B, C and D', leaving teachers to choose the set of criteria that feels most appropriate to their pupils, regardless of age or year-group.

Some of their suggested criteria could be used to assess evidence collected on a short timescale, for instance:

'Join in and stop as appropriate' (from Stage B).

Other criteria would need to be used over a longer timescale, or separated into smaller components, such as:

'Use voice, sounds, technology and instruments in creative ways' (from Stage C).

Figure 7.4 Assessment criteria from the first of the four stages (Daubney and Fautley, no date)

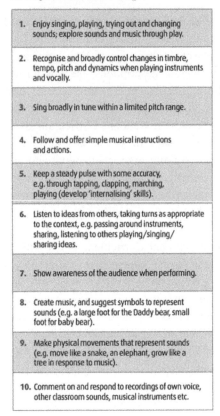

Example statements stage A

1.	Enjoy singing, playing, trying out and changing sounds; explore sounds and music through play.
2.	Recognise and broadly control changes in timbre, tempo, pitch and dynamics when playing instruments and vocally.
3.	Sing broadly in tune within a limited pitch range.
4.	Follow and offer simple musical instructions and actions.
5.	Keep a steady pulse with some accuracy, e.g. through tapping, clapping, marching, playing (develop 'internalising' skills).
6.	Listen to ideas from others, taking turns as appropriate to the context, e.g. passing around instruments, sharing, listening to others playing/singing/ sharing ideas.
7.	Show awareness of the audience when performing.
8.	Create music, and suggest symbols to represent sounds (e.g. a large foot for the Daddy bear, small foot for baby bear).
9.	Make physical movements that represent sounds (e.g. move like a snake, an elephant, grow like a tree in response to music).
10.	Comment on and respond to recordings of own voice, other classroom sounds, musical instruments etc.

Teachers can be confident that if their pupils learn in and through music in ways that fulfil all the Daubney and Fautley criteria, they will also meet the expectations of the current National Curriculum.

The second example framework (see Figure 7.5) was mentioned as good practice in an OFSTED report on music in schools (OFSTED 2012a, p. 50). Many schools have something similar. This frame of reference is a straightforward chart containing the individual musical dimensions of pitch, dynamics, etc. Suggested progression in relation to understanding and using each dimension is outlined.

Unlike the Daubney and Fautley framework, this one makes no mention of how children might demonstrate their understanding and use of these dimensions, though OFSTED commended 'the teaching approach ... founded on practical, creative activities where pupils explored and created music using these ideas' (OFSTED 2012a, p. 50). This framework focuses on an important core of musical understanding rather than on specific aspects of musicianship. It is easy for teachers to assimilate so they can keep the 'big picture' of the musical elements in mind at all times, making it easier to assess and support children's musical understanding. In addition to using this framework, it would be important to assess children's musicianship skills, that is, what they actually *do* with their musical understanding, when playing, discussing, creating, singing and listening.

Figure 7.5 Assessment frame of reference based on musical dimensions (OFSTED 2012a, p. 50)

	Key Stage 1 → →→ →→→→→→ Lower Key Stage 2 →→ → → → → → → Upper Key Stage 2→→→→					
Pitch	High/low	➡	Steps Leaps	Pentatonic Patterns	➡	Major & minor
Duration	Long/short Steady beat	Rhythmic patterns	Strong beats Weak beats	Metre Crotchets Quavers	2, 3, 4	5, 6, 9 Dotted and swung rhythms
Dynamics	Loud/quiet	Graduation	➡	Strong contrasts	➡	Accents & articulation
Tempo	Fast/slow	Graduation	➡	Comparing tempi	➡	Tempo for mood effects
Timbre	Exploring	Wood, metal, strings	➡	Orchestral family timbres	➡	Electronic sounds
Texture	One sound Several sounds	Layers	Melody Accompaniment	➡	Weaving Parts	Chords
Structure	Beginnings Endings	Simple repeated patterns	Question & answer	Ostinato	Rounds	Ternary Forms

The third exemplar frame of reference (see Figure 7.6) again focuses on underlying musical understanding, which can be evidenced through children's involvement in a variety of musical activities. It was developed by Swanwick (1997) and takes a more holistic view of musical understanding than the previous example. Swanwick's proposal is that children develop their understanding in four cumulative phases. In the first phase they are focused on the *sonic material* that all music is made of. This would presumably encompass the various dimensions of sounds mentioned previously. Building on this, in the second phase children develop their understanding and control of the *expressive shaping* of sounds. In the third phase, children come to understand how simple sound-structures (such as short rhythms or melodic phrases) are combined into more substantial *compositions*. The final phase concerns children's abilities to *evaluate and improve upon* musical work. As each phase begins, the earlier phases continue, developing in depth, breadth and subtlety of understanding.

Although Swanwick's focus was on older children and he published this framework a long time before the current National Curriculum, it provides manageable guidance in assessing more holistic aspects of children's musicality over the medium to long term.

Any of the frameworks described, or a combination of them, or another similar framework, can offer valuable support to help answer assessment questions such as:

'What can this child do, musically?'

'What musical understanding does this child demonstrate?'

'How well do they do/know this?'

The frameworks help to fill in the developmental detail that the current National Curriculum does not include. From such frameworks, real-time and short-term assessment criteria can be developed. Let us see how.

The frame of reference for making assessments on a lesson by lesson basis is the *learning objective* of each lesson. Each musical learning objective should constitute

Figure 7.6 A more holistic frame of reference from Swanwick (1997, p. 211)

Assessing Musical Quality in the National Curriculum Keith Swanwick

	PERFORMING	COMPOSING	APPRAISING
	GENERAL CRITERIA FOR ASSESSING MUSICAL UNDERSTANDING		
D	Pupils *control voices / instruments*	Pupils *organise musical materials*	Pupils *distinguish between sound qualities and/or instruments*
C	Pupils control voices / instruments *with expressive shaping*	Pupils organise musical materials *with expressive shaping*	Pupils distinguish between different sound qualities and/or instruments and *they identify expressive features*
B	Pupils control voices / instruments with expressive shaping and *are aware of the structural relationships between musical ideas*	Pupils organise music materials with expressive shaping and *create structural relationships between musical ideas*	Pupils distinguish between different sound qualities and/or instruments, they identify expressive features and *are aware of structural relationships*
A	Pupils control voices / instruments with expressive shaping, they are aware of structural relationships between musical ideals and *they autonomously evaluate and develop their performance*	Pupils organise musical materials with expressive shaping, they create structural relationships between musical ideas and *they autonomously evaluate and refine their composition*	Pupils distinguish between different sound qualities and/or instruments, they identify expressive features, they are aware of structural relationships *and they make independent critical appraisals*

a tiny contribution towards achieving one of the elements of the National Curriculum and should be chosen to be relevant to the current needs of the class, perhaps with reference to one or more of the example frameworks just described. The clearer and sharper the learning objective, the easier it is to 'translate' it into one or more success criteria against which children's learning can be assessed – see below. (Also, the easier it is to develop meaningful musical activities that will support children's learning and achievement of the objective, as advocated by OFSTED [2009b] – see Chapter 8.)

As an example of how to develop a useful learning objective and related assessment criteria, suppose a teacher in Key Stage 1 decides to focus on dynamics. From the three frameworks outlined above, the teacher chooses the following:

- from Daubney's and Fautley's Stage A: 'Recognise and broadly control changes in timbre, tempo, pitch and dynamics when playing instruments and vocally'
- from the second framework it can be seen that 'loud' and 'quiet' are going to be the main focus, but there is the possibility that some children may also be ready to work on gradual changes of dynamics
- from Swanwick's framework, Row D suggests a number of musical activities focusing on awareness of dynamics and perhaps some children might understand and use the expressive possibilities of changing dynamics as in Row C

In the light of this guidance, the teacher develops the following learning objective and success criteria for the lesson:

> Learning objective: To recognize and play loud and quiet music.
> Success criterion 1: Demonstrates awareness of loud and quiet passages when listening to music.
> Success criterion 2: Plays an instrument with deliberate control to produce loud and quiet sounds.

It is only after having developed these that the teacher plans the musical activities. A mix of activities is chosen:

- listening and physically responding to Bjork's 'It's Oh So Quiet' (1995)
- playing by copying loud and quiet rhythmic patterns
- composing in response to pictures of a playground at different times of day

As the lesson itself unfolds, the teacher focuses on 'taking in' evidence relating to children's awareness and control of loud and quiet sounds. The evidence is used formatively, in real time, guiding the teacher's actions to help the children achieve the two-part learning objective. It is also used summatively when, at the end of the lesson, the teacher quickly annotates the lesson plan with children's initials to indicate who met/didn't yet meet/exceeded the two criteria. The teacher also notes the unexpected observation that one child invented a piece of music in which she played loud/quiet/loud while her partner played quiet/loud/quiet: this shows an understanding of structural relationships as described in Swanwick's (1997) Row B.

For more on how to plan music lessons, see Chapter 8.

The assessor – or assessors

The teacher is the most obvious assessor of children's musical learning and development. As discussed earlier, assessment is a skill that improves with practice. If music lessons are practical and fully involve the children, there will be a wealth of tiny pieces of evidence of musical understanding, but it takes time to begin to notice them and 'take them in'. With carefully constructed learning objectives and success criteria, the search for evidence can be more selective, which helps. However it is important to be open to incidental, unexpected evidence too (and, therefore, to plan activities that allow scope for children to excel and surprise). Develop the habit of asking, 'What do I notice? What does it mean in terms of this child's musicality?' and more and more evidence will indeed be noticed.

Children can also be highly effective assessors. They often have an enormous capacity to notice all sorts of astonishing detail. What they may need support with is making judgements on the basis of musical evidence, as they do not have 'teacherly' frames of reference and their opinions can seem erratic. They can be very stern critics at times, while at other times seeming happy with anything. Non-musical factors are often influential in their judgements: such things as self-esteem, peer pressure and mood. Once again, learning objectives and success criteria are the solutions. If children are clear about the focus and purpose of their musical learning activities, their judgements can be very astute. Note that it is not always necessary to share the objective verbally. Musical demonstrations often make the point better, perhaps by modelling what *isn't* wanted as well as what is.

Assessment is an important aspect of being a musician and therefore something that all children should be engaged in and developing. The current National Curriculum's Purpose of Study describes how children should develop their 'talent as musicians' and their 'critical engagement with music', both of which rely on the ability to make informed musical judgements.

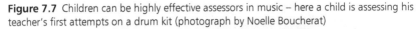

Figure 7.7 Children can be highly effective assessors in music – here a child is assessing his teacher's first attempts on a drum kit (photograph by Noelle Boucherat)

Figure 7.8 Practising and self-assessing go hand in hand as this child works on using alternate hands on a djembe

Figure 7.9 Peer assessment in action

A good strategy is to make – or ask the children to make – frequent audio or video recordings during lessons. Children should be encouraged to play back the recordings and ask the usual assessment questions: 'What do I notice? What else? What can I see? What can I hear? What is surprising to me, or impressive?' And with reference to the success criteria: 'Are these musicians showing that they understand X/know how to do Y?'

Recordings of work in progress also allow teachers to take a later, unhurried look for more evidence of musical understanding to use formatively and/or summatively. There are two added benefits of carrying out assessment away from the actual lesson. It allows the teacher to assess 'discreetly', which can be useful when real-time observation by the teacher might interrupt a child's musical flow or cause anxiety. It also affords the teacher more time to consider what strategies to use to help children's musical learning. It is good practice to keep such recordings of musical work-in-progress as well as finished projects, as evidence of musical learning.

Other adults can also be involved in assessing musical learning and understanding and it can help to have other pairs of eyes and ears. If they are not involved in teaching, they may be assessing for purely summative (descriptive) purposes. However their judgements can also be used formatively by the teacher in future music lessons.

Summary

The main purpose of assessment in primary music is a formative one: to 'listen critically to pupils' musical responses and spot what needs to be improved' (OFSTED 2009b, p. 7). It takes time to develop the skills of doing this, but it is perfectly possible to become an astute assessor of children's musical understanding. Two skills are needed: to deliberately notice and 'take in' musical evidence as children are engaged in primary music; and to design clear learning objectives and success criteria, based on a suitable longer-term framework, against which to make judgements. Children too should be supported to develop as assessors of their own and their peers' musicianship and musical understanding, using success criteria as their guide.

The current National Curriculum for Music is a description of children's 'expected' musical understanding and musicianship at the *end* of each Key Stage. The musical learning and development that children need in order to meet the expectations will occur over time if they are offered varied, engaging, meaningful, practical and creative musical experiences and activities throughout the Key Stage. Short-term and longer-term summative assessments, based on evidence collected during normal lessons, will enable teachers to see how children's musical understanding and musicianship skills are increasing, widening and consolidating in a non-linear but cumulative manner over time.

This chapter is designed to support cautious, less experienced teachers of music. It sounds solemn at times. But assessment is a natural part of the pleasure of music-making and in time you will realize that you are getting to know your pupils as musicians, that is, making musical assessments. These will mainly be used formatively to guide your support of children's further learning. You will devise manageable systems for recording the most important summative outcomes of your – rightly – informal assessments.

Recommended reading

Daubney, A. and Fautley, M. (no date). *The National Curriculum for Music: An Assessment and Progression Framework*. Available at: http://www.ism.org/images/files/An_Assessment_and_Progression_Framework_Primary_Music.pdf (Accessed 11 May 2016).

Fautley, M. (2010). *Assessment in Music Education*. Oxford: Oxford University Press.

Murphy, R. (2013). 'Assessing creatively'. In Burnard, P and Murphy, R. (eds), *Teaching Music Creatively*. Oxon: Routledge, pp. 141–52.

Office for Standards in Education, Children's Services and Skills (2009b). *Making More of Music: Improving the Quality of Music Teaching in Primary Schools*. Available at: http://webarchive.nationalarchives.gov.uk/20141124154759/http://www.ofsted.gov.uk/resources/making-more-of-music-improving-quality-of-music-teaching-primary (Accessed 5 May 2017).

Swanwick, K. (1997). 'Assessing Musical Quality in the National Curriculum'. *British Journal of Music Education*, 14, pp. 205–15.

Wiliam, D. (2011). 'What is Assessment for Learning?'. *Studies in Educational Evaluation*, 37, pp. 3–14.

Chapter 8
Practical Issues

Chapter objectives

- to understand the basic principles of good planning
  - how to choose and phrase musical learning objectives
  - how to choose suitable musical activities that start and finish with sound
  - sources of ideas for activities
- to have strategies for including every child
  - those with special educational needs or disabilities
  - those with particularly low or high levels of musicality
  - those with musical and cultural backgrounds different from your own
  - the importance of continually assessing children's musical responses, as the basis for providing motivating levels of musical challenge
- to find ways around a lack of musical instruments in school
  - know what *is* available
  - body and voice
  - found sounds and 'junk' instruments
  - digital technology
  - borrowing from elsewhere
- to consider how to improve one's own singing

What is important to consider when planning primary music?

When teachers plan, they need to consider many things. But the three most important ones are:

1 **what** the musical learning aim is (the learning objective)
2 **how** it might be achieved (activities)
3 **who** the lesson is for (your particular pupils)

(N.B. These are not the same as the 'how, what and why' of the music curriculum – see p. 20!)

Everything else follows. This section will look at the first two considerations – how to fashion a worthwhile and *musical* learning objective, and how to choose activities that will enable children to achieve the objective in musical ways. Later we focus on who your particular pupils are and how to make sure your music lessons cater for each of them.

Learning objectives

In a music lesson, the learning objective needs to be a musical one. This sounds obvious, but OFSTED has repeatedly found that 'in too many cases there was not enough music in music lessons' (OFSTED 2012a, p. 4). (See also Chapter 2.)

How do we develop good, musical learning objectives? Shirley Clarke has written extensively about setting effective objectives generally (e.g. Clarke 2008) while OFSTED (2009b) gives helpful guidance specifically for music planning. Here are the essentials:

- take account of what your pupils already know and can do (see Chapter 7) as far as you can, though you may not have detailed information to begin with
- know your way around the music curriculum (see Chapter 1)
- make your objective specific
- state what you want the children to *learn* not what you want them to *do*
- be clear about what the musical benefit will be of achieving the objective
- keep it simple – one single objective to guide your planning for one music lesson or even a longer unit of work in music.

The three aspects of the music curriculum – skills, knowledge and purposes – go hand in hand (see Chapter 1), so allow any one of them to lead in the brewing of a learning objective. On another occasion, let a different aspect be your inspiration. You might find the tracking document in Figure 7.2 helpful when selecting a focus. Here are some examples of musical learning objectives:

skill-inspired

- to learn to listen to another part while playing your own, so that an audience has a clear sense of the beat/pulse
- to learn to listen to another part while singing your own, so that an audience has a clear sense of the pitch of the tune/melody
- to learn to control your breathing while singing, so that a song is well shaped into expressive phrases
- to learn to control the way an instrument/beater is held, so that the loudness (or pitch, or duration) of the sound can be controlled effectively

- to select sounds according to their timbre, to enhance the mood/emotional tone of a piece of music (either an existing piece or one being newly created)
- to audiate (have in your head) a previously heard (or newly imagined) tune (or chant, or rhythm)

knowledge-inspired

- to understand that music can communicate mood/emotional state
- to understand that music can have a steady pulse/beat
- to understand the verse/chorus structure of many songs, in order to compose a new song *or* in order to make decisions about how to highlight a song's structure when performing it
- to understand that changes in dynamics (or, on another occasion, tempo or texture or timbre) in a piece of music help the music to communicate
- to know what a chord is
- to know what a musical motif is
- to understand the basics of blues music (or reggae, or rap, or Klezmer, or soul, or Indian classical raga music, or English folk, or early choral church music, or West African polyrhythmic music, or ...)

purpose-inspired

- to sing well in a concert (as a group/on your own)
- to play well for an audience
- to create an effective piece of music for a specific occasion
- to enjoy and understand the style/genre of music played by a group of visiting musicians
- to accompany the singing/dancing of another class/group appropriately
- to celebrate musically
- to choose/use music appropriately to calm down/energize/feel ...

Many of these objectives are actually quite substantial and will therefore need revisiting on occasion to consolidate, deepen and refine the children's learning.

Notice that in each case, the learning objective is focused on music but 'content-free' – it says nothing about how it will be achieved. This means you can choose which musical activities will take place in your class to enable children to work towards the objective, depending on the opportunities available, the context of the work and the interests and prior experiences of your pupils. The teacher next door might plan a totally different lesson that still achieves the same objective: there are many paths up the mountain, as they say.

To illustrate this point, imagine that the objective was to make someone feel special on their eightieth birthday. This objective could be achieved by cooking, singing, telling jokes, doing a dance, singing a song, giving a present, making a card, looking at old photographs together, going out in the car, etc.

Choosing activities

This is my favourite part of lesson planning. Having decided what the musical learning objective is, I get to choose – usually with children's help – engaging activities that will motivate and support learning, cumulatively, towards achieving the objective. I can consider individual children's needs and strengths, making sure the activities give scope for every child to be included and to contribute (see next section).

In music lessons the most important criterion for choosing activities is this: will the children be operating as musicians here? Sitting at desks colouring in pictures of Mozart won't do. But any of the activities described in chapters 3, 4, 5, 6 and 7 will do nicely – as would many others. In the same way that even young children are already readers, writers, speakers and artists – but with beginner-level skills – so they are already musicians in your classroom, only needing the opportunity and support to develop their musicianship over time. So, treat them as such.

Whether planning for ten minutes or sixty, an important principle is to start and finish with sound (OFSTED 2009b, p. 6). In a longer lesson, I would also try to include a mix of singing, listening, playing and creating. The proportions can vary. Remember to integrate assessment opportunities, using success criteria based directly on the learning objective (see next section). And always ask yourself, 'Will the children be thinking, feeling and acting as musicians, while engaged in these activities?'.

Figure 8.1 Children are already musicians, gradually increasing their skills and knowledge – here a girl explores the sounds of an octachime

Pause for thought

Choose one of the learning objectives from the list above. How many different activities can you think of that could be used to achieve this objective? Consider activities that involve selecting and creating, singing and playing, rehearsing and performing, listening and expressing: that is, children being musicians.

To illustrate the point that any given learning objective can be achieved in numerous alternative ways, using different activities to work towards the same end, let us take an example:

example learning objective

• to understand that music can have a steady pulse/beat

Here are some ideas for activities that would help children – as musicians – in achieving the objective:

possible activities

• <u>listen</u> to music/sounds with a strong beat and other music/sounds which flow freely, without any particular pulse
• <u>respond</u> to the music by moving
• <u>respond</u> to the music by representing it on paper
• <u>respond</u> to the music by discussing the contrasts between beat and 'free-flow'
• <u>play</u> a steady beat, keeping in time with some recorded/live rhythmic music
• <u>chant</u> a simple piece to a rhythmic backing
• half the class <u>chant</u> rhythmically while the other half <u>play</u> a steady beat/a repeating rhythm pattern (and then swap over!)
• <u>sing</u>, with backing and later without, focusing on keeping time as a group (perhaps using simple actions/movements in support) and later perhaps, solo
• <u>sing</u> a simple round, first with an audible beat and later with a feel for the beat
• <u>create and play</u> a piece of freely flowing music with no pulse
• <u>create and play</u> a piece of music with a strong pulse and repeated rhythm patterns (perhaps using untuned instruments only, so the focus is not on melodies or note pitches)
• <u>compose and perform</u> a piece of music that has some 'metric' sections with a clear pulse, while other sections are free-flowing with no pulse

You can see that there is plenty of scope for choosing activities appropriate to your class at a particular time, each of which will support learning towards your desired ends, musically.

Let us follow the example further, to see how some of the possible activities might unfold into music lessons. One choice for a longer lesson (or sequence of lessons) might be to work on a creative project (see Chapter 6, too):

Using the idea of composing and performing rhythmic/'free' music, perhaps start with sound by listening to some of the first of Britten's 'Four Sea Interludes' (miljkmi 2012), or by creating a tranquil sea soundscape with soft, quiet sounds made by whispering soft syllables and stroking different classroom surfaces.

Then challenge small groups of children to compose peaceful, non-rhythmic music inspired by a tranquil scene (a garden/a lake/a forest/the sea), creating soundscapes with a timeless feel. Once they have 'set the scene' in this way, ask the children to choose something to happen there, that has a steady beat. Perhaps someone comes to dig/rake/jump rope in the garden. Perhaps someone rows or swims steadily across the lake. Perhaps a horse and rider clop along a forest lane, or someone saws logs. Perhaps a fishing trawler glides past with a throbbing engine.

Each group can develop a piece of music structured like a sandwich, beginning and ending 'timelessly' and with the rhythmic event as its middle section. (This structure is known as ABA or 'ternary form'.) Will this middle part be introduced gradually or suddenly? Will it fade out or stop abruptly to leave the scene peaceful once more? There are lots of creative decisions for children to make during the composition of their music. Who will hear the children's completed music? How will you ensure that the session finishes with sound? Can listeners sense a steady beat in the central section?

Alternatively, singing could be the main activity. Make sure you have space for everyone to sit or stand as one big group (see Chapter 4, too):

Start with sound from the teacher, speaking the following as natural, non-rhythmic speech rather than words from a song, with appropriate gestures: 'Frère Jacques, dormez-vous? Sonnez les matines! "Ding, ding dong!"' Can the children recognize the language? What is being said? Let them learn and savour the phrases, interchanging their friends' names for 'Jacques'. Develop a little role-play where one child goes around whispering the phrases while others make noises of the sleeping – and then waking – frères.

Now let the children hear a steady 'ding, dong, ding, dong' on notes F C F C (the C lower than the F) – played at walking-speed. This could be the teacher playing, or someone who is good at keeping a steady beat. Or the teacher could have pre-recorded a minute of this to use as a backing-track. Use a metallophone, or whatever you have that is most 'bell-like'. Notice which children automatically move in time to the beat, nodding or shifting rhythmically.

Use gestures to indicate 'my turn, your turn'. Show how each French phrase can be spoken rhythmically to the sound of the 'bells'. Gradually put phrases together, doubling the first two, so that you all end up chanting the lyrics of the round 'Frère Jacques' in rhythm.

From here, you could do a number of things:

- You could get the whole class singing 'Ding, ding, dong' over and over in time to the 'bells'. Gesture for them to keep this going, then gesture with your arms to 'carve out' half the class and signal for this group to stop singing 'ding, ding, dong' and start singing the song 'Frère Jacques, Frère Jacques'. When they get to the last line, gesture for them to repeat 'Ding, ding, dong' over and over. Now repeat the process with the other half of the class. It helps children to keep one part going while hearing others. Are they keeping a steady beat?

- You could invite children to choose just one line of the song to sing, over and over, while walking and mingling among the others. This is good practice for holding one part when hearing others. Are they keeping a steady beat?

- You could teach all the children to sing the entire song, then divide the class in half and stagger the start so you get it going as a two-part round, to the beat of the 'bells'. You could fade out the 'bells' and manage without that audible pulse.

- You could get some children to make up simple rhythm patterns on Fs and Cs or on untuned instruments, using these patterns to accompany the rest singing. Swap around so every child has an opportunity to use the instruments at some point. Are they keeping a steady beat?

- You could develop a short performance which starts with the role-play and then moves into singing the round with the accompanying rhythm patterns. (This two-part structure is known as AB or 'binary form'.)

Notice that both these example lessons start and finish with sound (OFSTED 2009b). This is a very useful principle which will help to ensure that your music lessons are musical. Incorporate it into your PCK for music!

Sources of ideas

Here are some likely places to find ideas for musical activities:

- This book is one good source, as are other books about teaching music. Choose an activity that appeals to you and make it your own.

- Many schools have purchased commercial 'schemes' for music and you can dip into those to pick up good ideas. Don't be afraid of adapting ideas to fit your learning objectives. Often ideas work for different age groups too, with a tweak!

- A handful of songs are all you need for most learning objectives (see below).

- Lots of schools subscribe to the Sing Up resource online which has extensive and accessible teaching ideas and a useful bank of songs and backing-tracks.

- Find out who the music coordinator or subject leader is in your school and talk to them about ideas for activities (and learning objectives). Other colleagues in school will often be good sources of ideas, too.

- Every area of the country has a Music Hub which will be able to help and also to 'signpost' you to further sources of support and ideas.

- The children can be a great source of ideas. Which songs do they suggest as an inspiring focus for work on singing quality? What music interests them and might make a good basis for understanding more about structure or timbre or texture? What musical purposes do the children want to direct their efforts into?

- Investigate the instruments that the school has and let them inspire you. (More on this later in the chapter.)

- What online resources might you draw on? (More on this later in the chapter.)

Pause for thought

Do you know any potentially useful-for-the-classroom songs off by heart?

Make a list of songs you know that might come in handy.

It is useful to develop a small repertoire of songs that you can manage without having to look them up. Just a handful of songs can take you a long way. Hang on to ones you particularly like and that go down well with your class. Feel free to include current hits and songs in different languages (see next section too). You can explore different dimensions of music through any song, or use a song as a starting point to create something new. Here's my list of 'everyday' songs, built up over the years:

SOME USEFUL EVERYDAY SONGS

1, 2, 3, 4, 5, Once I Caught A Fish Alive

Aiken Drum

Alice The Camel

Ally Bally Bee

Apples And Bananas

B A Bay *or* Swingin' The Alphabet (*It's a cracker! Learn it here: https://youtu.be/bgmdnxtz3Bo*)

Five Little Ducks Went Swimming One Day

Five Little Speckled Frogs

Frère Jacques

Go Tell Aunt Rosie

Grandma Rap

Happy Birthday To You

Heads, Shoulders, Knees And Toes

Hello, Hello, It's Good To See You

Humpty Dumpty

I Know An Old Lady Who Swallowed

A Fly
If You're Happy And You Know It
Incy Wincy Spider
London Bridge is Falling Down
London's Burning
Mama Don't Allow
Michael Row The Boat Ashore
Nanuma
Oats And Beans And Barley Grow
Oh When The Saints Go Marching In
Oh My Darling Clementine
Old MacDonald Had A Farm
One Finger, One Thumb, Keep Moving
One Man Went To Mow
Row, Row, Row Your Boat
She'll Be Coming Round The Mountain
Swing Low, Sweet Chariot
Ten Green Bottles
The Animals Went In Two By Two

The Bear Went Over The Mountain
The Grand Old Duke Of York
The Wheels On The Bus
There's A Hole At The Bottom Of The Sea
There's A Hole In My Bucket
There Were Ten In The Bed
This Old Man
Tomorrow's Another Day
Twinkle Twinkle
Viva La Musica
We're All Going To The Zoo Tomorrow
What Shall We Do With The Drunken
  Sailor?
When I First Came To This Land
When I'm On My Journey
Where Oh Where Has My Little Dog
  Gone?
You Are My Sunshine

Figure 8.2 It is fun to sing old favourites together

How can I make sure every child feels included and valued?

Music is perhaps the ideal curriculum subject when it comes to inclusion (also see Chapter 3). If you maintain the firm belief that music is for everyone, not for a talented few, and that it is all about participation, with each person contributing in whatever way they can, then it naturally engages and motivates children. It is multisensory and invites physical responses too, so there is something for everyone and this engenders a powerful feeling of inclusion and belonging.

In this section, we look at the educational, physical, linguistic and musical needs of individual children and how you can find out about these, so that you can fully accommodate them in music lessons. To begin with you may not know much at all about your children's needs. But music is a versatile thing. Approach your class lessons with an attitude of valuing whatever your pupils contribute. Assume that there will be a range of individual differences such as those described below and plan ahead for how you can adapt your lesson to accommodate whatever arises. Keep asking yourself how you can assist individual children so that they can contribute more and better. Have high expectations of every child, combined with a growing understanding of 'where they are now' in terms of their musical achievements so far.

In Chapter 3 we looked at how to accommodate the kinds of special educational needs and disabilities that typically present within a class of children. Adamek and Darrow (2010), writing in the United States, give further detailed and helpful advice about strategies for including children with cognitive, emotional, behavioural and physical needs in music sessions specifically.

Music offers powerful opportunities for including children for whom English is an additional language (EAL). Plan some musical activities that do not have words as their focus. When singing, choose songs with language content that will help children with EAL to develop their English. Make up new verses, so that children are applying their learning of English. Consider translating some or all of an English-language song into the first language/s of your pupils. Try to find popular songs in their first language/s too. Everyone benefits from exploring language in this way.

We should pay attention, too, to the 'special *musical* needs' of those children who have particularly high or low levels of musicality compared with their peers. There is no shortcut to acquiring musical knowledge and skills, so for low levels of musicality the solution is: more music! At the other extreme, you may well have children in your class with singing, playing, listening or creative skills or musical knowledge far in advance of their peers, perhaps as a result of individual music tuition and/or a home-life rich in musical experiences. How do you ensure that these children are sufficiently challenged in the context of your whole-class music?

- Use the things they are good at in more challenging contexts. For instance, if they can already keep a steady beat unaided, can they provide a 'live' rhythmic backing for others to sing/play along to? If they have begun to read staff notation, can they work out how to play an unfamiliar piece from printed music, in order to share it 'by ear' with others?

- Focus on the things they are less good at, to 'round out' their musicality. For instance, if they are good at playing a certain instrument, ask them to work on a different one. If they are good at playing existing music, challenge their creative capacities, so they apply their 'technical' skills as singers or players in the development of new musical material and ideas. If they are good at solo performance, challenge them to participate in, coach, encourage or direct a group. If they are good at sight-reading (reading from printed music), work on their ability to learn new music 'by ear' and memorize it.

Children will also come to class music with different kinds of musical experience, so it is useful to find out what music children are engaged in outside school. Think in terms of musical skills, knowledge and purposes. For instance, music is often part of family social and cultural occasions: try to get a sense of children's 'sound-worlds' so that you can be more aware of what you are connecting with and building on in your music lessons.

Figure 8.3 Challenge those children with higher levels of skill on instruments to use their skills in different contexts

It is my belief that teachers' success depends primarily upon the quality of relationships in the classroom. The better you can get to know each of your pupils as human beings through developing genuine person-to-person relationships, the more effectively you can plan lessons that fully value and engage them. Jellison (2015) also stresses the importance of getting to know each of your pupils individually, adapting your developing practice to meet each child's unique profile of needs and capabilities.

Getting-to-know is, if you think about it, assessing. Inclusion depends on knowing your pupils, so that you can support and challenge them appropriately (see Chapter 5). And the way to know *how the children are doing* as musicians is to assess this continually.

Continually assessing to ensure engagement and learning

Chapter 7 discusses the principles and techniques of musical assessment. It is important that you build assessment into all parts of your lesson planning, as follows:

before the lesson: Consider children's starting points: their *'prior attainment'*. What can they already do? What do they already know? What have they already experienced?

during the lesson: How are the children doing, moment by moment? Are they finding the activity easy or hard? How do you know? How can you respond to what children are doing in such a way that they can engage more fully/get better at what they are doing? Would it help to get a child/group to listen and feed back their comments? Would it help to audio-record or video-record something at this moment and use the recording with the children?

after the lesson: To what extent was the learning objective achieved? Who by? Did any child surprise you with unexpected musicianship? What else did you notice? What do you think the class/pupil/group might usefully do next in their music?

Remember that in music lessons assessment is not about marking books or administering tests. Instead, we observe, listen and notice evidence of musicianship and indications of musical understanding, as the lesson is happening. This is a skill that develops over time (see Chapter 7) and can be assisted greatly by building assessment into your lesson plans:

1 Ensure your planning 'template' includes a prompt, at the top, about the *prior attainment* of the class and of individual pupils/groups.

2 a) Develop a 'ladder' of success criteria based on your chosen learning objective. This helps you to prepare yourself to support the children's musical learning. Based on our earlier example, success criteria might be:

<u>All</u> children have experienced music with a steady beat

<u>Most</u> children show that they can hear and feel the steady beat

<u>Some</u> children can keep a steady beat in movement or sound without a 'backing-track'

<u>Surprisingly</u> … [Here, you encourage yourself to notice unexpected outcomes. Your expectations may be exceeded – great!]

b) In the main 'body' of your lesson plan, include specific prompt questions to ask yourself, *as the lesson unfolds*, to support your minute-by-minute assessment of learning as it happens. For example:

○ What am I noticing?

○ How are the children doing?

○ What are children bringing to this activity, in terms of musicality?

○ How can children be helped at this point?

○ Would an audio-recording be useful here?

○ What do children think about their work at the moment?

○ Are children meeting any of the success criteria? Which children? Which criteria?

○ What should I focus on now, to help make a difference? (The success criteria can support you here.)

○ Who is exceeding the most demanding criterion? How do I know this?

○ What else is happening that is interesting, in terms of children's musical development? (Think about all the skills covered in chapters 4, 5 and 6, as well as the attitudes and knowledge described in Chapter 3.)

(It will take a while, but if you keep referring to this list of prompts you will gradually internalize it and begin to make continual assessment a natural part of your minute-by-minute teaching, enhancing it greatly.)

If your children were working towards the example learning objective discussed earlier, your prompts to yourself might include

• Is there evidence here that children can feel a steady beat? What evidence? Which children? What do I notice? (Maybe jot down initials of children and a brief word about how you know, e.g. 'JD, MR, SS swaying rhythmically')

• How can I further challenge the children who have definitely 'got it'?

• How can I support the children who haven't 'got it'?

(These last two are about differentiation and relate to the success criteria. You can plan some potentially useful challenges and simplifications in advance, so you have some ideas 'up your sleeve'.)

3   As soon as possible *after the lesson* while it is fresh in your mind, reflect on the learning objective and summarize the extent to which it was achieved. Make brief notes about particular children, against the success criteria. Also note what else you have learnt about individual children, to support improved inclusion next time.

Pause for thought

What do you notice about the way the beaters are being held in Figure 8.4? (See chapter 5.) What might you say or do to help this child improve?

Figure 8.4 Imperfect grip

Why should I draw on the environment, the social world and other subjects in primary music?

Environment

One important reason for drawing on the environment is to help children become aware of, and discriminating about, the sonic dimensions of their world.

Help children to focus on their listening by inviting them to position themselves in an interesting spot and to draw or write down everything they can hear. They can make a subjective judgement about how far away each sound-source is and in which direction, and record their ideas on a sheet of paper with a set of concentric circles printed on it like an archer's target. Their own position is represented by the centre of the circles (and they might want to indicate which way they are facing). Nearby sound-sources would be noted in the central circles while faraway sounds would be added to the peripheral ones.

Focused, active listening can also be encouraged by asking children to go and search for suitable sounds for a creative project. This immediately raises awareness of the sounds in the environment, so often unheeded. They can record these sounds on digital devices and use them as 'samples' in their own music. (Every time I run such an activity with student teachers, at least one group comes back with the sound of a flushing toilet, mixed with giggles.)

If your pupils are lucky enough to spend time outside the classroom, take the opportunity to explore the acoustic environment and its possibilities. In town, listen to footsteps on the pavement, car tyres on gravel or cobbles, engine sounds when idling or changing speed, background music in shops and malls, splashing puddles and sighing automatic doors. On a beach, listen to waves while lying down: do they sound different when you stand up to hear them? Click stones together. Listen to shells. Find somewhere quiet outdoors to lie looking at the stars at night, savouring the silence. Conga through a forest singing. Whack long logs with stiff sticks. Hum an invented tune accompanied by raindrops on a tent roof. Explore echoes in a valley or between high walled buildings. Listen to birdsong, the wind, the buzz of insects, water dripping, machines working rhythmically. Find ways to mimic some of these sounds, or compose lyrics for songs inspired by them.

Thinking about sounds in an imagined environment can also develop audiation (auditory imagination). For instance, when focusing on a geographical or historical context, can children think about the kinds of sounds that might be heard? Can they build up a real soundscape from their ideas? How might a Roman trumpet have sounded? What might you hear in a rainforest? What sounds might there be at night, camping in the countryside? In a cave? In a Tudor palace? This kind of activity can help children to think themselves deeply into a context and can trigger very thoughtful historical, geographic and environmental questions.

The social world

Since music is primarily a social phenomenon, the social world offers all-important *purposes* for active music-making (see Chapter 4). Every special occasion can be enhanced with music. As well as learning suitable songs, why not use some of the opportunities as springboards for creative work?

As part of learning about the nature and functions of music in different times and places (see Chapter 3), encourage children and families with a variety of cultural and religious backgrounds to share the ways that music features in their social and personal lives. Handled with due respect and a positive attitude to celebrating and understanding cultural diversity, such sharing can offer profound learning experiences for all pupils (and adults!). It is also a powerful strategy for including those who might often feel like 'outsiders', since music is an accessible language-without-words through which people can feel a common bond of enjoyment and belonging, overcoming any feelings of separation due to language or cultural practices.

Other subjects

Barnes (2015, pp. 272–74) outlines a variety of ways in which different subjects can be combined in a cross-curricular approach to learning. Although the ideal would be for music to feature as a major player in the school curriculum, in reality linking music with other subjects can be a way to ensure that there is at least some music in children's school lives.

One way to achieve this is to use singing as a teaching strategy within other subjects. Singing the alphabet or the nine-times table is using music as the servant of English or mathematics. (There are some great song suggestions online. Try Alan Peat Ltd [2015], Jack Hartmann Kids Music Channel [2015] or Gore [2015], for example.) Barnes (2015, p. 272) describes such cross-curricular links as 'tokenistic' if no heed is paid to musical learning at the time. However, with a slight tweak to the lesson planning to include a musical learning objective (e.g. keeping steady time, or articulating words clearly, or exploring tempo) some musical progress can be made and the relationship of the subjects would be described as 'hierarchical' (Barnes 2015, p. 272).

This fits well with the current emphasis on 'depth of learning' in the core curricular subjects. Children need opportunities to demonstrate that they have assimilated what they have been learning in English and mathematics and can use, apply and explain their learning in new contexts. There are many ways to link music in here, for instance:

- applying early counting skills when taking part in music-making and listening activities (see Chapter 3 mention of beats/metres)
- using multiplication facts to work out how many times to repeat a musical phrase
- applying ideas of pattern and repetition in composing rhythmic material
- using understanding of ratio, proportion and fractional amounts in developing rhythm patterns
- using understanding of ratio, proportion and fractional amounts to grasp how note durations and tempi (speeds) are represented in staff notation
- applying knowledge of time measurement in operating recording/ playback equipment

- using calculations to support understanding of chronology in music history
- using phonic knowledge to invent rhyming lyrics
- using phonic knowledge to develop onomatopoeic vocal sounds
- using knowledge of onomatopoeia in developing lyrics
- using spoken language in various functional ways (see Chapter 4).

At other times, it is important to allow music to take an equal share of the limelight in terms of learning objectives, within a project/theme/topic that involves more than one curricular subject. Such projects usually evolve over many hours of curriculum time. Seek advice within your school as to how to plan such a project and how to include the children's ideas and interests within the planning. Stick to the planning principles mentioned earlier in this chapter, across all the subjects linked with the project. Consider whether music can play a significant part in the final project outcome. (See also Chapter 4.)

CASE STUDY

Every other year, my class of mixed Year 5 and Year 6 pupils studied the language of Shakespeare and brought an abridged version of one of his plays to an audience. To do this we incorporated History, Design and Technology, English, Music, and Personal, Social and Health Education into a cross-curricular project.

One year 'Macbeth' was our focus. A costume designer from the Royal Shakespeare Company brought in a rail of full-sized costumes and talked about the research and design needed in their production. As well as rehearsing the play itself, children were immersed in researching, designing and creating key props and costumes for themselves, as well as suitable music from the period. Families were invited to come to the performance at Stokesay Castle in Shropshire, which had kindly given permission for our play to be performed 'on location' in a medieval castle.

The idea was to rehearse in the castle in the morning, grab a quick lunch and then perform for our invited guests in the afternoon. Somewhere along the line a step had been missed and our coach did not arrive to take us to the castle. After a desperate appeal on the local radio, another coach company came to the rescue and scooped up three dozen anxious Tudor folk who ate their non-Tudor lunches en route.

With no time for rehearsal, just a quick walk-around, the play commenced. It was a riotous success, with the three witches intoning in the atrium, Banquo's ghost appearing at a banquet in the medieval great hall, Lady MacBeth wringing her hands as she came down a set of eleventh-century stairs and a gory finale in the central courtyard.

Music, played by different children at different times and supported by a specialist in Tudor music, was heard first as a prelude, then to enhance various scenes and finally as the cast took their bows. Children developed their musical knowledge, skills and understanding of purpose through this aspect of the project.

What do I do about the lack of instruments in my school?

Are you sure there are no instruments in school? If no one has championed music for a while, they may be imprisoned in the back of a cupboard somewhere. If they are nowhere to be found, they may gradually have dispersed to various corners. Perhaps you can set up an 'instrument amnesty' and see what appears mysteriously from around the school. You could even put out a call to your school community for unused, easy-to-play instruments and see what turns up.

In all seriousness it is worth checking, since most schools will have some instruments. New instruments are expensive: however, if there is a budget for buying new resources, do go for quality. You will then have instruments that sound good and last well, though it is important to teach everyone how to handle each instrument sensibly, and to reinforce this consistently. Sticks should be used parallel to drum-heads. If notes are to be removed from xylophones, lift them off horizontally rather than levering them off. Avoid dropping instruments.

It is good if there are enough untuned percussion instruments for every child to have one, with a few left over so no child gets 'last choice'. Make a teaching habit of asking children to swap instruments frequently so that everyone gets opportunities to play everything, over time.

Figure 8.5 It is good to have enough instruments for everyone, but not essential

Ideally you should have at least ten tuned percussion instruments too, so that half the class can play them at the same time (sharing one between two children) and so that small groups of children can each have one when working creatively. (See Chapter 3 for a reminder of what kinds of instruments we are talking about.)

You will also need a range of sticks and beaters to go with your instruments. Softer, more muffled sounds require soft-headed beaters which are quite expensive, so look after them.

However, never let a lack of instruments prevent you from teaching music! There are several ways of circumventing the issue.

Body and voice

A surprising proportion of the curriculum can be achieved through making sounds with voice, mouth and body percussion (stamping, clapping, patting, stroking, clicking, tapping, etc). Our bodies are our 'oldest' and most portable instruments and many musicians spend their lifetimes mastering them at a high level. One of the 'Ten Pieces' recently featured by the BBC was 'Connect It' by Anna Meredith, composed entirely for body percussion and vocal sounds (Reich-Storer 2016). The group Stomp is also inspirational (e.g. tonynsyde 2012), as are beat-boxers such as Thom Thum (FIVEaa Radio 2013).

The pitch range of the voice can be used for singing, humming, yodelling, wordless tunes, instrument impersonations. ... Experiment with the effect of playing body percussion at the same time, like the legendary Bobby McFerrin (KTS Broadcast 2012).

Found sounds and 'junk' instruments

If our own bodies are our 'oldest' instruments, then making sounds using things around us must be the second oldest source. Experiment with whatever you have at hand. The kitchen is a good place to look: bang pots and pans with wooden spoons, click metal spoons together, shake tubs of rice, ping elastic bands over empty boxes, blow across the necks of bottles, shake a bag of metal bottle-tops. If you have a metal mixing-bowl, explore what happens when you 'ding' it and then part-submerge it in water!

You can extend these ideas to create a wide variety of 'junk' instruments. Here are a few possibilities (the setting-up of many of them is best done by an adult):

- collect hollow things, such as metal bowls, plastic drainpipes and kitchen containers, that sound interesting when tapped with wooden beaters or sticks

- hang a simple metal object (a bicycle part? a piece of plumbing pipe? part of some disused metal furniture?) with sewing thread and tap it with a metal stick such as a large, long nail

- construct a 'mobile' with upside-down earthenware plant pots hung up with knotted rope – different shapes and sizes will give sounds of different pitches
- you can also take large nails of different lengths and hang them with sewing thread, then play them with another large nail (or lay them across the open top of a suitably shaped rigid box rimmed with draft-excluder tape for the nails to rest on, for a home-made metallophone)
- with a metal drill-bit, make holes in metal bottle-tops, then loosely nail them in pairs or threes to a long stick that can be shaken or tapped like a walking stick
- make a collection of different-sounding shakers using a variety of (safe if spilled!) contents (sand, dry pasta, rice) in different containers
- hold a single layer of tissue paper folded over the teeth of a comb, then press the covered comb lightly to your lips and sing a wordless tune – it sounds like a kazoo (and makes your lips tickle: a good opportunity to talk about sound and vibration!)
- if you can procure the inner tube of a tractor tyre, it is a good material for home-made drum-heads – cut a large circular shape, punch circular holes (not too close to the edge) to minimize tearing and lace the drum-head to an empty catering tin
- giant balloon rubber can also be used for drum-heads, secured with elastic bands
- make a 'shoe-box harp' (devineDiY 2013) with elastic bands, then, if you wish, experiment with 'tuning' the notes by matching them with notes played on a piano or a xylophone
- make a set of pan-pipes from drinking straws, or lengths of plastic plumbing pipe if you can get it (Armin Hirmer 2016)
- then there's the perennial ruler-twanging sound – why not line a set of rulers up at the edge of a desk, each protruding by a different amount, and clamp them down with something to create an instrument with several different notes?

Digital technologies

Perhaps your school is better resourced for ICT than music. If so, make use of that: there are digital ways to support every aspect of the music curriculum. The speakers provided with classroom whiteboards deliver good sound quality. Portable devices such as laptops and ipads are particularly useful in music lessons.

singing

- use YouTube, Sing Up (2016), etc., to provide backing-tracks and visual lyrics
- link with other schools for singing projects

playing

- use GarageBand, Bebot, Loopseque, Singing Fingers and suchlike as simple-to-play instruments (see Chapter 3), just as you would use tambourines and xylophones

- an advantage of such digital instruments is that children can work on them using headphones, which bypasses problems of sound interference

- to balance the dynamics when playing with others, use small high-quality speakers plugged into the headphone sockets of portable digital devices.

listening

- 'Minute of Listening' (Sound and Music 2016) was mentioned in Chapter 3 but there are also millions of other great audio recordings, of everything under the sun, accessible these days via the internet

- ask children to record their own sounds.

creating

- use 'found sounds', recorded voices, recorded instruments and/or digital sounds to create new pieces, using simple composition software such as GarageBand and Audacity

- use the software to distort and change the initial sounds: change the pitch, the dynamics, the timbre

- copy and paste sections of sound to repeat them, or use the 'loop' facility to play a section of sound over and over

- consider mixing live sounds and sounds developed using digital means.

practising, rehearsing, performing

- use recording and playback to enhance assessment and improvement in a learning–feedback loop of 'do – review – adjust – do – review – adjust …' (see Chapter 7 too)

- over time, children will become better able to self-assess and improve *without* the recording, having become better able to notice subtle aspects of their own work through using recordings

- consider the use of microphones in certain contexts.

Borrowing instruments

Another way to bypass a shortage of instruments is to look beyond the school. Do any neighbouring schools have class sets of ukuleles, drums or keyboards that they

Figure 8.6 Can you borrow instruments for a period of time, if you plan ahead?

would be willing to lend for a time? Make contact with local secondary schools as they tend to be better off in this regard. (It is excellent practice to develop music links with children's future schools in any case, to support transition and help ensure your good work is built upon.) The local Music Hub is another likely option for borrowing/renting class sets of instruments at a very reasonable price.

How can I improve my own singing?

It takes time to master the skills of controlling the voice, just as it does with acquiring any skill. Most adults who profess to being unable to sing have the potential, as children do, if they give time to learning gradually.

Improving your own singing skills can be done informally by singing along to recorded material. Choose any songs you like. Songs that do not leap around wildly between very high and low notes are the easiest to begin with. Try one of these:

'Because the Night' (BruceSpringsteenVEVO 2010)

Bobby McFerrin's 'Don't Worry Be Happy' (emimusic 2009)

'Happy' (PharrellWilliamsVEVO 2014)

Nancy Sinatra's 'These Boots Are Made For Walkin' (VideosVariosOfficial 2013)

An internet search for 'easy songs to sing' will quickly yield more ideas. Concentrate on trying to match the note your voice is making to the note of the online singer. This can be easier if you ignore the words for a while and hum or 'lah' the tune. Keep the volume of the recording down low enough that you can hear your own voice too.

You might find that an online video or audio version of a song is difficult to sing along with because it feels physically uncomfortable for your voice. This is probably because the note pitches (the range of notes used in the song) are too high or too low for your voice. You may well be able to find a different version that starts on a higher or lower note (which is called 'being in a different key') and that is easier to join in with.

Once you have the song firmly in your head (which is 'audiation' – see Chapter 5), sing it by yourself. Again, start by humming or using 'neutral syllables', focusing on reproducing the pitches of the notes that make up the tune. The more you do it, the better it will become. Sing in the shower. Sing in the car. Sing while you are cooking. Join an informal local choir. Just sing!

Recommended reading

Adamek, M. S. and Darrow, A.-A. (2010). *Music in Special Education.* Silver Spring, Maryland: American Music Therapy Association.

Alan Peat Ltd (2015). *The Literacy Jukebox by Mr A, Mr C & Mr D.* (Version 1.0) [Mobile app]. Available at: itunes App Store. (Downloaded 4 December 2016).

Armin Hirmer (2016). *How to Build a Pan Flute Out of Drinking Straws* Available at: https://www.youtube.com/watch?v=sglOT1J80Ss. (Accessed 9 December 2016).

Barnes, J. (2015). 'An introduction to cross-curricular learning'. In Driscoll, P., Lambirth, A. and Roden, J. (eds), *The Primary Curriculum: A Creative Approach*, 2nd edn. London: Sage, pp. 260–83.

BruceSpringsteenVEVO (2010). *Bruce Springsteen & The E Street Band – Because the Night.* Available at: https://www.youtube.com/watch?v=HcqUSi8QPN0 (Accessed 21 July 2016).

Clarke, S. (2008). *Active Learning Through Formative Assessment.* London: Hodder Education.

devineDiY (2013). *DiY – How to make a shoebox harp.* Available at: https://youtu.be/i6Iug6cMAq8 (Accessed 9 December 2016).

ElvisPresleyVEVO (2013). *Can't Help Falling in Love.* Available at: https://www.youtube.com/watch?v=vGJTaP6anOU (Accessed 21 July 2016).

emimusic (2009). *Don't Worry Be Happy.* Available at: https://www.youtube.com/watch?v=d-diB65scQU (Accessed 21 July 2016).

FIVEaaRadio (2013). *Tom Thum – Adelaide Fringe.* Available at: https://youtu.be/5HEz3SUDmS4 (Accessed 9 December 2016).

Gore, J. (2015). *Introduction to the Musical Times Tables Project.* Available at: https://musicalmaths.com/ (Accessed 4 December 2016).

Jack Hartmann Kids Music Channel (2015). *Count by 5's | Exercise and Count By 5 | Count to 100 | Counting Songs | Jack Hartmann.* Available at: https://www.youtube.com/watch?v=amxVL9KUmq8 (Accessed 12 December 2016).

KTS Broadcast (2012). *Bobby McFerrin & Crowd – I Can See Clearly Now (LIVE in Kaunas).* Available at: https://www.youtube.com/watch?v=pO_LV-yInc8 (Accessed 9 December 2016).

miljkmi (2012). *Benjamin Britten – Four Sea Interludes from "Peter Grimes"* Available at: https://www.youtube.com/watch?v=VTd2aXLTA84 (Accessed 10 December 2016).

PharrellWilliamsVEVO (2014). *Happy.* Available at: https://www.youtube.com/watch?v=ZbZSe6N_BXs (Accessed 21 July 2016).

Robert Reich-Storer (2016). *Anna Meredith and Radio 1s Dev Introduce her Body Percussion Piece Connect It.* Available at: https://youtu.be/Ai6yGKB3obY?list=PL7zwV8Yqy_M5Ae9t0gjify7RbPHqqkdue (Accessed 6 December 2016).

tonynsyde (2012). *Stomp Live – Part 3 – Just Clap Your Hands.* Available at: https://www.youtube.com/watch?v=l0XdDKwFe3k (Accessed 6 December 2016).

VideosVariosOfficial (2013). *These Boots Are Made For Walkin.* Available at: https://www.youtube.com/watch?v=yQG4bLFQkIY (Accessed 21 July 2016).

Bibliography

Adamek, M. S. and Darrow, A.-A. (2010). *Music in Special Education.* Silver Spring, Maryland: American Music Therapy Association.

Adams, P., McQueen, H. and Hallam, S. (2010). 'Contextualising Music Education in the UK'. In Hallam, S. and Creech, A. (eds.) *Music Education in the 21st Century in the United Kingdom: Achievements, Analysis and Aspirations.* London: Institute of Education, University of London, pp. 18–34.

Alan Peat Ltd (2015). *The Literacy Jukebox by Mr A, Mr C & Mr D.* (Version 1.0) [Mobile app]. Available at: itunes App Store. (Downloaded 4 December 2016).

Apple Inc. (2016). *Garageband.* Available at: http://www.apple.com/uk/mac/garageband/ (Accessed 31 July 2016).

Armin Hirmer (2016). *How to Build a Pan Flute Out of Drinking Straws* Available at: https://www.youtube.com/watch?v=sglOT1J80Ss. (Accessed 9 December 2016).

Arts Council England (no date) *Music Education Hubs.* Available at: http://www.artscouncil.org.uk/music-education/music-education-hubs (Accessed 21 December 2016).

Associated Board of the Royal Schools of Music (2015). *Classical 100.* Available at: www.abrsm.org/classical100 (Accessed 14 July 2016).

Austin, J., Renwick, J. and McPherson, G. (2006). 'Developing Motivation'. In McPherson, G. (ed.), *The Child as Musician: A Handbook of Musical Development.* Oxford: Oxford University Press, pp. 213–38.

Bandura, A. (1977a). *Social Learning Theory.* Englewood Cliffs: Prentice-Hall.

Bandura, A. (1977b). 'Self- efficacy: Toward a unifying theory of behavioral change'. *Psychological Review*, 84 (2). pp. 191–215.

Barnes, J. (2012). 'Integrity and autonomy for music in a creative and cross-curriculum'. In *Debates in Music Teaching.* Abingdon: Routledge.

Barnes, J. (2015). 'An introduction to cross-curricular learning'. In Driscoll, P., Lambirth, A. and Roden, J. (eds), *The Primary Curriculum: A Creative Approach*, 2nd edn. London: Sage, pp. 260–83.

Barrett, M. S. (2012). 'Preparing the mind for musical creativity: Early music learning and engagement'. In Odena, O. (ed.), *Musical Creativity: Insights from Music Education Research.* Surrey: Ashgate.

Barton, P. (2016). 'Aquarium' from *Carnival of the Animals*, edited by Camille Saint-Saëns. Available at: https://www.youtube.com/watch?v=_sN3Xmnd5cs (Accessed 19 July 2016).

BBC (2016). *Ten Pieces: Teaching Resources for Educators Working with 7–11 Year Olds.* Available at: http://www.bbc.co.uk/programmes/articles/3xWSYQhHfM9dZYfmRmTwVqN/teaching-resources-for-educators-working-with-7-11-year-olds (Accessed 31 December 2016).

Benedict, C. (2010). 'Methods and approaches'. In Abeles, H. and Custodero, L. (eds), *Critical Issues in Music Education: Contemporary Theory and Practice.* Oxford: Oxford University Press, pp. 194–214.

Biasutti, M., Hennessy, S. and de Vugt-Jansen, E. (2015). 'Confidence development in non-music specialist trainee primary teachers after an intensive programme'. *British Journal of Music Education*, 32(2), pp. 143–61.

Biesta, G. and Burbules, N. C. (2003). *Pragmatism and Educational Research*. Lanham, MD: Rowman & Littlefield.

Bjork (1995). 'It's Oh So Quiet'. *Post* [CD]. London: One Little Indian Records.

Blake, Q. (1992). *All Join In*. London: Random House.

BruceSpringsteenVEVO (2010). *Bruce Springsteen & The E Street Band — Because the Night*. Available at: https://www.youtube.com/watch?v=HcqUSi8QPN0 (Accessed 21 July 2016).

Bruner, J. (1966). *Towards a Theory of Instruction*. Massachusetts: Harvard University Press.

Bruner, J. (1977). *The Process of Education*. Massachusetts: Harvard University Press.

Campbell, M. R. (2014). 'Inquiry and Synthesis in Pre-service Music Teacher Education: A close look at cultivating self-study research'. In Kaschub, M. and Smith, J. (eds), *Promising Practices in 21st Century Music Teacher Education*. Oxford: Oxford University Press, pp. 149–74.

Carlile, O. and Jordan, A. (2012). *Approaches to Creativity: A Guide for Teachers*. Maidenhead: Open University Press.

Casual Underground (no date) *LoopsequeKids*. ipad edition. [Mobile app]. Available at: Apple itunes Appstore (Downloaded 6 February 2013).

Clarke, S. (2008). *Active Learning Through Formative Assessment*. London: Hodder Education.

Cohen, L., Manion, L. and Morrison, K. (2011). *Research Methods in Education*, 7th edn. London: Routledge.

Conway, C. (2003). 'Good Rhythm and Intonation from Day One in Beginning Instrumental Music'. *Music Educators Journal*, 89(5), pp. 26–31.

Cox, G. (2010). 'Britain: Towards 'A Long Overdue Renaissance'?'. In Cox, G. and Stevens, R. (eds), *The Origins and Foundations of Music Education: Cross-cultural Historical Studies of Music in Compulsory Schooling*. London: Continuum, pp. 15–28.

Craft, A. (2001). 'Little c Creativity'. In *Creativity in Education*, edited by Craft, A., Jeffrey, B. and Leibling, M. London: Continuum, pp. 45–61.

Craft, A. (2010). 'Possibility thinking and wise creativity: Educational futures in England?'. In Beghetto, R. A. and Kaufman, J. C. (eds), *Nurturing Creativity in the Classroom*. Cambridge: Cambridge University Press.

Craft, A., Cremin, T., Burnard, P., Dragovic, T. and Chappell, K. (2013). 'Possibility thinking: Culminative studies of an evidence-based concept driving creativity?'. *Education 3–13*(5), pp. 538–56.

Cremin, T. (2015). 'Creative teachers and creative teaching'. In Wilson, A. (ed.), *Creativity in Primary Education*, 3rd edn. Exeter: Learning Matters, pp. 33–44.

Cremin, T., Burnard, P. and Craft, A. (2006). 'Pedagogy and possibility thinking in the early years'. *Thinking Skills and Creativity*, 1(2), pp. 108–19.

Cross, I. (2011). 'The nature of music and its evolution'. In Hallam, S., Cross, I. and Thaut, M. H. (eds), *Oxford Handbook of Music Psychology*. Oxford: Oxford University Press, pp. 3–13.

Csikszentmihalyi, M. (1999). 'If We Are So Rich, Why Aren't We Happy?' *American Psychologist*, 54(10), pp. 821–7.

Daubney, A. and Fautley, M. (no date) *The National Curriculum for Music: An Assessment and Progression Framework*. Available at: http://www.ism.org/images/files/An_Assessment_and_Progression_Framework_Primary_Music.pdf (Accessed 11 May 2016).

Daubney, A. and Mackrill, D. (2015). 'Planning music in the national curriculum'. In Sewell, K. (ed.), *Planning the Primary National Curriculum: A Complete Guide for Trainees and Teachers*. Exeter: Learning Matters, pp. 249–61.

Definite Article (1996). Directed by Ed Bye [Video cassette]. London: Vision Video.

Department for Education (2013). *Music Programmes of Study: Key Stages 1 and 2 National Curriculum in England*. Available at: https://www.gov.uk/government/uploads/system/

uploads/attachment_data/file/239037/PRIMARY_national_curriculum_-_Music.pdf (Accessed 19 December 2016).

Department for Education & Department for Culture, Media and Sport (2011). *The Importance of Music: A National Plan for Music Education.* Available at: https://www.gov.uk/government/uploads/system/uploads/attachment_data/file/180973/DFE-00086-2011.pdf (Accessed 19 December 2016).

devineDiY (2013). *DiY – How to Make a Shoebox Harp.* Available at: https://youtu.be/i6Iug6cMAq8 (Accessed 9 December 2016).

DoReMiworld (no date) *NoteWorks.* Available at: http://www.doremiworld.com/ (Accessed 31 July 2016).

Dweck, C. (2016). *Mindset: The New Psychology of Success,* 2nd edn. New York: Ballantine Books.

Eisner, E. W. (2005). *Reimagining Schools: The Selected Works of Elliot W. Eisner.* London: Routledge.

Elliott, D. J. and Silverman, M. (2015). *Music Matters: A Philosophy of Music Education,* 2nd edn. Oxford: Oxford University Press.

Ellison, J. and Creech, A. (2010). 'Music in the primary school'. In Hallam, S. and Creech, A. (eds), *Music Education in the 21st Century in the United Kingdom: Achievements, Analysis and Aspirations.* London: Institute of Education, University of London, pp. 211–27.

emimusic (2009). *Don't Worry Be Happy.* Available at: https://www.youtube.com/watch?v=d-diB65scQU (Accessed 21 July 2016).

Fautley, M. (2010). *Assessment in Music Education.* Oxford: Oxford University Press.

Finney, J. (2011). *Music Education in England, 1950–2010: The Child-Centred Progressive Tradition.* Farnham, Surrey: Ashgate.

Finney, J. (2015). 'Music Education without a centre'. In *Music Education Now.* 2016. Available at: https://jfin107.wordpress.com/2015/03/13/music-education-without-a-centre/ (Accessed 20 April 2016).

Fischer, M. H. and Zwaan, R. A. (2008). 'Embodied language: A review of the role of the motor system in language comprehension' *The Quarterly Journal of Experimental Psychology,* 61(6), pp. 825–50. DOI:10.1080/17470210701623605.

FIVEaaRadio (2013). *Tom Thum – Adelaide Fringe.* Available at: https://youtu.be/5HEz3SUDmS4 (Accessed 9 December 2016).

Gordon, E. (1999). 'All about audiation and music aptitudes'. *Music Educators Journal,* 86(2), pp. 41–4.

Gore, J. (2015). *Introduction to the Musical Times Tables Project.* Available at: https://musicalmaths.com/ (Accessed 4 December 2016).

Green, L. (2008). *Music, Informal Learning and the School: A New Classroom Pedagogy.* Aldershot: Ashgate.

Hallam, S. (2006). 'Musicality'. In McPherson, G. (ed.), *The Child as Musician: A Handbook of Musical Development.* Oxford: Oxford University Press, pp. 93–110.

Hallam, S. (2015). *The Power of Music: A Research Synthesis of the Impact of Actively Making Music on the Intellectual, Social and Personal Development of Children and Young People.* London: Music Education Council.

Hallam, S. and Prince, V. (2003). 'Conceptions of musical ability'. *Research Studies in Music Education,* 20(1), pp. 2–22.

Hallam, S., Creech, A. and Papageorgi, I. (2008). *EMI Music Sound Foundation: Evaluation of the Impact of Additional Training in the Delivery of Music at Key Stage 1.* Available at: http://eprints.ioe.ac.uk/2299/1/Hallam2008_FinalEMI_Music_FoundationEvaluation.pdf (Accessed 20 April 2016).

Hammerton, R. (2014). 'Music in schools: where words finish, music begins'. *TES Connect,* 16 June. Available at: https://www.tes.com/blogs/ofsted/music-schools-where-words-finish-music-begins (Accessed 11 May 2016).

Happylander/Abstract Alien (no date) *Isle of Tune.* ipad edition. [Mobile app]. Available at: Apple itunes Appstore (Downloaded 6 February 2013).

Hargreaves, D., MacDonald, R. and Miell, D. (2012). 'Musical identities mediate musical development'. In McPherson, G. and Welch, G. (eds), *The Oxford Handbook of Music Education.* Oxford: Oxford University Press, pp. 125–42.

Hedden, D. (2012). 'An overview of existing research about children's singing and the implications for teaching children to sing'. *Update: Applications of Research in Music Education,* 30(2), pp. 52–62.

Henley, D. (2011). *Music Education in England.* Department for Education: Department for Culture, Media and Sport. Available at: https://www.gov.uk/government/publications/music-education-in-england-a-review-by-darren-henley-for-the-department-for-education-and-the-department-for-culture-media-and-sport. (Accessed 19 December 2016).

Henley, J. (2016). 'How musical are primary generalist student teachers?'. *Music Education Research,* pp. 1–15 DOI:10.1080/14613808.2016.1204278 [Online]. Available at: http://dx.doi.org/10.1080/14613808.2016.1204278.

Hennessy, S. (2000). 'Overcoming the red-feeling: The development of confidence to teach music in primary school amongst student teachers'. *British Journal of Music Education,* 17(2), pp. 183–96.

Hennessy, S. (2015). 'Creativity in the music curriculum'. In Wilson, A. (ed.), *Creativity in Primary Education.* London: Sage, pp. 219–33.

Jack Hartmann Kids Music Channel (2015). *Count by 5's | Exercise and Count By 5 | Count to 100 | Counting Songs | Jack Hartmann.* Available at: https://www.youtube.com/watch?v=amxVL9KUmq8 (Accessed 12 December 2016).

Jellison, J. (2006). 'Including everyone'. In McPherson, G. (ed.), *The Child as Musician: A Handbook of Musical Development.* Oxford: Oxford University Press, pp. 257–72.

Jellison, J. (2015). 'Including everyone'. In McPherson, G. (ed.), *Including Everyone: creating music classrooms where all children learn.* Oxford and New York: Oxford University Press.

JessiesFund (2014). *Jessie's Fund intro 2014.* Available at: https://www.youtube.com/watch?v=IiH7n4rNUeg (Accessed 5 July 2016).

Jesson, J. (2012). *Developing Creativity in the Primary School.* Maidenhead: McGraw-Hill Open University Press.

Johnson, R. and Swain, M., eds (1997) *Immersion Education: International Perspectives.* Cambridge: Cambridge University Press.

Kaschub, M. (2014). 'Where it all comes together: Student-driven project-based learning in music teacher education'. In Kaschub, M. and Smith, J. (eds), *Promising Practices in 21st Century Music Teacher Education.* Oxford: Oxford University Press, pp. 125–48.

Kaschub, M. and Smith, J. (2009). *Minds on Music: Composition for Creative and Critical Thinking.* Lanham, MD: Rowman & Littlefield Education.

Kirschner, S. and Tomasello, M. (2010). 'Joint music making promotes prosocial behavior in 4-year-old children'. *Evolution and Human Behaviour,* 31, pp. 354–64.

Kolb, D. A. (1984). *Experiential Learning: Experience as the Source of Learning and Development.* New Jersey: Prentice-Hall.

Krathwohl, D. R. (2002). 'A revision of bloom's taxonomy: An overview'. *Theory into Practice,* 41(4), pp. 212–18.

KTS Broadcast (2012). *Bobby McFerrin & crowd — I Can See Clearly Now (LIVE in Kaunas).* Available at: https://www.youtube.com/watch?v=pO_LV-yInc8 (Accessed 9 December 2016).

Lamont, A., Daubney, A. and Spruce, G. (2012), 'Singing in primary schools: case studies of good practice in whole class vocal tuition'. *British Journal of Music Education,* 29(2), pp. 251–68.

Lave, J. and Wenger, E. (1991). *Situated Learning: Legitimate Peripheral Participation.* Cambridge: Cambridge University Press.

Layton Music (no date). *Games and Resources.* Available at: https://laytonmusic.wordpress.com/2007/12/19/rhythm-flashcards/ (Accessed 31 July 2016).

lirbugler (2012). *British Army Routine Bugle Calls Part 2.* Available at: https://www.youtube.com/watch?v=1UkW9aEP4fI (Accessed 12 December 2016).

Lougheed, J. (1997). *Signposts to Music: Pitch.* Oxford: Oxford University Press.

lucpebo (2012). *Mussorgsky/ Pictures at an exhibition – Bydlo – Karajan.* Available at: https://www.youtube.com/watch?v=vOvIbfaUjIw. (Accessed 12 December 2016).

Malloch, S. and Trevarthen, C. eds (2010). *Communicative Musicality: Exploring the Basis of Human Companionship.* Oxford: Oxford University Press.

Marsh, K. and Young, S. (2006). 'Musical play'. In McPherson, G. (ed.), *The Child as Musician: A Handbook of Musical Development.* Oxford: Oxford University Press, pp. 289–310.

MashupZone (2015). *Funny Babies Dancing — A Cute Baby Dancing Videos Compilation 2015.* Available at: https://www.youtube.com/watch?v=ZiV4KhvuQJw (Accessed 5 July 2016).

Matthews, C. (2014). *Hook, Line and Singer: 125 Songs to Sing Out Loud.* London: Penguin Books.

Melody Cats (no date). *Rhythm Cat.* Available at: http://melodycats.com/rhythm-cat/ (Accessed 31 July 2016).

miljkmi (2012). *Benjamin Britten – Four Sea Interludes from "Peter Grimes"* Available at: https://www.youtube.com/watch?v=VTd2aXLTA84 (Accessed 10 December 2016).

Mithen, S. J. (2006). *The Singing Neanderthals: The Origins of Music, Language, Mind and Body.* London: Phoenix.

Murphy, R. (2013). 'Assessing creatively'. In Burnard, P and Murphy, R. eds, *Teaching Music Creatively.* Oxon: Routledge, pp. 141–52.

Music Mark (2014). Making the Most of Music in Your School. Available at: http://www.nottsmusichub.org.uk/site/files/2014/07/Making-the-most-of-music-in-your-school-Music-Mark-July-2014.pdf (Accessed 5 May 2017).

Musical Futures (2015). Available at: https://www.musicalfutures.org/ (Accessed 10, July 2016).

National Advisory Committee on Creative and Cultural Education [NACCCE] (1999). *All Our Futures: Creativity, Culture and Education.* London: Department for Education and Employment. Available at: http://www.readyunlimited.com/wp-content/uploads/2013/02/all-our-futures1.pdf (Accessed 5 May 2017).

National Foundation for Educational Research (2016). *Key Data on Music Education Hubs 2015.* Available at: http://www.artscouncil.org.uk/sites/default/files/download-file/MEH%202015%20report%20final%20October%202016.pdf (Accessed 21 December 2016).

Normalware (2008). *Bebot.* ipad edition. [Mobile app]. Available at: Apple itunes Appstore (Downloaded 6 February 2013).

Office for Standards in Education, Children's Services and Skills (2009a). *Making More of Music: An Evaluation of Music in Schools 2005-8.* Office for Standards in Education, Children's Services and Skills.

Office for Standards in Education, Children's Services and Skills (2009b). *Making More of Music: Improving the Quality of Music Teaching in Primary Schools.* Available at: http://webarchive.nationalarchives.gov.uk/20141124154759/http://www.ofsted.gov.uk/resources/making-more-of-music-improving-quality-of-music-teaching-primary (Accessed 5 May 2017).

Office for Standards in Education, Children's Services and Skills (2010). *Learning: Creative Approaches that Raise Standards.* Manchester: Crown copyright. Available at: http://www.creativitycultureeducation.org/wp-content/uploads/learning-creative-approaches-that-raise-standards-250.pdf (Accessed 21 May 2016).

Office for Standards in Education, Children's Services and Skills (2012a). *Music in Schools: Wider Still, and Wider.* Available at: https://www.gov.uk/government/publications/music-in-schools (Accessed 25 April 2016).

Office for Standards in Education, Children's Services and Skills (2012b). *Music in Schools: Promoting Good Practice.* Available at: https://www.gov.uk/government/publications/subject-professional-development-materials-music-in-schools-promoting-good-practice (Accessed 25 April 2016).

Office for Standards in Education, Children's Services and Skills (2012c). *Music in Schools: Sound Partnerships.* Available at: https://www.gov.uk/government/uploads/system/uploads/attachment_data/file/413216/Music_in_schools_sound_partnerships.pdf (Accessed 24 December 2016).

Office for Standards in Education, Children's Services and Skills (2013). *Music in Schools: What Hubs Must Do.* Available at: https://www.gov.uk/government/uploads/system/uploads/attachment_data/file/413107/Music_in_schools_what_hubs_must_do.pdf (Accessed 20 December 2016).

Orffsite.com (no date). Available at: www.orffsite.com (Accessed 21 October 2016).

Overy, K. (2012). 'Making music in a group: Synchronization and shared experience'. *Annals of the New York Academy of Sciences*, 12521(1), pp. 65–8.

Parncutt, R. (2006). 'Prenatal development'. In McPherson, G. (ed.), *The Child as Musician: A Handbook of Musical Development.* Oxford: Oxford University Press, pp. 1–32.

Paynter, J. (2002). 'Music in the school curriculum: Why bother?'. *British Journal of Music Education*, 19(3), pp. 215–26.

Perkins, D. and Blythe, T. (1994). 'Teaching for Understanding', *Educational Leadership*, 51(5), pp. 4–7.

PharrellWilliamsVEVO (2014). *Happy.* Available at: https://www.youtube.com/watch?v=ZbZSe6N_BXs (Accessed 21 July 2016).

Phillips-Silver, J. and Keller, P. (2012). 'Searching for roots of entrainment and joint action in early musical interactions'. *Frontiers in Human Neuroscience*, 6(26). doi:10.3389/fnhum.2012.00026.

Philpott, C. (2001). 'The body and musical literacy'. In Philpott, C. and Plummeridge, C. (eds), *Issues in Music Teaching.* London: Routledge Falmer.

Piaget, J. and Inhelder, B. (1969). *The Psychology of the Child.* London: Routledge & Kegan Paul.

Pitts, S. (2000). 'Reasons to teach music: Establishing a place in the contemporary curriculum'. *British Journal of Music Education*, 17(1), pp. 32–42.

Pitts, S. (2016). 'What is music education for? Understanding and fostering routes into lifelong musical engagement'. *Music Education Research*, pp. 1–9. doi:10.1080/14613808.2016.1166196.

Qualifications and Curriculum Authority (2004). *Creativity: Find It, Promote It.* London: QCA Publications. Available at: https://www.literacyshed.com/uploads/1/2/5/7/12572836/1847211003.pdf (Accessed May 20 2016).

Reddish, P., Fischer, R. and Bulbulia, J. (2013). 'Let's dance together: Synchrony, shared intentionality and cooperation'. *PLoS One*, 8(8). doi:10.1371/journal.pone.0071182.

Reich-Storer, R. (2016) *Anna Meredith and Radio 1s Dev Introduce her Body Percussion Piece Connect It.* Available at: https://youtu.be/Ai6yGKB3obY?list=PL7zwV8Yqy_M5Ae9t0gjify7RbPHqqkdue (Accessed 6 December 2016).

Robinson, K. (2001). *Out of Our Minds: Learning to be Creative.* Oxford: Capstone.

Robinson, K. and Aronica, L. (2010). *The Element: How Finding Your Passion Changes Everything.* London: Penguin

Rogers, L., Hallam, S., Creech, A. and Preti, C. (2008). 'Learning about what constitutes effective training from a pilot programme to improve music education in primary schools'. *Music Education Research Journal*, 10(4), pp. 485–97.

Rogoff, B. (2012). 'Fostering a new approach to understanding: Learning through intent community participation'. *Learning Landscapes*, 5(2), pp. 45–53.

Rogoff, B., Paradise, R., Arauz, R. M., Correa-Chávez, M. and Angelillo, C. (2003). 'Firsthand learning through intent participation'. *Annual Review of Psychology*, 54, pp. 175–203.

Rosenbaum, E. and Silver, J. (no date). *Singing Fingers*. Available at: http://singingfingers. com/ (Accessed 10 July 2016).

Saunders, J., Varvarigou, M. and Welch, G. (2010). 'The role of singing'. In Hallam, S. and Creech, A. (eds), *Music Education in the 21st Century in the United Kingdom: Achievements, Analysis and Aspirations*. London: Institute of Education, University of London, pp. 69–84.

Schön, D. A. (1987). *Educating the Reflective Practitioner: Toward a New Design for Teaching and Learning in the Professions*. San Francisco, California: Jossey-Bass.

Schön, D. A. (1991). *The Reflective Practitioner: How Professionals Think in Action*. Aldershot: Avebury.

Sewell, K. (2015). *Planning the Primary National Curriculum: A Complete Guide for Trainees and Teachers*. Exeter: Learning Matters.

Shulman, L. (1987). 'Knowledge and teaching: Foundations of the new reform'. *Harvard Educational Review*, 57(1), pp. 1–22.

Sing Up (2016). *Sing Up*. https://www.singup.org/ (Accessed 9 July 2016).

Small, C. (1998). *Musicking: The Meanings of Performing and Listening*. New Hampshire: University Press of New England.

Smith, J. (2006). 'Every child a singer: Techniques for assisting developing singers'. *Music Educators Journal*, 93(2), pp. 28–34.

Sound and Music (2016). *Minute of Listening*. Available at: http://www.minuteoflistening. org/ (Accessed 3 July 2016).

Stunell, G. (2010). 'Not Musical? Identity perceptions of generalist primary school teachers in relation to classroom music teaching in England'. *Action, Criticism, and Theory for Music Education*, 9(2), pp. 79–107.

Swanwick, K. (1997). 'Assessing musical quality in the national curriculum'. *British Journal of Music Education*, 14, pp. 205–15.

Swanwick, K. (2008). 'The 'Good-Enough' Music Teacher'. *British Journal of Music Education*, 25(1), pp. 9–22.

Swanwick, K. (2012). *Teaching Music Musically*. Abingdon: Routledge.

Tafuri, J. (2006). 'Processes and teaching strategies in musical improvisation with children'. In Deliege, I., Wiggins, G. (ed.), *Musical creativity: multidisciplinary research in theory and practice*. Hove, East Sussex: Psychology Press, pp. 134–58.

Tafuri, J. (2008). *Infant Musicality: New Research for Educators and Parents,* edited by Welch, G., SEMPRE studies in the psychology of music. Farnham: Ashgate.

Taylor, A. (1993). *Notes and Tones: Musician-to-Musician Interviews*. New York: Da Capo Press.

The Visitor (2007). Directed by Tom McCarthy [Film]. New York City: Groundswell Productions, Participant Productions and Next Wednesday Productions.

The Yip Harburg Foundation (no date). *The Yip Harburg Foundation*. Available at: http:// yipharburg.com/ (Accessed 12 December 2016).

This is Global Ltd (2016). *Classic FM*. Available at: www.classicfm.com (Accessed 3 July 2016).

tonynsyde (2012). *Stomp Live – Part 3 – Just clap your hands*. Available at: https://www. youtube.com/watch?v=l0XdDKwFe3k (Accessed 6 December 2016).

Trehub, S. E. (2006). 'Infants as musical connoisseurs'. In McPherson, G. E. (ed.), *The Child as Musician: A Handbook of Musical Development*. Oxford: Oxford University Press, pp. 33–50.

UK Music (2014). *Measuring Music: September 2014*. Available at: http://www.ukmusic. org/assets/general/UK_MUSIC_Measuring_Music_September_2014.pdf (Accessed 7 June 2016).

uke3453 (2009). *I'm Yours (Ukulele)*. Available at: https://www.youtube.com/ watch?v=ErMWX--UJZ4 (Accessed 5 July 2016).

ukroyalpriesthood (2012). *FEROmedia presents Khaliyl Iloyi rapping at 2years old with father Femi*. Available at: https://www.youtube.com/watch?v=tZh1_aaFqTQ (Accessed 5 July 2016).

VideosVariosOfficial (2013). *These Boots Are Made For Walkin*. Available at: https://www. youtube.com/watch?v=yQG4bLFQkIY (Accessed 21 July 2016).

Watson, S. (2011). *Using Technology to Unlock Musical Creativity*. Oxford [England]: Oxford University Press.

Webster, P. (2012). 'Towards pedagogies of revision: Guiding a student's music composition'. In Odena, O. (ed.), *Musical Creativity Insights from Music Education Research*. Burlington, VT: Ashgate, pp. 93–112.

Webster, P. R. and Hickey, M. (2006). 'Computers and Technology'. In McPherson, G. (ed.), *The Child as Musician: A Handbook of Musical Development*. Oxford: Oxford University Press, pp. 375–95.

Welch, G. F. (2006). 'Singing and vocal development'. In McPherson, G. E. (ed.), *The Child as Musician: A Handbook of Musical Development*. Oxford: Oxford University Press, pp. 441–61

Welch G. F. and Adams, P. (2003). 'How is music learning celebrated and developed?: A Professional User Review of UK and related international research undertaken for the British Educational Research Association'. pp. 1–24 [Online]. Available at: https:// www.researchgate.net/publication/237478043_HOW_IS_MUSIC_LEARNING_ CELEBRATED_AND_DEVELOPED (Accessed 17 June 2016).

Welch, G. F. and Ockelford, A. (2010). 'Music for all'. In Hallam, S. and Creech, A. (eds), *Music Education in the 21st Century in the United Kingdom: Achievement, Analysis and Aspirations*. London: Institute of Education, University of London, pp. 36–52.

Welch, G. F. and Henley, J. (2014). 'Addressing the challenges of teaching music by generalist primary school teachers'. *Revista da Abem*, 22(32), pp. 12–38.

Welch, G. F., Himonides, E., Saunders, J., Papageorgi, I., Rinta, T., Preti, C., Stewart, C., Lani, J. and Hill, J. (2011). 'Researching the first year of the National Singing Programme Sing Up in England: An initial impact evaluation'. *Psychomusicology: Music, Mind and Brain*, 21(1–2), 83–97.

Wiliam, D. (2011). 'What is Assessment for Learning?', *Studies in Educational Evaluation*, 37, pp. 3–14.

Wood, Marion (2013). *Woodchuck Rhythm* [ipad app]. Available at: http://woodchuck-rhythm.moonfruit.com/ipad-app/4575573291 (Downloaded 31 July 2016).

Young, V. (2011). 'An introduction to music'. In Lambirth, A., Driscoll, P. and Roden, J. (eds), *The Primary Curriculum: A Creative Approach*. London: SAGE Publications, pp. 157–75.

Young, V. (2015). 'An introduction to music'. In Driscoll, P., Lambirth, A. and Roden, J. (eds), *The Primary Curriculum: A Creative Approach*, 2nd edn. London: SAGE Publications, pp. 173–93.

Index